THRIVE AFTER RETIREMENT

A Woman's Guide to Health, Purpose, and Longevity

Debra Barrios

AIMQWEST BOOKS
AIMQWESTBOOKS.COM

First Edition

ISBN: 979-8-9921762-2-3

Published by AIMQWEST CORPORATION

Foreword

By Debra Barrios

Retirement is often portrayed as an ending, a slow descent into leisure, a winding down of ambitions and aspirations. But for the modern woman, retirement is not a retreat—it is a rebirth. It is an awakening to a life that is no longer dictated by career obligations, familial responsibilities, or societal expectations. It is a chance to reclaim time, rediscover passions, and redefine what it means to thrive.

When I embarked on my own journey beyond the traditional workforce, I was met with a mix of excitement and apprehension. Like many women, I had spent decades balancing professional endeavors with the intricate demands of family and personal growth. The transition to retirement was not merely a shift in routine; it was a profound transformation of identity. I found myself asking: Who am I now? What will give my life purpose? How do I ensure that these years are not just restful, but meaningful?

As I searched for guidance, I realized that the prevailing narrative around aging often lacked the vibrancy and empowerment that women deserve. So many resources focused on financial security, but so few addressed the deeper questions: How do we maintain our health with strength and dignity? How do we remain relevant in a rapidly changing world? How do we cultivate joy, connection, and a lasting legacy?

That is why I wrote Thrive After Retirement: A Woman's Guide to Health, Purpose, and Longevity—to offer not just practical advice but a new paradigm for what retirement can be. This book is not about fading into the background; it is about stepping forward with wisdom, confidence, and an unshakable sense of purpose. It is about embracing aging not as an obstacle, but as an invitation—to explore, to give back, and to live with vitality.

In the pages ahead, you will find insights and strategies to sustain physical and mental well-being, foster social connections, and cultivate financial stability in ways that align with your evolving aspirations. You will be encouraged to see this stage of life not as an endpoint, but as a powerful new beginning—one where you can contribute, create, and grow in ways you never imagined.

To every woman holding this book, know this: Your greatest chapters are not behind you. They are waiting to be written, full of new discoveries, adventures, and joys. Together, let us redefine what it means to thrive after retirement.

Debra Barrios
Author, Mentor, and Advocate for Lifelong Growth

TABLE OF CONTENTS

Introduction

Retirement once evoked images of quiet days and a slower pace, yet in modern times, it has become something entirely different: an opportunity to reshape one's life and explore paths that might have previously seemed elusive. No longer should this phase be dismissed as a mere conclusion to decades of professional service. Instead, many individuals discover that, upon stepping away from their primary careers, they possess a wealth of knowledge and experience that can be harnessed for personal growth and societal contribution. The notion of reaching a certain age and simply retreating from the world may seem foreign in an era of vibrant longevity and boundless possibility. Where once people quietly bowed out to reflect on past achievements, now they find themselves at the cusp of new beginnings, poised to embrace untried pursuits and passions.

This new perspective on retirement offers an opportunity to delve into endeavors that ignite curiosity, purpose, and fulfillment. By redefining what it means to move beyond traditional working years, people can harness a renewed sense of autonomy and authenticity. The search for meaning often intensifies as careers wind down, and many notice that the sense of purpose cultivated during their professional lives can evolve into passions that flourish during these newfound hours of freedom. Rather than considering the post-career stage an endpoint, it can be viewed as a catalyst for reinvention. This mindset shift invites individuals to explore unfamiliar experiences, connect with like-minded communities, and challenge long-standing assumptions about age and its associated limitations.

At the core of this evolving attitude is a commitment to staying active, remaining intellectually relevant, and nurturing overall well-being. Maintaining physical health grows increasingly important with each passing year, and the benefits of regular exercise, wholesome nutrition, and mental stimulation become impossible to ignore. Equally critical is the recognition that people need more than just a strong body; they also deserve opportunities for mental engagement, creative expression, and social interaction. Whether it is through traveling, volunteering, pursuing artistic pursuits, or joining discussion groups on everything from literature to technology, modern retirees find that cultivating a balanced life is not just a luxury but a necessity. By tapping into the potential for continued learning and growth, individuals can remain vital contributors to their communities, dispelling long-standing stereotypes about aging and inactivity.

In the pages that follow, readers are guided through a fresh way of thinking about life after leaving the workforce. Emphasis is placed on transforming fear or uncertainty into a sense of excitement, fueled by knowledge, introspection, and proactive preparation. Through this lens, retirement becomes an ongoing journey rather than a final resting point, rich with the possibility of designing a life reflective of personal values and evolving interests. The ideas presented here aim to uplift, empower, and encourage readers as they chart their own course, relying on both a profound respect for the wisdom gleaned from past experiences and a willingness to greet the unknown with curiosity. This approach underscores the importance of remaining purposeful, energetic, and open-minded, showing that the best chapter might unfold precisely when it is least expected.

For many, the realization that traditional notions of aging are rapidly changing can be both liberating and intimidating. There was a time when popular culture glorified a grand finale, a moment when one would simply depart from a long-held position and fade into the quiet comforts of personal life. However, that model rarely accounts for the fluid nature of human ambition, curiosity, and connection. Individuals are more complex than a single career path or role, and this deeper intricacy becomes fully apparent when faced with the open horizon of life after full-time employment. People often speak of a newfound opportunity to revisit dreams left behind in youth, to rediscover talents and interests put aside for the demands of a routine schedule. It is an occasion to explore the intersection between accumulated wisdom and personal fulfillment.

Yet, the process of embracing this transformation does not always happen effortlessly. Many retirees experience a period of adjustment that can feel disorienting, particularly when their sense of identity was closely tied to professional status or responsibilities. When the social rhythms of the workplace disappear, it can be challenging to maintain the same level of drive and purpose. In these moments, it helps to remember that the mind craves engagement, and one of the surest ways to stay motivated is to seek out projects and activities that resonate with core values. It could be mentoring a younger generation, offering expertise to a nonprofit, or studying an entirely new field. What matters most is sustaining a sense of relevance, which, in turn, nourishes self-confidence.

This approach to a post-career life also reshapes social dynamics. Whereas once friendships might have revolved around colleagues and shared professional experiences, new connections can form through clubs, volunteer groups, and even online platforms that bring together people with common interests. Fostering these relationships often demands stepping out of established comfort zones, but the rewards are numerous and lasting. Engaging regularly with peers in pursuit of shared goals counters the isolation sometimes associated with aging. Many find that by merging altruism with curiosity, they not only help others but also invigorate their own spirits. This sense of collective purpose provides a buffer against the downsides of inactivity and invites a healthier, more optimistic outlook.

Physical well-being is likewise integral to the redefinition of retirement. Whether it involves frequent walks, gardening, recreational sports, or more structured exercise regimens, staying mobile supports mental acuity and emotional resilience. By integrating movement into daily life, individuals maintain vitality and reduce the risk of common health challenges. Proper nutrition complements these efforts, fueling the body and mind with the strength required to remain active and alert. Meanwhile, attentiveness to mental health deserves equal recognition. Meditation, mindfulness, and other therapeutic practices can soothe the stress that arises during any significant life change. Adopting a flexible mindset, one that balances rest with engagement, is key. Rather than viewing these practices as mere tasks to be checked off, they become cornerstones for sustaining a fulfilling new chapter, reinforcing the notion that this stage is not about decline but about growth and perpetual reinvention.

Yet another perspective arises when one considers the interplay between past accomplishments and future aspirations. Many people realize that the stories they have collected during their professional lives are not merely remnants of a time gone by but stepping stones toward new forms of personal growth. In embracing this change, individuals often rediscover a sense of possibility that once drove their most creative endeavors. This sensation can be incredibly energizing, as it situates the experiences of one's life on a broader continuum rather than seeing them as a closed chapter. Indeed, the skills, insights, and network acquired over many years can be redirected toward novel pursuits that cultivate meaning and connection.

Embracing this transition is not without challenges. Feelings of doubt and apprehension commonly emerge when familiar routines and external validation suddenly recede. It can become tempting to linger in nostalgia for professional roles that once defined a sense of purpose, or to focus solely on the material rewards of a career that are no longer part of daily life. However, those who successfully navigate this period of uncertainty learn the value of reflection, giving themselves time to acknowledge their emotions while also avoiding the trap of becoming mired in regret or longing. Learning to appreciate the past without allowing it to overshadow the potential of the present is a delicate but essential balance.

In the face of such adjustments, it becomes clearer than ever that people are not designed to exist in a state of stagnation. Activity, whether intellectual, physical, or social, serves as a powerful agent of well-being. While careers may have once provided an automatic sense of momentum, post-work life requires a more proactive approach to staying engaged. One might decide to learn a new language or instrument, to take up painting or creative writing, or to delve deeper into a subject that was always intriguing but never fully explored. These efforts need not be bound by preconceived notions of proficiency or career-based outcomes;

the genuine reward lies in the sense of achievement and continual growth they foster.

Yet, even as individuals cultivate these new skills and interests, they are also expanding their horizons in ways that support physical and mental health. Active learning has been linked to a slower cognitive decline, reinforcing the idea that the mind thrives on stimulation and novelty. In parallel, remaining physically active through various forms of exercise—everything from gentle yoga and tai chi to brisk walks or more rigorous workouts—can significantly improve quality of life. This holistic approach to personal development generates a positive feedback loop, where a healthier body encourages a sharper mind, and a sharper mind motivates one to remain physically engaged.

Equally significant in this new reality is the ongoing support of community and family. Far from retreating into isolation, many individuals find that retirement, when approached conscientiously, can result in a profound reinforcement of social ties. Whether through volunteerism, neighborhood initiatives, or intergenerational projects, retirees often discover that they have an expanded capacity to give back, to teach, and to lead by example. Indeed, forging these deeper bonds underscores the notion that stepping out of a professional role is not about disengagement, but about renewing one's focus on what truly matters in life.

In learning to value the future as much as the legacy of the past, it becomes essential to acknowledge how one's sense of self can flourish through the right combination of deliberate exploration and introspection. Some people find it productive to engage in a reflective practice, such as journaling or quiet contemplation, that allows them to take stock of where they have been and where they wish to go. In doing so, they often uncover a renewed sense of direction that bridges life's prior seasons with the adventures that lie ahead. This forward-looking attitude does not diminish the accomplishments already attained; instead, it honors them by transforming their lessons into building blocks for even greater personal realization.

One of the most significant insights to emerge from this method of reflection is that purpose need not be singular or static. Over the course of a long career, individuals might have grown accustomed to a specific function or title that lent structure to their everyday routines. Without that anchor, it can initially feel as though one has been set adrift. Yet, the freedom from strict schedules and clearly defined obligations can also be liberating, enabling a more expansive view of what truly enriches one's days. Some discover new facets of themselves, whether through creative hobbies or unexpected collaborations, while others find that the volunteer work they began as a casual pursuit blossoms into a profound commitment to service. This fluidity of purpose underscores the idea that, with each passing year, there is room for reinvention and fresh perspectives.

As part of this reimagining process, it helps to recognize that retirement provides a unique platform for personal development. With fewer constraints on time, individuals have a remarkable chance to step back and assess which values resonate most powerfully. They may find that connecting more deeply with family and friends becomes a priority, whether through scheduled gatherings, shared travels, or smaller, thoughtful gestures that keep relationships strong. Others may focus on contributing to their communities in ways that align with their sense of social responsibility, tackling challenges such as environmental conservation or youth empowerment. This capacity to invest one's energy where it feels most impactful is not simply a substitute for professional ambition; it is often an even more meaningful application of accumulated knowledge and abilities.

Moreover, the approach to well-being during these years shifts to a more holistic view that accounts for physical, mental, emotional, and even spiritual aspects of health. Engaging with a broader circle of peers and mentors can reveal creative strategies for maintaining balance. Sometimes, this involves setting realistic goals for exercise and adopting novel ways to remain active, like group fitness classes that foster camaraderie or learning a new sport that doubles as a social outlet. Other times, it involves carefully monitoring emotional wellness, reaching out for support when needed, and sharing personal insights so that others, too, feel less alone. Introspection does not need to be solitary; there is immense benefit in leaning on the wisdom of those who have ventured along a similar path and reaching out to encourage those who are just beginning.

Expanding on the idea of purposeful engagement, it becomes increasingly apparent that nurturing creativity and intellectual curiosity are pillars of a fulfilling later stage in life. Rather than perceiving this period as one of diminished drive, it can be approached as a season of exploration, fueled by a curious mind and a willingness to attempt what may previously have seemed out of reach. By learning a new craft, studying an unfamiliar culture, or even embarking on an entrepreneurial venture, individuals demonstrate that vitality is not exclusively a feature of youth but rather the result of consistently tending to inquisitiveness and inspiration.

Such pursuits also carry psychological benefits, as they encourage the brain to forge new pathways, expanding neural plasticity and boosting cognitive resilience. The joy that emerges from trying something fresh—whether it is a creative hobby, an academic interest, or a social cause—provides a sense of dynamism and possibility. This sense of dynamism, in turn, fosters resilience against life's inevitable ups and downs. Even when progress seems gradual or success uncertain, there is meaning in the daily act of cultivating one's abilities, a reward that no external measure can replicate.

Central to this perspective is the understanding that retirement, far from signaling withdrawal from society, can open doors to deeper community engagement. Many find themselves inspired to examine broader social questions and to channel their energies into projects that address real human needs. Whether these efforts involve grassroots activism, educational mentorship, environmental stewardship, or cultural preservation, they instill a reassuring sense that one's presence and wisdom continue to matter. This alignment of personal growth with community betterment can elevate a routine day to something significant, weaving individual passion together with collective well-being.

At the same time, finding the right balance between action and rest is crucial. Retirees who throw themselves zealously into numerous activities without mindful pacing may risk burnout or neglect their own mental and emotional health. The process of self-discovery in this new phase includes recognizing personal limitations and adapting schedules accordingly. A gradual approach to new projects can be more sustainable, particularly when it allows one to savor each moment of learning and development. By choosing engagements carefully, focusing on quality rather than quantity, and honoring the natural rhythms of body and mind, it is easier to remain both enthusiastic and energized over the long term.

Hand in hand with this outlook is the realization that the definition of "staying active" extends well beyond physical exercise. It is equally a matter of staying alert, staying curious, and staying connected to the wider world. Building relationships across generations can be particularly inspiring in this regard. Younger people often gain invaluable insights and direction from those who have navigated similar challenges, and in return, they share fresh perspectives that can reinvigorate older adults' sense of relevance. This reciprocal dynamic enriches both sides, underscoring that retirement, rather than being a one-sided retreat, can spark intergenerational dialogue, mutual learning, and enduring friendships.

By cultivating a lifestyle grounded in continuous discovery and open-hearted engagement, individuals stand poised to transform assumptions about aging. What begins as a quest for meaning after a career concludes can quickly expand into a fulfilling and vibrant next chapter, one in which each day brings an opportunity to learn, create, and contribute.

Envisioning this phase of life as a fresh horizon involves not only embracing new interests but also confronting questions that may have remained sidelined for years. This includes an honest reckoning with one's own desires, fears, and hopes. Such introspection can unfold gently, revealing layers of aspiration that once felt unrealistic or far-fetched in the midst of demanding careers. Now, freed from the necessity to perform within rigid professional structures, many feel emboldened to direct their energy toward personal passions, which can range from scientific inquiry and artistic experimentation to humanitarian outreach. In seizing these possibilities, individuals uncover a vitality they may never have known they possessed.

Another powerful element in this transformative period is the reshaping of daily routines. Instead of being bound to schedules dictated by external demands, retirees can craft rhythms that align with their natural inclinations. For example, early risers might devote peaceful morning hours to reading, writing, or meditation, while night owls discover newfound joy in quiet, creative pursuits under starlit skies. This freedom from conventional timetables creates mental space for deeper reflection and fosters a sense of ownership over one's time. Far from feeling idle, this intentional way of living can illuminate fresh insights about priorities, relationships, and self-care.

It is also important to remember that, even with purposeful planning, unpredictable hurdles may arise. Financial or health concerns, familial responsibilities, and even shifts in personal motivation can complicate the picture. Yet these challenges should not be viewed as reasons to shy away from life's potential. Instead, acknowledging and preparing for inevitable obstacles paves the way for resilience and adaptation. By staying informed and flexible, individuals can navigate uncertainties with greater ease, transforming potential setbacks into learning opportunities. It is precisely this blend of preparedness and openness that empowers people to view aging not as a decline but as an ongoing evolution.

A crucial element in maintaining this mindset is the cultivation of meaningful social connections. While some may worry about becoming disconnected from their professional networks, the reality is that stepping away from a full-time career can free up time to strengthen existing bonds and develop new ones. This might involve participating in regular gatherings, forming reading groups, or simply reaching out to old friends who have drifted apart over the years. True fulfillment frequently hinges on the sense of belonging that arises from shared experiences, laughter, and mutual understanding. Modern technology has made it simpler than ever to stay connected, yet face-to-face interactions and genuine expressions of empathy remain invaluable. Whether through small acts of kindness, shared community efforts, or candid conversations about life's joys and struggles, these human exchanges feed the soul and reinforce a profound sense of purpose.

In this newly shaped world, the pursuit of healthy living continues to be a cornerstone. Physical strength, psychological well-being, and emotional balance are interdependent strands within the tapestry of overall health. Engaging in activities that boost each aspect—through gentle stretches, mind-body exercises, social games, spiritual reflection, or time spent outdoors—can fortify one's resilience. The process is less about following rigid regimens than about adopting a lifestyle that promotes ongoing vitality. The capacity to flourish in later years depends on one's willingness to blend self-discipline with joy, recognizing that well-chosen habits can lay the foundation for a life rich in meaning and endeavor.

Another valuable insight during this phase is the potential for forging deeper, more resonant relationships with oneself and with others. As time opens up, individuals gain the chance to listen to their inner voices more intently, to acknowledge what excites them or stirs them to action, and to confront the lingering questions that once lay buried beneath professional obligations. These personal inquiries often yield a heightened sense of authenticity, one that encourages honest communication with family members, neighbors, friends, and even casual acquaintances. By being true to evolving interests and values, and by voicing those truths openly, retirees often inspire others to do the same, fostering a network of support and understanding that transcends age boundaries and expectations.

Naturally, it is impossible to ignore the practical side of forging a fulfilling life after a career. Financial stability plays a crucial role, as it ensures that individuals can pursue their goals without constant worries about basic necessities. However, the path toward security need not be a source of undue stress; prudent planning, a willingness to adapt, and a measured approach to living expenses can help safeguard peace of mind. Meanwhile, recognizing that each person's circumstances are unique allows for personalized strategies that accommodate different levels of income, family situations, and health conditions. The important point is that financial preparedness, while essential, should not overshadow the profound opportunity for growth that this chapter in life represents.

Hand in hand with these practical considerations comes the need for nurturing one's emotional and spiritual core. The confidence to step outside of traditional boundaries stems partly from an inner belief that one's life purpose continues to unfold. This belief often solidifies through self-reflection, dialogue with trusted confidants, and a willingness to engage with varied ideas, whether through books, workshops, or meaningful conversations. As people become comfortable speaking about their experiences and future goals, they frequently discover that their stories resonate with others in surprising ways. Such exchanges highlight the universal quest for purpose and validation, reminding retirees that they are integral contributors to the collective narrative of their communities and beyond.

Central to this collective narrative is the conviction that wisdom is a currency of vast importance. Far from being relegated to history books or confined to the memories of loved ones, the accumulated insights of a lifetime hold immense potential to shape future endeavors. When shared generously, these perspectives can spark innovation, deepen empathy, and guide others through obstacles they may not yet know how to overcome. Moreover, they serve to affirm an essential truth: that growth is a continuum, existing at every point of life, and those who have traveled far along that path are invaluable mentors and visionaries.

Taken as a whole, this outlook illuminates the transformative power of redefining retirement. By refusing to accept the narrative that aging equates to stepping away from life's main stage, individuals claim a new form of ownership over their days, their relationships, and their aspirations. They become architects of their destinies, guided by curiosity, mindful self-care, and the conviction that every chapter remains open to infinite possibility. The result is a richly woven tapestry of learning, connection, and self-expression that transcends old limitations and ushers in a future defined by renewed purpose and enduring vitality.

Part I: Laying the Foundation for a Healthy and Fulfilling Retirement

Chapter 1: Mindset Matters – A Positive Approach to Retirement

Stepping into a later phase of life brings with it a mix of emotions, often intensified by the uncertainty that accompanies any major transition. For many, these emotions include excitement about new possibilities, coupled with trepidation about leaving behind a familiar sense of structure and identity. Such mixed feelings can manifest in subtle ways, influencing day-to-day thoughts and behaviors. Yet it is precisely this interplay between apprehension and optimism that underscores the power of perspective. By adopting a constructive mindset, individuals can transform uncertainties into stepping stones that lead toward personal growth. This process involves understanding the psychological landscape of moving on from a long-held role, recognizing the innate ability to adapt, and harnessing the motivation that arises from a renewed sense of purpose.

The first step in easing into this stage of life is acknowledging that fear, doubt, and even restlessness are perfectly natural reactions. Our minds, shaped by years of habit, tend to cling to what is known and predictable. The routine of daily work and its associated responsibilities become ingrained, forming a comfortable cocoon that can be difficult to discard. When that anchor disappears or changes drastically, some experience an unsettling loss of direction, which can cause anxiety about the future and regret over choices made in the past. In these vulnerable moments, deliberate efforts to practice self-compassion and maintain a hopeful outlook can help soothe the initial turmoil. With patience and an openness to self-exploration, the tension between longing for what was and yearning for what might be eventually yields an inner balance.

As part of this emotional recalibration, the recognition that personal growth does not cease with the end of a professional career emerges as an essential component of well-being. Growth can take many forms: expanding intellectual horizons, deepening social connections, or exploring new creative or spiritual interests. The possibilities are as varied as the individuals themselves.

Some discover that the same problem-solving prowess once used in the workplace can be directed toward a beloved pastime or community initiative. Others may realize that qualities overlooked during their years of labor—an artistic flair, a compassionate nature, a quiet knack for leadership—can blossom when given sufficient time and space to flourish. What unites these experiences is the empowering realization that development is an ongoing process, unbound by any specific age or life event.

At the heart of this new chapter lies a purposeful approach to managing thoughts and emotions. Instead of interpreting the end of a career path as a loss of status or value, one can perceive it as a chance to refocus on personal aspirations and deeper contentment. Exploring ideas, whether through reading or thoughtful conversation, can spark a renewed sense of curiosity and lead to the discovery of unfamiliar yet exciting worlds. Just as importantly, the practical strategies for thriving in this stage reflect universal truths about how the mind and spirit function best: by continually seeking meaning, fostering connections, and staying receptive to transformative learning. A clarity of mind and confidence of heart, once achieved, make the transition into new routines feel like an opportunity rather than a burden.

In moments of hesitation, it is helpful to look more closely at the underlying beliefs that shape reactions to major life changes. Sometimes, these beliefs stem from deeply ingrained cultural ideals that equate productivity with worth, leading individuals to wonder if they will remain useful or valued once their professional duties are no longer at the forefront of their daily existence. Confronting these ingrained notions calls for an honest exploration of identity: what it means to be accomplished, how contributions can be measured beyond a paycheck or job title, and why human dignity transcends any single external role. By reframing one's perspective in this way, the unsettling feeling of stepping out of a familiar sphere gradually transforms into a clarion call for self-discovery.

This approach can also temper the fear of the unknown that often accompanies transitions. When faced with abrupt shifts in routine, the mind may magnify worries about future security, companionship, and personal fulfillment. One strategy to alleviate those anxieties involves constructing clear objectives that reflect renewed priorities. These objectives need not be grand in scope; rather, they can be realistic, incremental goals tailored to personal interests and values. For instance, someone long intrigued by the outdoors might begin by committing to a simple habit of daily walks, gradually moving toward more challenging activities like extended hikes or nature photography. Another individual, drawn to the idea of giving back to the community, might begin with a few hours of volunteer work each week, discovering new dimensions of purpose in the process. With each small step, uncertainty loses its edge, replaced by the motivation that arises from meaningful engagement.

This mindset shift is further enriched by a willingness to embrace growth at every stage. Many people once believed that their capacity for learning peaked years ago or that substantial personal evolution was reserved for the young. Recent findings in neuroscience and psychology, however, affirm that the human brain retains its ability to form new connections and adapt throughout life. This phenomenon, often referred to as neuroplasticity, demonstrates that older adults can still acquire new skills, perspectives, and modes of creativity. By acknowledging this innate capacity for reinvention, one can expand the boundaries of what is deemed possible beyond customary retirement age. Undertaking a project that stretches the mind and touches the heart is a potent antidote to stagnation and self-doubt, opening channels for the discovery of unexplored talents.

Of equal importance is the recognition that vitality stems from more than just intellectual engagement. Spiritual reflection, shared laughs over a meal with close friends, moments of solitude that provide clarity of thought—these experiences contribute to a holistic sense of well-being that underpins any outward pursuit. Fostering strong personal relationships can be especially supportive during times of change, as trusted confidants offer reassurance and fresh perspectives that disrupt cycles of unhelpful self-talk. Although uncertainty may still linger, it becomes more manageable when balanced by the warmth of connection and the comforting knowledge that personal identity need not hinge on professional identity alone. By redefining what it means to thrive, individuals begin to see the transformation before them not as a descent into irrelevance but as a chance to illuminate new dimensions of their potential.

Another revealing aspect of this stage involves discovering how one's mindset can directly influence physical and emotional well-being. Researchers have found that individuals who harbor optimistic views of aging and personal potential often experience better health outcomes than those who brace themselves for a steady decline. This finding reinforces the idea that adopting a hopeful stance transcends mere wishful thinking; it can tangibly shape how the body and mind respond to the demands of everyday life. When people welcome change with curiosity and determination, their efforts to stay active, engaged, and socially connected gain a deeper resonance, becoming more than just measures against boredom or isolation. They morph into part of an overarching philosophy that champions resilience, self-efficacy, and the ongoing pursuit of fulfillment.

This shift in attitude also prompts a reevaluation of how one navigates inevitable setbacks. Challenges that arise during this new phase—whether related to health, finances, or interpersonal dynamics—can seem magnified without the daily anchors that once provided structure. A constructive mindset does not deny the existence of such obstacles; rather, it encourages a perspective that views them as chapters in a broader story of personal growth. By reframing setbacks as lessons in adaptability, individuals strengthen their capacity to face future trials with composure. This approach aligns with the widely accepted principle that emotional flexibility supports lasting mental health. The person who can calmly adjust to unexpected changes is often the one who emerges not only intact but stronger for the experience.

The adoption of a more open, exploratory mindset has the further benefit of inviting a broader, more nuanced interpretation of self-worth. When defining who they are, people often realize that they are more than a résumé or a series of professional accomplishments. The shift away from a workplace identity highlights other qualities—compassion, creativity, humor, empathy, perseverance—that may have played a secondary role in their careers but now have room to flourish. This transformation in self-perception can have a liberating effect, allowing retirees to see themselves as multifaceted individuals whose value radiates across domains of life, rather than being confined to a single role.

Family and community relationships also stand to benefit from this new perspective. When the focus is on growth and discovery, there is an opportunity for more authentic interaction with loved ones. Conversations may delve deeper into shared values, personal philosophies, and long-held dreams, creating a richer emotional tapestry that knits people closer together. Equally, many find that connecting with like-minded peers or local community groups can expand their sense of belonging. Surrounding oneself with supportive companions who share a belief in ongoing growth can act as a powerful motivator, reinforcing the positive habits and attitudes that sustain a balanced life. The realization that one's thoughts and actions can spark reciprocal inspiration in others can be transformative, nurturing a sense of purpose that stretches far beyond personal goals.

In this framework, moments of introspection become an essential pillar of well-being, serving as checkpoints for mental clarity and emotional steadiness. Reflective practices—such as quiet meditation, self-guided journaling, or even deep discussion with trusted allies—offer valuable opportunities to reassess priorities, recalibrate efforts, and consciously acknowledge incremental progress. Rather than drifting aimlessly, one consistently reorients toward purposeful living, guided by inner reflections that validate the journey.

Cultivating gratitude can serve as a powerful ally in this realignment of thoughts and feelings. Making a habit of noticing moments of beauty or kindness can gradually reshape one's emotional landscape, highlighting the abundance that remains when professional obligations conclude. This does not mean ignoring life's trials; rather, it encourages a shift of focus toward the positive aspects that frequently go unnoticed. As days become less regimented, there is room to awaken to small, meaningful experiences: witnessing the morning light dancing on a windowsill, sharing a warm exchange with a neighbor, or relishing a freshly prepared meal. A regular practice of recognizing and giving thanks for such events can act as a subtle yet profound reinforcement of optimism.

At the same time, fear and uncertainty can be tamed by acknowledging that they are, in fact, natural responses to any significant upheaval. Rather than trying to deny or suppress these feelings, one can practice accepting them as part of the broader emotional tapestry. By allowing these emotions to surface, individuals can then examine their origins, unravel them with self-compassion, and transform them into catalysts for growth. Recognizing that apprehension and eagerness often coexist underpins the transition toward a dynamic and constructive stance. New beginnings rarely arrive without a degree of unease, but this initial unease can stimulate creativity and fuel the determination needed for meaningful progress.

In this context, maintaining a steady sense of agency becomes crucial. Feeling in control of one's choices and actions fosters resilience, especially when grappling with unknown outcomes. Whether it involves embarking on a fitness routine, undertaking a community project, or learning a new skill, each intentional step underscores that one's trajectory remains in their own hands. When this sense of control converges with an expansive mindset, it helps create a powerful protective barrier against the paralyzing effects of self-doubt. This synergy also improves emotional equilibrium, as the combination of choice and openness nurtures a belief that personal transformation is both feasible and worthwhile.

Alongside bolstering a sense of agency, self-awareness plays a prominent role in preserving well-being. Making room for introspection in daily life—through reflective dialogue, meditative walks, or quiet moments of prayer—encourages a gentle yet thorough appraisal of personal aspirations, anxieties, and values. This form of self-examination, undertaken with kindness and patience, lays the foundation for a more purposeful existence. Rather than moving through new activities on autopilot, individuals remain conscious of their deeper motivations, continually aligning actions with authentic goals. Over time, this habit of internal check-ins strengthens the link between what one does and why it matters, guarding against a sense of drift in this uncharted stage of life.

A final ingredient in this evolving perspective is the spirit of experimentation. While the notion of trial and error might seem reminiscent of youth, it is never too late to adopt a flexible approach to learning and living. Pursuing fresh experiences with curiosity builds upon the recognition that people have the capacity to change, regardless of age or circumstance. Each foray into uncharted territory not only hones specific skills but also bestows a newfound confidence in navigating the unknown. It is in these moments—when novelty meets a willingness to adapt—that the true spirit of growth emerges, revealing that the horizons of possibility remain as wide as ever, even when the parameters of daily life have fundamentally shifted.

At the core of this ever-evolving mindset is the understanding that one's sense of identity is not confined to any single stage or label. Rather, identity grows and transforms over time, shaped by the blend of experiences, insights, and aspirations that accumulate with each passing year. Individuals who gracefully manage this transition often remark on a newfound fluidity of self-concept, wherein the boundaries of what they thought possible gently recede to make room for emerging interests and talents. By recognizing that personhood evolves alongside circumstances, it becomes easier to release old narratives about who one should be, replacing them with a more flexible and exciting vision of who one can become.

Letting go of previous self-definitions does not imply discarding cherished memories or achievements. Instead, it invites an appreciation for the richness of one's past, acknowledging that those experiences serve as building blocks for further growth. Observing this continuity can illuminate unexpected links between past achievements and current endeavors. A detail-oriented skill that once enhanced job performance might now be invaluable in organizing a charitable event, or an aptitude for diplomacy that once facilitated business negotiations could be repurposed to mediate community disputes. In this way, the carefully honed abilities from a former career continue to enrich life, repackaged in ways that keep both body and mind engaged and purposeful.

The concept of change, once framed as a source of unease, can begin to assume a more positive hue. Many discover that if they meet alterations to routine or environment with an attitude of inquiry—asking what lessons might be gleaned or what doors might be opening—they find themselves less afraid and more inclined to consider alternatives that might not have entered their thinking before. This perspective echoes the broader human capacity for resilience: the ability to adapt to shifting conditions while holding onto an abiding sense of direction and self-regard.

Inseparable from this journey is the willingness to carve out personal space where genuine contentment can flourish. While some may relish the opportunity for total immersion in a new project, others might prefer devoting more time to contemplative pursuits or fostering deeper family relationships. There is no singular, universally correct formula for achieving fulfillment; individual preferences guide a medley of activities and pursuits. The essential thread lies in tuning into one's own rhythms, respecting personal inclinations, and steadily weaving these elements into a fabric of daily life that feels balanced, stimulating, and meaningful. Even small adjustments, like dedicating the first hour of the day to a calm, centering practice, can create a domino effect that sets a positive tone for the hours that follow.

Maintaining this balance can be further enhanced by understanding how thought patterns shape emotional realities. Alongside exploring new passions, deliberately cultivating gentle, constructive mental dialogue can minimize the drain of negative rumination. Engaging in regular self-talk that emphasizes capability and potential can counteract the persistent voice of doubt. By regularly reminding oneself of past accomplishments and future possibilities, an undercurrent of confidence can become woven into the daily experience. This internal reassurance, when combined with measurable steps toward personal goals, encourages a steady momentum forward. It is in this synthesis of thoughtful introspection, self-supporting language, and targeted action that one discovers the potent synergy necessary for genuine transformation.

When placed in a broader sociocultural context, this transformation of mindset also has a ripple effect that extends well beyond the personal sphere. By choosing to remain curious, resilient, and actively engaged, individuals challenge the prevailing stereotypes that aging inevitably leads to passivity or withdrawal. The renewed vigor radiating from such a mindset can be an inspiration to those who might otherwise view later life through a more limiting lens. Younger generations, often uncertain about their own paths, can look to these examples of self-directed growth as models of adaptability and creative problem-solving. In a world where change is a constant and no one remains in the same role indefinitely, the willingness to continuously evolve stands as a universal asset.

Social relationships also benefit from the intentional optimism that underlies this new approach. When embracing ongoing growth, individuals are more likely to be open and spontaneous, ready to participate in shared endeavors that enhance community cohesion. Whether it is by leading a workshop in a local center, volunteering at a school, or initiating a reading club that bridges different age groups, the spirit of collaboration forged in later life can be a force for intergenerational learning. By stepping outside the boundaries of age-defined activities, people discover fresh viewpoints that spark mutual enrichment. The synergy that emerges from these collective interactions reinforces the notion that everyone, regardless of where they stand in life's timeline, has wisdom, creativity, and energy to offer.

In parallel, the pursuit of a mentally receptive mindset can pave the way for deeper self-understanding, prompting individuals to untangle longstanding emotional knots that might otherwise linger. Those who once directed their full attention to external responsibilities may now turn inward to examine unresolved personal issues or dormant aspirations. This introspection can lead to greater emotional maturity, allowing people to communicate more authentically and build healthier, more compassionate ties with friends and family. Moreover, by acknowledging hidden dreams or past regrets, retirees reclaim the power to respond in new ways. What may have seemed impossible decades ago might now be approached with a combination of wisdom, resourcefulness, and life experience that unlocks unanticipated success.

Part of nurturing this environment of self-discovery involves challenging internal narratives that limit one's sense of possibility. For some, the idea that time is running short can stand in stark contrast to the desire to embark on new adventures. While it is true that certain physical or logistical constraints might arise, it is equally true that every individual holds the innate capacity for creativity, innovation, and perseverance. By contrasting negative internal monologues with tangible evidence of personal triumphs—both large and small—one systematically weakens the hold of skepticism. Every hurdle cleared, no matter how mundane or trivial it might appear from the outside, can serve as a building block for self-belief. These incremental victories, in turn, accumulate into a robust conviction that fuels further endeavors.

In the process of clarifying this sense of agency, it becomes ever more evident that purposeful action and reflective thought must intertwine. Immersion in a meaningful project—such as writing a personal memoir, tackling a long-deferred scholarly pursuit, or launching a local environmental campaign—demands the synergy of intellectual stamina and passionate commitment. Reflective thought ensures that these endeavors do not become mere busyness but remain rooted in heartfelt convictions. Over time, every well-chosen endeavor nurtures a more integrated self, a person whose vision for the future harmonizes with an acceptance of the present and a reverence for the lessons of the past.

Another facet of this introspective process involves recognizing how personal fulfillment arises when purposeful effort aligns with one's internal values. This alignment becomes especially clear when the drive to keep learning and creating rests on an authentic commitment to growth. Rather than chasing purely external markers of success, individuals begin to appreciate the intrinsic rewards that come with perseverance, curiosity, and an open heart. They also realize that certain aspirations may be met by lending support to the endeavors of others, be it through mentorship, collaboration, or unwavering moral encouragement. In these moments, the ethos of shared humanity comes to the forefront, revealing that one's own flourishing naturally contributes to a broader collective uplift.

Overcoming fear and uncertainty is often aided by developing healthy coping strategies that address emotional, physical, and spiritual dimensions. On the emotional front, honest dialogue— whether with a trusted confidant, a professional counselor, or a reflective journal—helps clarify the root of lingering anxieties, transforming them from nebulous worries into tangible concerns that can be tackled. Physically, even small commitments to regular movement, balanced nutrition, and restorative rest build a foundation of resilience, preparing both body and mind to handle the unexpected. Spiritually, many find solace in contemplative practices or the quiet marvel of nature, tapping into a sense that life's transitions, however daunting, are part of a natural cycle of renewal.

Within this tapestry of adaptive strategies, the ability to cultivate deep psychological well-being emerges as a central theme. The sense of purpose that once revolved around profession-based tasks refocuses on endeavors that nurture both self and community. Some might initially feel uncertain about how to contribute once the routines of the workplace have disappeared. Yet by reframing the question from "Am I still useful?" to "How can I express my values and passions?" the path forward becomes more apparent. This shift in inquiry underlines the principle that genuine purpose stems from the interplay between personal interests and societal needs. In searching for that balance, individuals often uncover reserves of creativity and determination that exceed their own expectations.

Equally significant is the emotional enrichment that accompanies belonging to a cause greater than oneself. Whether it involves volunteering at a shelter, starting a local garden, or raising awareness about social issues, the act of devoting time and energy to benefit others can elicit a profound sense of fulfillment. Research consistently links altruistic behavior to increased happiness, reduced stress levels, and stronger social bonds—all of which bolster confidence and help dispel feelings of loneliness or disconnection. Thus, engaging in purposeful acts can prove transformative, showing that it is not only feasible but immensely worthwhile to keep making a difference, no matter one's chronological age or employment status.

By continually learning, adapting, and embracing change, people discover that a new season of life need not be shrouded in apprehension but can instead bloom into a vivid, expansive landscape of possibility. In forging meaningful connections with the self and the world, in daring to aspire and evolve, and in recognizing that innate potential remains evergreen, individuals affirm that emotional vitality and a sense of purpose are available at any juncture. The mind, like the human spirit, is remarkably adept at renewal, ensuring that each transition—far from being an ending—heralds an unfolding horizon of growth and fulfillment.

Chapter 2: Designing Your Ideal Retirement Lifestyle

Creating a rewarding way of life beyond traditional work often begins with a clear, introspective examination of one's true goals and aspirations. After years of adhering to set schedules and fulfilling professional obligations, the freedom to shape a personal timetable offers enormous potential for discovery. It can be both exhilarating and daunting to recognize that the ultimate shape of each day now rests primarily in one's own hands. Yet by taking time to reflect carefully on what truly brings satisfaction, meaning, and growth, individuals can begin crafting a framework for daily life that is as purposeful as it is enjoyable. This gradual unveiling of personal priorities is a worthwhile endeavor, as it serves to highlight the experiences that most consistently ignite a sense of wonder and accomplishment.

Such realizations often emerge when people scrutinize their long-held dreams, reflecting on creative pursuits or curiosities they might have postponed. Revisiting these interests can reveal fertile ground for establishing new routines and commitments. Whether the dream involves learning a musical instrument, exploring a latent passion for organic gardening, or diving into the study of linguistics, these seeds of aspiration can flourish once given the time and space to grow. This willingness to examine the content of one's day-to-day life from the vantage point of personal desire rather than professional necessity awakens possibilities that might once have seemed out of reach. In the process, people discover that retirement is not merely an intermission but an opportunity to curate experiences that lead to deeper fulfillment.

Equally significant in this phase is the ability to cultivate structure without stifling spontaneity. While the absence of a rigid work calendar brings relief, an entirely unstructured existence can leave individuals feeling disoriented. Striking a balance between planned activities and flexible downtime allows for a sense of continuity that supports emotional equilibrium. It is entirely feasible to map out segments of the day devoted to fitness, study, social connection, or volunteering, while also reserving a generous margin for rest, creativity, and the unexpected joys that materialize when the mind is free to wander. This interplay of discipline and freedom nurtures a harmonious daily rhythm that neither burdens nor bores, meeting the human need for variety, growth, and intervals of repose.

Equally important is discovering what everyday activities spark genuine delight. There can be wisdom in approaching even simple tasks—such as preparing breakfast or tidying a workspace—with renewed attention to detail and appreciation for the present moment. In the rush of earlier professional life, small pleasures may have gone unnoticed or were swiftly overshadowed by looming deadlines. By slowing the pace and focusing on sensory details or mindful awareness, individuals can transform simple chores into a source of calm satisfaction. This does not trivialize the importance of grand ambitions or new endeavors; instead, it reinforces the essential truth that everyday life is woven from small acts of care and attentiveness. Weaving meaning into these ordinary routines fosters a sense of gratitude and presence that resonates well beyond the confines of any single day

An essential element in designing a more fulfilling way of life during this phase lies in periodically reassessing priorities. Over the course of a career, many individuals develop a shorthand for what matters most, yet these mental hierarchies can become entrenched, even as personal values evolve. Recognizing the shifts that have occurred—perhaps in health needs, family responsibilities, or intellectual interests—can clarify which pursuits now deserve center stage. Some may find themselves increasingly drawn to artistic outlets they long admired but had no time to explore. Others might feel a new pull toward mentoring younger generations or engaging in environmental initiatives. Whatever the inclination, examining the nuances of personal goals helps clear the path for more deliberate, energizing decisions about how each day should unfold.

In this spirit of introspection, it can be particularly helpful to adopt a mindset of ongoing experimentation. Even if a certain pursuit initially seems promising, it may not always deliver the expected sense of reward. By allowing oneself to move fluidly from one endeavor to the next, responding naturally to curiosity and feedback from the experience, a larger tapestry of fulfilling activities emerges. This adaptable approach preserves a sense of openness, reminding people that there is no single blueprint for success. Indeed, the question "What does my ideal day look like?" may be revisited multiple times as interests grow and transform. The freedom to refine and adjust ensures that a sense of vitality remains, regardless of how many new directions one may choose to explore.

Within this evolving framework, it is also important to pay attention to the body's cues. The rhythms of energy and rest change over the years, and designing a suitable routine requires an honest appraisal of those needs. If early mornings no longer feel natural or if the body demands more frequent intervals of rest, it is wise to honor those messages. A balanced daily rhythm often includes some form of physical activity, whether it is a brisk walk, a gentle yoga session, or a nature hike that combines exercise with aesthetic enjoyment. The mind, similarly, may flourish with intervals devoted to reading, writing, or studying a favorite subject, interspersed with conversations that spark creativity and laughter. By blending movement, reflection, and social interaction in a way that respects individual energy patterns, people create a healthy, dynamic routine that sustains them from dawn to dusk.

Finding gratification in day-to-day living can benefit from a touch of playfulness. Breaking away from rigid definitions of what it means to be mature or productive leaves room for spontaneity and whimsy. Perhaps there is a local dance class that offers a fun challenge, or an opportunity to explore a new style of cooking that stimulates the senses. These lighthearted engagements nourish the spirit, loosening any lingering tension around the idea of having to prove oneself after leaving a more traditional work environment. They also enrich social circles, as laughter and shared merriment often lead to connections that transcend generational boundaries. By giving oneself permission to savor the eccentric and the unexpected, one keeps joy and curiosity at the forefront of each new experience.

Moments of calm introspection can further enhance this shift in perspective. Setting aside time to unwind, whether through a short meditation, a walk in a quiet park, or simply savoring the silence of morning coffee, ensures that the pace of the day does not become frantic. These intervals of stillness open a window into the deeper layers of thought and feeling, promoting clarity about where to direct one's efforts. Thoughtful reflection can also help in detecting patterns of frustration or restlessness that may signal a need to adjust the daily routine. It is within these unhurried spaces that the spark of inspiration often arises, guiding the mind toward fresh ideas for learning, creating, and contributing.

A crucial realization during this phase is that not every aspiration needs to revolve around large, transformative goals. Sometimes, profound contentment stems from modest achievements woven into the daily fabric of life. Tending a small vegetable garden, learning a few new chords on a musical instrument, or taking the time to appreciate a tranquil sunset can all represent meaningful progress. By cultivating these smaller pleasures with intention and reverence, individuals broaden their concept of success beyond traditional metrics. What was once measured in promotions or accolades now finds expression in personal enrichment and the unwavering delight of discovering unknown facets of one's own capacities.

Mindful consumption of time and resources further supports a lifestyle that prioritizes purpose over compulsion. Without the rigid framework of a nine-to-five schedule, there arises the potential to examine habits that may have been on autopilot for years. From shopping routines to television viewing, it is possible to gauge whether these activities still bring satisfaction or merely fill unoccupied space. In this more fluid state of living, each choice about how to spend an hour or a dollar can be carefully evaluated. Many find that by shedding the unnecessary—be it excess possessions or commitments that no longer resonate—they unlock a fresh sense of spaciousness that makes room for new passions.

At the same time, fostering social engagement remains indispensable. The value of meaningful connections cannot be overstated in ensuring a sense of belonging and emotional equilibrium. Friends and family can serve as sounding boards for emerging ideas, partners in shared experiences, or simply sources of companionship when unexpected difficulties arise. Engaging in clubs, community gatherings, or intergenerational volunteer opportunities expands these bonds beyond established circles, creating a richer network of support. Even digital platforms, if used thoughtfully, can help retirees discover local interest groups or connect with individuals who share similar pursuits around the globe. What matters is finding a balance between savoring solitude and maintaining the social ties that enliven and inspire.

In designing a balanced approach to daily life, flexibility proves vital. Even the most carefully planned schedule can benefit from occasional spontaneity—deviating on a whim to explore a new café, attend an impromptu cultural event, or indulge in a last-minute day trip. These breaks from routine can provide a sense of adventure that invigorates the mind, reminding it that novelty and excitement are not limited to a single age bracket. Indeed, those who embrace a spirit of adaptability often find that their days feel neither cluttered nor monotonous, but alive with potential and open to unexpected pathways of fulfillment.

Within this framework of exploration, each person is encouraged to set healthy boundaries that safeguard well-being. This might include limiting screen time, carving out dedicated periods for quiet reflection, or being intentional about staying active in ways that align with individual fitness levels. The temptation to undertake too much too quickly can lead to burnout, just as idling without focus can lead to stagnation. By maintaining a keen awareness of personal limits and aspirations, individuals can pace themselves in a way that preserves stamina for the long run. This balanced approach promotes not just physical endurance but also a heightened sense of emotional and mental clarity.

Every day thus becomes an opportunity to refine the interplay between structure and freedom, to discover activities that align with heartfelt aims, and to cherish moments of simple gratification. Guided by self-knowledge, curiosity, and the desire to live fully, one can craft a lifestyle that nurtures both stability and growth. In doing so, each person sets the stage for a retirement experience that stands as a testament to resilience, adaptability, and the enduring human capacity for renewal and creativity.

Another valuable consideration in shaping a new daily rhythm involves taking stock of personal strengths, experiences, and resources in ways that promote sustained self-confidence. In the workplace, many acquire clear markers of competence—job titles, performance evaluations, or accolades—that can fade into the background once those positions no longer define one's sense of purpose. Replacing that external validation with a more internalized appreciation of one's abilities paves the way for a healthier, self-directed motivation. By reflecting on past accomplishments, untapped skills, and inherent talents, individuals can pinpoint endeavors that align naturally with their interests and aptitudes. This self-awareness not only guides the selection of meaningful pursuits but also reinforces a sense of resilience and capability, qualities that are indispensable when navigating unexplored territory.

Within this framework of self-discovery, it becomes fruitful to set targets that combine challenge with enjoyment, thereby maintaining an element of excitement. While certain goals might be large and long-term—writing a collection of short stories, planting a community garden, or undertaking a major fitness milestone—it is often the short-term objectives that keep everyday momentum alive. The satisfaction of overcoming small hurdles on a daily or weekly basis can create a rewarding cycle of accomplishment, fueling motivation to tackle progressively more ambitious undertakings. Because these more immediate objectives are frequently linked to personal growth rather than external demands, their fulfillment resonates more deeply, reinforcing the belief that life beyond a profession can continue to expand in both breadth and depth.

Awareness of the world around us also gains new significance during this shift in focus from work obligations to voluntary commitments. Freed from the tight constraints of a busy professional calendar, retirees are better positioned to observe community needs, environmental concerns, and social injustices that might once have gone unnoticed. For some, engagement might take a highly local form, such as volunteering at a nearby school or cultural center. Others might direct their curiosity toward broader global issues, seeking to understand and address problems through digital channels or by partnering with international organizations. In all such instances, the act of stepping forward to contribute tangibly affirms the notion that retirement is neither retreat nor inertia, but a repurposing of energies guided by one's moral compass.

Equally vital to this reimagined way of life is acknowledging that fulfillment does not follow a single trajectory. A transition from a structured work environment to a more autonomous daily routine has the potential to sharpen awareness of what truly matters. Over time, it may become apparent that certain social connections encourage new ways of thinking, while others remain anchored in patterns no longer conducive to personal growth. Reevaluating the quality of each relationship in the context of mutual respect and shared enthusiasms can help shape a social network that remains dynamic, supportive, and enriching. Even the manner of communication might evolve—from traditional in-person gatherings to increasingly versatile digital platforms—reflecting the diversity of individual preferences and connections available in a rapidly changing world.

Meanwhile, discovering joy in everyday activities calls for a willingness to slow down and appreciate small wonders, unhurried moments, and quiet acts of creation. This could entail cultivating a garden, immersing oneself in an art project, or exploring nearby nature trails with no destination in mind. Through these endeavors, the ordinary becomes extraordinary, less defined by external measures of success and more by the personal delight derived from each fleeting moment. It is precisely this capacity to convert habitual tasks into mindful, fulfilling experiences that can transform life after a formal career, releasing older adults from the belief that their most significant contributions are behind them. Instead, they gradually realize that each day delivers fresh opportunities for beauty, insight, and a deeper understanding of themselves and their place in the wider community.

A further dimension of refining one's daily routine emerges when considering the impact of technology on how time is spent. Modern innovations offer a wealth of resources that can enrich the post-work environment, from online educational platforms and virtual forums for shared interests to digital tools that facilitate creative expression. Video tutorials, interactive workshops, and live-streamed performances can extend horizons far beyond what was once possible, enabling older adults to connect with experts, enthusiasts, and peers scattered across the globe. When approached mindfully, technology becomes an ally in the pursuit of continual learning, helping to bridge physical distances and expand one's intellectual and cultural palette.

Nevertheless, the allure of digital devices can become a double-edged sword. The ease of constant connectivity may encourage overreliance on passive entertainment or social media scrolling, gradually eroding the sense of enrichment one initially sought. Maintaining a deliberate approach to screen time helps preserve the purposeful, self-directed spirit that defines this stage of life. By setting boundaries—whether that entails designating specific times for online exploration or regularly logging off to engage in hands-on activities—retirees safeguard the integrity of their newfound freedom. In so doing, they transform technology from a potential distraction into a versatile tool that augments learning, creativity, and social interaction on their own terms.

In parallel, reevaluating how space is utilized can further foster an environment of inspiration and clarity. Whether living in a sprawling family home or a smaller apartment, every environment holds possibilities for small but meaningful modifications that resonate with personal aspirations. A quiet corner can be outfitted with comfortable seating and good lighting for reading or meditation. A formerly underused dining table might become a crafting station, its surface strewn with art supplies that beckon spontaneous creative activity. If one's passion lies in the culinary arts, the kitchen can be rearranged to accommodate specialized tools that simplify adventurous recipes. These tweaks help transform living quarters into a supportive haven where the act of simply being at home encourages exploration and self-expression.

Equally powerful is the growing recognition of the therapeutic value of nature. Studies have shown that spending time in green spaces positively affects mood and mental clarity, reducing stress and enhancing emotional equilibrium. People who once spent their days confined to office settings may now embrace this renewed opportunity to step outdoors, even if it involves nothing more than tending a few potted plants on a balcony or gazing at the sky during leisurely walks. Breathing fresh air, feeling the warmth of the sun, and observing the quiet rhythms of wildlife can gently remind us that life unfolds in cycles, and that each new day brings subtle transformations. This awareness serves as a counterpoint to any lingering sense of urgency or apprehension, unveiling a perspective that appreciates both the fleeting and the enduring aspects of one's surroundings.

All the while, cultivating social connections remains as vital as ever. Some might choose to begin hosting casual gatherings, inviting neighbors or friends to share meals and ideas. Others could join community workshops, fostering new acquaintances who share their passion for fine arts, athletics, or civic engagement. In the course of these interactions, an invaluable sense of belonging emerges, revealing that social ties need not dwindle after the conclusion of a professional life. Rather, the absence of competing workplace commitments opens a door to forging friendships on the basis of shared personal values and pursuits. These relationships often develop a depth and authenticity that can be harder to achieve under the pressure of managing long work hours. Over time, they become a cornerstone of support, offering encouragement and solidarity in the face of life's inevitable twists and turns.

In this newly emerging tapestry of daily life, people often find renewed confidence in their capacity to shape their surroundings and experiences. They discover that many of the qualities once associated with professional advancement—discipline, innovation, collaboration—can now be redirected toward personal enrichment and service to others. Where once deadlines and office hierarchies imposed structure, retirees can invent their own system that reflects the rhythms of their energy, interests, and relationships. This self-directed lifestyle, shaped by reflection and guided by purpose, grants a level of autonomy that can feel simultaneously freeing and surprisingly profound.

Alongside freedom, however, arises the responsibility of discerning which pursuits merit investment. Without the boundary of a job description, one could scatter attention among numerous ideas and social commitments, risking overextension. The balance lies in allowing enough space to entertain fresh possibilities, while also practicing discernment to focus deeply on the endeavors that evoke genuine enthusiasm. This approach resonates with the principle of quality over quantity, where purposeful engagement in a few well-chosen activities yields far more gratification than a breathless scramble to do everything at once. By learning to pause, evaluate, and then commit, individuals ensure that their time unfolds in alignment with their truest values.

Such intentional living finds an additional anchor in the pursuit of intellectual stimulation. Gone are the days when learning was confined to formal classrooms and rigidly structured lessons. Instead, the curiosity that fuels personal growth can lead to self-paced study of a newly acquired language, the challenge of mastering a complex piece of music, or in-depth discussions in book clubs dedicated to exploring literature, history, or philosophy. This sustained engagement with ideas, stories, and theoretical frameworks can not only sharpen cognitive abilities but also deepen empathy and cultural awareness. Each layer of understanding resonates in one's conversations and creative output, demonstrating that the thirst for knowledge does not wane with age; rather, it gains new dimension as it becomes fueled by passion rather than obligation.

Emotionally, the cultivation of a calm yet purposeful disposition helps ward off the undercurrent of malaise that sometimes accompanies dramatic life transitions. By adopting contemplative practices such as journaling, guided visualization, or regular mindfulness exercises, retirees learn to keep a finger on the pulse of their emotional states, observing how shifts in routine or environment affect their overall sense of peace. In the process, they strengthen emotional awareness and cultivate resilience, giving them the internal resources necessary to greet challenges with clarity. This combination of external participation—through vibrant, enriching activities—and internal reflection—through deliberate, focused introspection—strengthens an appreciation for the interplay between personal well-being and broader purpose.

An outgrowth of this process is the discovery that seemingly small modifications in outlook can have profound consequences for daily contentment. For instance, reinterpreting routine chores not as drudgery but as opportunities for gratitude shifts the emotional energy surrounding them. A mundane task like folding laundry becomes a moment to celebrate the simple comforts of a warm, safe home. A stack of dishes can be tackled as a personal meditation, each movement synchronized with measured breathing, transforming kitchen cleanup into a break from mental clutter. These subtle changes in attitude translate into a broader capacity to recognize and embrace the possibility for joy that resides in almost any aspect of the day.

There is also value in confronting any lingering perceptions that retirement equates to a diminished presence in the larger world. The absence of a professional title does not dissolve one's capacity to make a difference, whether by serving as a mentor, actively engaging in community initiatives, or using newfound leisure for creative or artistic contributions. In some cases, the simplest acts carry significant weight, as a willingness to listen attentively, express encouragement, or share expertise can have a tangible impact on those who may be in an earlier phase of their personal or professional journeys. Serving as a bridge between different generations or social circles deepens one's sense of connectedness, validating the idea that later life can indeed be a period of extraordinary influence and altruistic expression.

A final insight in shaping a richly layered lifestyle lies in recognizing that the process of deliberate living is never truly finished. While a profession may have had a clear endpoint, the journey of self-discovery unfolds continuously, shaped by both external events and the internal evolution of feelings, beliefs, and aspirations. With each passing season, the interplay between new challenges and one's existing knowledge fosters further refinement of goals and strategies. At times, this constant flux can spark unforeseen adjustments in how one spends their hours, whether due to shifts in physical well-being, family commitments, or changed interests. Yet this fluidity also safeguards against stagnation, reminding us that humans are innately adaptable and that true fulfillment stems from embracing transformation rather than resisting it.

Central to this approach is the principle of self-compassion. Mistakes and miscalculations may happen, particularly when individuals stretch beyond their comfort zones in pursuit of uncharted pursuits. But these experiences need not be viewed as failures; rather, they can serve as valuable lessons that reveal necessary pivots or inspire even bolder directions. Treating oneself with kindness amid experimentation fortifies the courage to continue exploring, unimpeded by the crippling fear of judgment or disappointment. This stance finds a healthy counterbalance in holding oneself accountable to certain standards of effort and follow-through, ensuring that kindness does not devolve into complacency. The dual presence of gentle self-acceptance and earnest dedication allows for sustainable growth that resonates with genuine aspiration.

The profound shift in priorities that can accompany this new life stage also paves the way for more deliberate assessments of what success truly means. Freed from corporate expectations or the relentless pace of achievement-driven environments, many older adults find themselves redefining success in more personal, holistic terms. It may mean cultivating a flourishing garden, deepening family bonds, or building a local legacy through volunteer work. By giving themselves permission to claim these milestones as accomplishments—just as significant as promotions or accolades once were—individuals honor the breadth and depth of their own evolution. They begin to see that real value resides in aligning day-to-day activities with heartfelt principles and in leaving a gentle yet enduring mark on the lives they touch.

In tandem with these realizations, the importance of celebrating one's progress becomes apparent. Whether it is a private acknowledgment of a weekly fitness improvement, a toast to the completion of a short story draft, or a quiet reflection on a newly discovered skill, these moments of recognition counterbalance the impetus to keep moving on to the next objective. They underscore that life is composed of present-tense accomplishments as well as long-term ambitions. Through thoughtful celebration, individuals grant themselves the grace to appreciate what they have attained thus far, fortifying the motivation to venture onward.

Ultimately, this period can stand as a testament to the power of design in living. Where once the domain of design might have referred to buildings or systems, it now includes the architecture of personal time, energy, and aspiration. By taking a methodical yet flexible approach—continually clarifying goals, creating a purposeful balance of structure and freedom, and tending to the genuine sources of joy that appear in everyday life—people reshape both their inner worlds and their outward engagements. Over time, the resulting lifestyle transcends earlier assumptions about retirement, revealing a space ripe with discovery and purpose. It is here, in the union of curiosity, adaptability, and a resolve to contribute meaningfully, that one finds a lasting wellspring of fulfillment, proving that the potential for growth remains boundless at any stage of life.

Part II: Health and Longevity – Staying Physically and Mentally Strong

Chapter 3: Maintaining Physical Strength and Vitality

Aging gracefully calls to mind not only the outward signs of vitality but also the inner fortitude that supports a fulfilling, independent life. Over time, muscles and joints need more deliberate attention, and the rhythms of daily existence may shift. Yet a well-considered approach to physical health can bolster energy levels, sharpen mental clarity, and reduce vulnerability to common ailments that emerge as the body accumulates years of experience.

Regular exercise occupies an essential role in preserving strength and protecting mobility, offering benefits that extend beyond aesthetics. A balanced plan that incorporates resistance work, targeted flexibility practices, and moderate yet consistent cardiovascular activity can do more than sculpt and tone. It supports bone density, supports optimal joint function, and sets the stage for a more robust lifestyle where daily tasks, from climbing stairs to carrying groceries, remain manageable.

Evidence from medical research highlights that consistent movement not only reduces the risk of chronic diseases but also elevates mood and resilience. As the body transitions through different phases of life, the capacity to adapt often depends on maintaining a solid foundation of muscular and cardiovascular endurance. Through mindful effort, individuals can enhance circulation, guard against osteoporosis, and even improve mental equilibrium, all of which promote a sense of optimism.

In exploring physical activity options, it helps to consider personal goals and limitations. Some find that walking outdoors yields immediate benefits, combining mild cardio with opportunities to soak in fresh air and natural scenery. Others may gravitate toward structured group classes or gentle forms of movement like yoga or tai chi, which cultivate stability and coordination. Regardless of the chosen approach, prioritizing safety and gradual progression fosters long-term adherence.

Strength exercises, which engage various muscle groups, prove indispensable in safeguarding healthy function. Even light resistance, performed consistently, preserves lean mass and supports overall balance. Rather than viewing this type of training solely through the lens of athletic ambition, one can appreciate its practical usefulness in everyday life. The ability to move furniture, lift bags, or pick up grandchildren without undue strain serves as a tangible reflection of preserved capability.

Where flexibility is concerned, gentle stretching or discipline-based modalities help preserve the range of motion that typically contracts with inactivity. Over time, a limber body not only reduces the likelihood of muscle strains but also promotes better posture and improved performance in casual sports or household tasks. Maintaining flexibility can be as simple as setting aside a few minutes each day for slow, deliberate movements, guided by mindfulness and proper breathing.

Cardiovascular health remains integral to overall wellness, influencing everything from circulation to energy levels. Activities that raise the heart rate, whether through brisk walks, swimming, or low-impact aerobics, reinforce the heart's efficiency and endurance. Even short intervals of sustained exertion can contribute positively to metabolic processes, sharpen mental clarity, and ease daily demands. By adjusting intensity according to personal capability, individuals safeguard themselves from undue strain while still reaping significant rewards.

In combining these elements with appropriate rest and recovery, one discovers a harmonious approach that respects both the aspirations and limitations inherent in the aging process. From bolstering resilience against injuries to supporting emotional balance, a well-rounded regimen can profoundly enhance overall day-to-day satisfaction and longevity.

Deliberate movement remains paramount when striving to maintain a healthy physique over the years. While some may recall their younger days as an era of unbounded energy, the mature body benefits from a gentler, more methodical approach to exercise. Rather than jumping straight into high-intensity routines, a process of gradual adaptation can ensure sustained progress while reducing the risk of overexertion. By taking small yet purposeful steps—beginning with short sets of resistance exercises, measured increments of distance in walking or swimming, and deliberate integration of balance work—one can systematically fortify the musculoskeletal framework without subjecting it to sudden strain. This pattern of gradual intensification recognizes that each person's starting point differs, reflecting individual histories of activity, health concerns, and preferences.

In addition, focusing on proper form can make all the difference in extracting maximum benefit from physical routines. Even a seemingly simple movement, such as a squat or lunge, holds potential for both strengthening and harm, depending on how carefully it is executed. Practicing correct alignment, sometimes with the guidance of a knowledgeable trainer or through carefully selected instructional resources, minimizes stress on joints and improves the efficiency of each repetition. Attention to detail also provides a mental anchor, shifting the experience of exercise from a mundane chore into an immersive, mindful pursuit. As each motion becomes more precise, confidence grows, and the body responds by building endurance and resilience.

Alongside careful form, selecting appropriate equipment or settings can significantly enhance safety and enjoyment. Investing in supportive footwear, opting for fitness spaces with slip-resistant surfaces, or choosing an exercise modality that feels comfortable for existing joint issues all contribute to a sense of security. This sense of security fosters consistency, as individuals are far more likely to continue with programs that do not trigger avoidable discomfort or aggravate underlying conditions. With a conscientious approach to the external environment, the body's signals can guide pacing and intensity, ensuring that the path toward better health remains constructive.

A commitment to moderation, deeply rooted in the principle of listening to one's own body, further refines this journey. Moderate workouts carried out consistently over months often produce lasting improvements in muscle tone, cardiovascular capacity, and joint flexibility. On the other hand, sporadic bursts of extreme effort interspersed with long periods of inactivity tend to yield diminished gains, along with an elevated risk of injury. Finding a middle ground that challenges the body without overwhelming it promotes steady adaptation. Periodically reassessing progress, perhaps by evaluating how certain activities have become easier or by noting improvements in balance, can reinforce motivation while allowing room for necessary adjustments.

Just as crucial as active movement is the process of cool-down and stretching, which helps the body transition smoothly from exertion back to rest. During these brief intervals of lower intensity, circulation remains elevated, carrying oxygen and nutrients throughout fatigued muscles and aiding recovery. Light stretching further alleviates tension, easing the tightness that can accumulate during workout sessions and everyday tasks. Over time, these understated yet essential practices contribute to a greater sense of comfort and fluidity, permitting individuals to advance their activities incrementally rather than succumbing to stiffness or strain. By weaving a thoughtful regimen of warm-up, activity, and cool-down into the fabric of daily life, even those who have been sedentary for years can gradually rediscover a realm of strength and vitality that encourages deeper engagement with the world.

Cultivating a stronger body in later years often involves weaving strength exercises into a more encompassing health strategy. Through deliberate, measured effort, the muscles and bones adapt, developing a capacity to support everyday movements with reduced strain. These improvements do not appear overnight; rather, they grow from a commitment to progression, where small increases in resistance or repetitions accumulate over time into considerable gains. Such developments extend beyond mere physical prowess, as the steady discipline of lifting weights or using one's own body mass as resistance also nurtures mental endurance. By confronting incremental challenges in a supportive environment, individuals discover renewed confidence in their capabilities, which can spill over into diverse facets of daily life. Familiar tasks become easier, and an improved sense of self-efficacy emerges, transforming the perception of aging from one of declining potential to one of continued growth.

In this context, flexibility work rises as a complementary pillar, ensuring that newfound strength is harmonized with range of motion and graceful movement. A dynamic interplay of tension and release through stretching helps alleviate everyday stiffness, preparing joints and connective tissues for both low-impact motion and more demanding exertions. Over time, sustained effort to elongate and relax muscles guards against the gradual tightening that often accompanies an increasingly sedentary lifestyle. The benefits include enhanced posture and balance, which not only reduce the likelihood of falls but also project an appearance of vitality and poise. Some individuals, particularly those unfamiliar with structured stretching, find it helpful to begin with simple routines that target major muscle groups in the shoulders, hips, and lower back. From there, one can explore mindfulness-based approaches, such as slow-flow movement or guided breathwork, to deepen the mind-body connection and foster a sense of serenity.

Cardiovascular fitness, closely intertwined with overall well-being, deserves equal attention. Even short sessions of moderate-intensity activities, undertaken regularly, can have a profound effect on heart health and metabolic function. For those concerned about joint stress, water-based exercises or gentle cycling can serve as suitable alternatives that lighten the load on sensitive areas. Meanwhile, individuals with more stamina may enjoy brisk walking, jogging, or a rhythmic dance practice that keeps the body in steady motion. By adjusting pace and frequency to align with personal comfort and current ability, it is possible to cultivate a routine that elevates energy levels without overwhelming the body's natural recovery processes. As the lungs and heart grow more efficient, this sense of vibrancy often fuels a greater desire for exploration, whether that means tackling a new hiking trail or joining a neighborhood group that meets for morning walks.

An additional layer of nuance arises when addressing the varying activity levels and health histories of older adults. Some carry the momentum of years spent engaging in physical pursuits, while others may be reintroducing themselves to exercise after a prolonged hiatus. The key lies in tailoring each routine to individual capacities and medical guidelines, recognizing that the overall aim is not to achieve a uniform performance standard but to sustain or improve functionality. Consulting a trusted healthcare provider or an experienced fitness professional can clarify any specific limitations or adjustments that might be beneficial. In this way, one's journey toward physical vitality remains both safe and deeply personal, respecting the body's wisdom and its call for attentive self-care. Over time, the consistent practice of mindful, balanced exercise habits paves the way for a future marked by autonomy, exuberance, and a profound sense of accomplishment.

Another significant factor in pursuing a vibrant lifestyle involves recognizing the social dimension of physical activity. Although exercise can be carried out independently with notable success, many find that forming or joining small groups enhances motivation and enjoyment. Perhaps it means meeting neighbors in a nearby park for walks at sunrise, gathering peers at a community center for low-impact aerobics, or organizing dance sessions in a shared space. In these contexts, camaraderie and mutual encouragement transform every workout into a communal celebration of well-being. This collective spirit can also provide a gentle layer of accountability, prompting individuals to remain faithful to their regimens even on days when personal resolve might waver. Moreover, the simple act of sharing progress or challenges contributes to a supportive environment that celebrates each milestone, however modest, in the quest for sustained health.

For many, an active social life may also converge with practical fitness choices, as volunteering in physical tasks can serve the dual purpose of contributing to the community while promoting personal vitality. Activities such as building community gardens, tidying local walking trails, or assisting in food distribution programs not only offer low to moderate levels of physical engagement but also provide the emotional fulfillment of purposeful service. This blend of altruism and exercise underscores the fact that movement is rarely an isolated effort; it can connect the individual to a network of like-minded participants, deepening a sense of belonging while establishing a more tangible reason to remain active.

In selecting the right variety of exercises, it helps to remember that variety itself can be a key ally. Alternating among different forms of training—such as gentle stretching on some days, brisk walking or swimming on others, and occasional strength-building sessions—keeps the body guessing and forestalls the stagnation that can come from repeating the same routine indefinitely. The principle of cross-training, long appreciated by athletes, applies equally to older adults. This approach offers the advantage of distributing stress across different muscle groups while ensuring that no single region of the body becomes consistently overworked. It also sustains mental engagement, since novelty wards off boredom and continually challenges coordination and balance.

Listening closely to feedback from the body remains fundamental in this ongoing process. While a mild sense of effort or muscle fatigue can be part of healthy progress, acute pain or long-lasting discomfort signals the need to adjust or scale back. Discerning between these sensations takes practice but becomes easier with experience, helping individuals proactively adapt their approach before problems escalate. Some may find it beneficial to maintain a brief exercise journal, noting each session's duration, intensity, and overall impact on energy levels or muscle soreness. Reviewing these records over time can highlight positive trends or expose patterns that call for change. Through this dynamic interchange between action and awareness, a flexible yet structured plan emerges, allowing each participant to evolve at a pace that respects the body's natural rhythms.

The role of consistency in nurturing longevity cannot be overstated. Even modest workouts, completed regularly over months and years, forge a foundation upon which future aspirations can be built. By acknowledging that transformation is incremental rather than instantaneous, one commits to a gentle but unwavering progression. This deepens the satisfaction found in every personal best, whether measured by heavier weights, longer walking distances, or the simple delight of feeling lighter on one's feet. Through patience, foresight, and a willingness to adapt, the path of steady, sustainable movement becomes a tangible means of honoring both the present moment and the potential to thrive in the future.

Cultivating a stronger body in later years often involves weaving strength exercises into a more encompassing health strategy. Through deliberate, measured effort, the muscles and bones adapt, developing a capacity to support everyday movements with reduced strain. These improvements do not appear overnight; rather, they grow from a commitment to progression, where small increases in resistance or repetitions accumulate over time into considerable gains. Such developments extend beyond mere physical prowess, as the steady discipline of lifting weights or using one's own body mass as resistance also nurtures mental endurance. By confronting incremental challenges in a supportive environment, individuals discover renewed confidence in their capabilities, which can spill over into diverse facets of daily life. Familiar tasks become easier, and an improved sense of self-efficacy emerges, transforming the perception of aging from one of declining potential to one of continued growth.

In this context, flexibility work rises as a complementary pillar, ensuring that newfound strength is harmonized with range of motion and graceful movement. A dynamic interplay of tension and release through stretching helps alleviate everyday stiffness, preparing joints and connective tissues for both low-impact motion and more demanding exertions. Over time, sustained effort to elongate and relax muscles guards against the gradual tightening that often accompanies an increasingly sedentary lifestyle. The benefits include enhanced posture and balance, which not only reduce the likelihood of falls but also project an appearance of vitality and poise. Some individuals, particularly those unfamiliar with structured stretching, find it helpful to begin with simple routines that target major muscle groups in the shoulders, hips, and lower back. From there, one can explore mindfulness-based approaches, such as slow-flow movement or guided breathwork, to deepen the mind-body connection and foster a sense of serenity.

Cardiovascular fitness, closely intertwined with overall well-being, deserves equal attention. Even short sessions of moderate-intensity activities, undertaken regularly, can have a profound effect on heart health and metabolic function. For those concerned about joint stress, water-based exercises or gentle cycling can serve as suitable alternatives that lighten the load on sensitive areas. Meanwhile, individuals with more stamina may enjoy brisk walking, jogging, or a rhythmic dance practice that keeps the body in steady motion. By adjusting pace and frequency to align with personal comfort and current ability, it is possible to cultivate a routine that elevates energy levels without overwhelming the body's natural recovery processes. As the lungs and heart grow more efficient, this sense of vibrancy often fuels a greater desire for exploration, whether that means tackling a new hiking trail or joining a neighborhood group that meets for morning walks.

An additional layer of nuance arises when addressing the varying activity levels and health histories of older adults. Some carry the momentum of years spent engaging in physical pursuits, while others may be reintroducing themselves to exercise after a prolonged hiatus. The key lies in tailoring each routine to individual capacities and medical guidelines, recognizing that the overall aim is not to achieve a uniform performance standard but to sustain or improve functionality. Consulting a trusted healthcare provider or an experienced fitness professional can clarify any specific limitations or adjustments that might be beneficial. In this way, one's journey toward physical vitality remains both safe and deeply personal, respecting the body's wisdom and its call for attentive self-care. Over time, the consistent practice of mindful, balanced exercise habits paves the way for a future marked by autonomy, exuberance, and a profound sense of accomplishment.

Another significant factor in pursuing a vibrant lifestyle involves recognizing the social dimension of physical activity. Although exercise can be carried out independently with notable success, many find that forming or joining small groups enhances motivation and enjoyment. Perhaps it means meeting neighbors in a nearby park for walks at sunrise, gathering peers at a community center for low-impact aerobics, or organizing dance sessions in a shared space. In these contexts, camaraderie and mutual encouragement transform every workout into a communal celebration of well-being. This collective spirit can also provide a gentle layer of accountability, prompting individuals to remain faithful to their regimens even on days when personal resolve might waver. Moreover, the simple act of sharing progress or challenges contributes to a supportive environment that celebrates each milestone, however modest, in the quest for sustained health.

For many, an active social life may also converge with practical fitness choices, as volunteering in physical tasks can serve the dual purpose of contributing to the community while promoting personal vitality. Activities such as building community gardens, tidying local walking trails, or assisting in food distribution programs not only offer low to moderate levels of physical engagement but also provide the emotional fulfillment of purposeful service. This blend of altruism and exercise underscores the fact that movement is rarely an isolated effort; it can connect the individual to a network of like-minded participants, deepening a sense of belonging while establishing a more tangible reason to remain active.

In selecting the right variety of exercises, it helps to remember that variety itself can be a key ally. Alternating among different forms of training—such as gentle stretching on some days, brisk walking or swimming on others, and occasional strength-building sessions—keeps the body guessing and forestalls the stagnation that can come from repeating the same routine indefinitely. The principle of cross-training, long appreciated by athletes, applies equally to older adults. This approach offers the advantage of distributing stress across different muscle groups while ensuring that no single region of the body becomes consistently overworked. It also sustains mental engagement, since novelty wards off boredom and continually challenges coordination and balance.

Listening closely to feedback from the body remains fundamental in this ongoing process. While a mild sense of effort or muscle fatigue can be part of healthy progress, acute pain or long-lasting discomfort signals the need to adjust or scale back. Discerning between these sensations takes practice but becomes easier with experience, helping individuals proactively adapt their approach before problems escalate. Some may find it beneficial to maintain a brief exercise journal, noting each session's duration, intensity, and overall impact on energy levels or muscle soreness. Reviewing these records over time can highlight positive trends or expose patterns that call for change. Through this dynamic interchange between action and awareness, a flexible yet structured plan emerges, allowing each participant to evolve at a pace that respects the body's natural rhythms.

The role of consistency in nurturing longevity cannot be overstated. Even modest workouts, completed regularly over months and years, forge a foundation upon which future aspirations can be built. By acknowledging that transformation is incremental rather than instantaneous, one commits to a gentle but unwavering progression. This deepens the satisfaction found in every personal best, whether measured by heavier weights, longer walking distances, or the simple delight of feeling lighter on one's feet. Through patience, foresight, and a willingness to adapt, the path of steady, sustainable movement becomes a tangible means of honoring both the present moment and the potential to thrive in the future.

Building upon this foundation of consistent, adaptable practice, it is equally important to recognize that exercise is only one facet of a more holistic approach to health. Nutritious eating habits, regular sleep patterns, and stress management techniques all play pivotal roles in how effectively the body responds to physical training. For individuals embracing a new fitness routine, adequate rest allows muscles to recover, while balanced meals rich in essential nutrients help replenish energy reserves and promote tissue repair. Likewise, strategies to mitigate stress—such as journaling, deep-breathing exercises, or gentle meditation—can enhance hormonal balance, reduce inflammation, and support a more resilient mind-body connection. When these elements synchronize, the momentum gained from any movement plan finds long-term stability, ensuring that the energy invested translates into enduring benefits.

This integrated view of well-being illustrates that fitness routines need not be lengthy or complicated to yield positive effects. Sometimes, short segments of stretching upon rising in the morning or a brisk stroll after lunch can provide a noticeable boost in alertness and mood. For those hesitant to engage in more formal or time-consuming workouts, incremental changes can be the starting point. Substituting a few minutes of light calisthenics for screen time, or walking part of a commute instead of driving, gradually adds up. Beyond the physical advantages, these consistent adjustments in daily habits serve as reminders of personal agency. Each small decision to move rather than remain sedentary reinforces a narrative of empowerment, cultivating a mindset that sees aging less as a decline and more as a sustained evolution of possibilities.

Adapting activities for varying levels of fitness also invites inclusivity. Some individuals may benefit from seated exercises that develop core strength and flexibility without straining joints, while others with moderate stamina might enjoy climbing gentle hills or embarking on short bike rides. A more advanced group, already accustomed to regular exercise, can challenge themselves with interval training, weight circuits, or advanced yoga flows. By considering the limitations and strengths of each participant, it becomes possible to tailor movements that are appropriately stimulating without causing undue risk. A willingness to adapt ensures that everyone, regardless of past athletic experience or health status, can find a path toward enhanced endurance and mobility.

Listening to healthcare professionals, especially if there are preexisting conditions, helps align chosen workouts with individual needs. Subtle variations in technique can ease pressure on the spine or protect vulnerable joints, and occasional screenings can track progress, verify that vital signs respond positively to increased activity, and confirm that any ongoing treatments remain effective. In many cases, healthcare providers welcome the proactive approach that involves regular movement, since such habits often support medication regimens, weight management, and emotional well-being in concert.

In the broader tapestry of daily life, these strategies pave the way toward a future that celebrates capability rather than limitation. No matter how modest or ambitious the specific goals may be, the underlying principle remains the same: each person holds a degree of power to shape their experience of aging through the choices they make every day. From the moment the alarm sounds in the morning to the last quiet thought before sleep, the body responds to kindness, diligence, and consistency. Over weeks and months, this accumulative effect of mindful movement expands the margins of what is feasible, reinforcing the notion that no door is irreversibly closed, and that the pursuit of strength is as much about cultivating hope as it is about building muscle.

Another dimension in maintaining strength and vitality involves aligning physical routines with a supportive mental framework. The discipline required to commit to regular exercise often dovetails with improved self-regulation in other areas, including healthier eating habits and more balanced emotional responses. When the mind recognizes the body's progress—be it a slight improvement in flexibility, greater ease in climbing stairs, or an uptick in energy upon waking—a sense of triumph and self-efficacy grows. This positive feedback loop can encourage adherence to broader wellness objectives, making it easier to sustain beneficial lifestyle changes over the long term. In essence, fortifying physical resilience fosters a reciprocal boost in mental resilience, underscoring that body and mind function best when mutually nurtured.

A key part of this nurturing process arises from setting realistic, purposeful milestones. Instead of measuring success by large-scale transformations, individuals can focus on smaller, attainable targets, such as maintaining a steady walking pace for a certain duration or achieving slight increases in weights lifted. These modest checkpoints can be celebrated and then periodically adjusted, serving as evidence of continuous progress. While it is natural to admire the achievements of others, personal metrics remain the most reliable compass. Everyone's baseline differs, and comparing one's pace to that of others may lead to discouragement or an unsafe desire to accelerate training. By embracing the principle of incremental advancement, each stage of progress becomes a building block for the next, reinforcing a sustainable, motivating journey rather than a fleeting burst of effort.

This perspective also clarifies that setbacks, when handled with understanding and patience, do not constitute defeat. Temporary disruptions, like minor illnesses or unexpected schedule conflicts, may interrupt a carefully established routine. Yet even during such pauses, the gains from prior workouts do not vanish overnight. Recognizing that the pursuit of better health is a continuum rather than a rigid timetable helps mitigate guilt or frustration. Once conditions improve, resuming activity at a suitable pace allows the body to regain its rhythm. This adaptable attitude extends grace to those moments when life's complexities momentarily sideline the best of intentions. By treating each interruption as a detour, not an endpoint, one preserves a sense of optimism that fuels the next round of structured movement.

In tandem with consistency, variety in exercise programs prevents both staleness and overuse of specific muscle groups. The body, much like the mind, thrives when stimulated in multiple ways. Rotating among resistance training, flexibility practice, and aerobic sessions reduces the likelihood of repetitive strain while keeping enthusiasm intact. For individuals who find traditional indoor routines uninspiring, the outdoors offers alternative forms of engagement. Trails, beaches, and public parks can become stages for walking, light jogging, or gentle calisthenics infused with fresh air and contact with nature. Shifting scenery brings a spark of novelty to exercise, while the presence of changing terrain challenges balance and coordination in beneficial ways. Many discover that these variables introduce an element of play into what might otherwise be purely mechanical repetition.

Mental engagement remains a vital ingredient in such explorations. When working out, directing attention to posture, breathing, and muscle activation can transform even the simplest exercise into a focused, meditative experience. This attentiveness offers two primary advantages: it enhances performance quality by ensuring each movement is performed with proper alignment, and it imparts a sense of presence that counters the tendency to treat exercise as a mindless task to be completed. In a broader sense, this immersion fosters a deeper appreciation for the body's abilities, reinforcing a respectful dialogue between mind and muscle. Over time, the consistent practice of mindfulness within physical activity can cultivate a lasting habit of self-awareness that spills into other parts of life, from day-to-day chores to moments of leisure.

Chapter 4: Nutrition for Longevity and Energy

Healthy eating patterns become increasingly important over time, particularly for women who may experience shifts in hormone levels and metabolic processes that influence overall well-being. Thoughtful attention to nutrients can make a measurable difference in energy levels, bone strength, and the body's capacity to recover from daily wear. For this reason, a balanced diet that emphasizes quality protein, wholesome carbohydrates, and essential vitamins and minerals becomes not just advisable, but foundational for a vibrant later phase of life.

Among the many nutritional elements to consider, calcium and vitamin D hold a place of particular significance. Over the years, the skeleton gradually loses density, and this process often accelerates during transitions such as menopause. Foods rich in calcium—milk, cheese, fortified plant-based alternatives, or leafy greens—nurture the bone matrix, helping to offset the natural decline in bone mineral content. Vitamin D, frequently acquired through sunlight exposure and certain dietary sources, furthers this process by ensuring that calcium can be absorbed and utilized effectively. When these two nutrients work in tandem, the chance of age-related fractures diminishes, allowing one to stay active and confident throughout daily activities.

Yet bone health represents only one dimension of longevity-oriented nutrition. Iron, a key component of healthy blood cells, also demands attention. While women's iron needs shift after certain life milestones, ensuring a consistent intake of this mineral assists in maintaining energy and resilience. Lean meats, legumes, and selected leafy vegetables can support hemoglobin synthesis, preventing fatigue and facilitating oxygen transport throughout the body. Pairing iron-rich foods with vitamin C sources like citrus fruits or bell peppers further enhances absorption, leveraging the synergy that exists among various dietary components.

Beyond these essential minerals, an array of vitamins plays a critical role in safeguarding the many systems at work in the maturing body. The B-complex vitamins, for instance, contribute to cellular metabolism and nervous system function. Specific varieties, such as B12, become more challenging to absorb with age, making them particularly important to monitor. By choosing lean proteins, eggs, dairy, or fortified cereals, one can reinforce cognitive clarity and maintain robust energy reserves. Antioxidants derived from colorful fruits and vegetables, including vitamins A and C, help mitigate the oxidative stress that accumulates over time, preserving cellular integrity and bolstering the immune system.

A practical approach to meal planning often begins with the mindful selection of whole, minimally processed foods, coupled with the recognition that each plate should harmoniously blend macronutrients and essential vitamins. Protein sources like fish, poultry, beans, and low-fat dairy can be complemented by whole grains to provide sustained energy. Generous servings of produce supply fiber, phytonutrients, and micronutrients without excessive calories. Thoughtful portioning of healthy fats from sources like avocados, nuts, and olive oil enhances both flavor and nutrient absorption. This gentle balance can help ward off blood sugar imbalances, reduce systemic inflammation, and cultivate a steady sense of vigor.

In tandem with the focus on core dietary components, hydration emerges as another critical factor. Water plays a role in lubricating joints, regulating body temperature, and assisting vital chemical reactions. Across seasons and lifestyles, clear signals like thirst or skin dryness offer reminders to drink enough fluids. When combined with appropriate supplementation—undertaken after careful assessment of individual needs—this holistic method lays the groundwork for a life stage that is both energized and adaptable.

Understanding how the body processes different categories of nutrients allows for more nuanced decisions about what to include in daily meals. Protein, for example, contributes significantly to tissue repair and muscle maintenance, a function that remains crucial even after the most physically demanding career phases have passed. Incorporating lean sources such as fish, poultry, beans, and low-fat dairy products not only bolsters strength but also promotes stable blood sugar. Furthermore, moderation in protein intake can prevent undue strain on the kidneys, an important consideration when balancing general wellness with specific individual factors. A measured approach—consuming sufficient amounts without excess—helps sustain vitality while minimizing potential complications.

Although carbohydrates sometimes receive criticism in certain dietary trends, their role in providing quick, accessible energy should not be overlooked. Rather than eliminating carbohydrates, one can focus on choosing those that break down more gradually, thereby offering a steady release of glucose into the bloodstream. Whole grains, nutrient-rich vegetables, and legumes fulfill this function, reducing sudden spikes and dips in energy. Pairing such foods with a bit of healthy fat or protein further tempers how quickly they are metabolized, supporting long-lasting stamina and stabilizing mood. By opting for complex varieties rather than overly refined options, it becomes easier to feel satisfied and maintain a nourishing equilibrium.

Healthy fats, found in foods such as avocados, nuts, seeds, and certain oils, also lend crucial support to many physiological processes. Beyond providing a concentrated source of calories that can aid in weight management when consumed mindfully, these lipids facilitate the absorption of fat-soluble vitamins, including A, D, E, and K. They likewise contribute to hormone synthesis, which remains a delicate balance during later years. Rather than fearing fats in general, focusing on those that demonstrate anti-inflammatory properties can protect heart health and perhaps even mitigate some age-related discomforts in the joints. Moderation remains a guiding principle, as all macronutrients have the potential to upset balance if taken in disproportionate quantities.

Committing to a pattern of mindful meal planning can further elevate the beneficial impact of a health-conscious diet. By shaping each plate to feature a vibrant selection of fruits and vegetables, thoughtful portions of lean protein, and unrefined carbohydrates, one cultivates a stable source of energy that extends through the day. This approach can be enriched by small measures of variety in color and flavor, transforming meals into opportunities for exploration and pleasure rather than rote tasks. Trying different spices and cooking methods also helps ward off dietary fatigue, ensuring that nutritious foods continue to hold appeal.

In seeking to bolster everyday energy, many find it advantageous to develop consistent eating patterns rather than relying on large, infrequent feasts. Consuming moderate-sized meals interspersed with nutrient-dense snacks can keep the metabolic fires burning steadily, preventing dramatic peaks and valleys in blood sugar. Some may benefit from breaking breakfast, lunch, and dinner into smaller segments, while others prefer a more standard framework. The optimal choice depends on personal rhythms and any underlying medical conditions. The overarching goal is to avoid extreme hunger that leads to hasty dietary choices, maintaining a sense of physical and emotional composure throughout the day.

Fluid intake, which may seem straightforward at first glance, deserves equally careful attention. Individuals who habitually drink water before thirst intensifies maintain better overall hydration, which in turn supports organ function and cognitive focus. For those who struggle to consume enough water, combining fluids with slices of fruit or mild herbal infusions can create a more enticing option. These little strategies help bridge the gap for individuals unaccustomed to drinking plain water regularly. At the same time, limiting beverages with high caffeine or sugar content can prevent the jitteriness or crashes that interfere with a balanced routine. By pairing these mindful hydration practices with a comprehensive approach to nourishment, one establishes a sturdy platform for enjoying both the simplest daily tasks and life's more demanding moments.

A balanced daily routine often calls for careful consideration of individual needs, particularly when the body undergoes subtle transitions that can alter how nutrients are absorbed or metabolized. As people embrace the idea of consistent, nourishing meals, it becomes prudent to remain attuned to the warning signs that certain vitamins or minerals might not be reaching adequate levels. For some, varying health factors or dietary restrictions may limit their ability to gain enough nutrients exclusively through food sources. Examples include complications with swallowing, chronic conditions that impede digestion, or a simple lack of appetite that can emerge at different life stages. Recognizing these challenges paves the way for sensible supplementation, chosen with professional guidance to ensure that any additional intake complements rather than replaces a wholesome diet.

When it comes to supplementation, calcium and vitamin D often stand at the forefront for those aiming to preserve bone integrity and reduce the risk of fractures. The natural decrease in estrogen, combined with other physiological changes, can accelerate bone loss unless mitigated by adequate nourishment. Rather than viewing supplements as a cure-all, however, it is often most effective to see them as part of a larger strategy that involves nutrient-rich meals, moderate weight-bearing exercise, and regular check-ins with healthcare providers. Taken in tandem, these measures encourage bone tissues to rebuild and remain robust. Similarly, iron supplements, when prescribed, can be vital for preventing anemia, but they work best when coupled with a thoughtful approach to everyday meals that supply enough complementary nutrients.

Individual variations also affect how the body interacts with dietary enhancements. Some nutrients, such as vitamin B12, become more difficult to absorb with advancing years, as stomach acid levels shift. A physician or registered dietitian may suggest specific forms of supplementation that bypass some digestive hurdles, especially for those noticing signs of fatigue, neurological changes, or low appetite. Likewise, the interplay between prescription medications and certain vitamins or minerals must be handled cautiously. By engaging in honest discussions about all substances being consumed—nutritional supplements, herbal remedies, and pharmaceuticals alike—one helps ensure safety and efficacy. This holistic mindset preserves the delicate balance on which vitality depends.

Consistently making informed food selections remains the bedrock of long-term health. Designing meals that are colorful, fresh, and based on whole foods offers the best defense against nutritional shortcomings. Vibrantly hued vegetables, such as carrots, bell peppers, and leafy greens, deliver a range of antioxidants that reinforce the body's natural defenses. Whole grains supply dietary fiber that can help regulate blood sugar and support healthy digestion. Lean proteins, carefully varied throughout the week, bolster muscle repair and immune function. To these staples, many choose to add occasional servings of fermented foods or probiotics, which nurture gut microbiota and improve nutrient absorption.

Even the ambience surrounding mealtimes can influence nutrient utilization and overall satisfaction. Sitting down to eat with minimal distractions, savoring the flavors and textures of each bite, and sharing conversation with family or friends can all enhance the digestive process by promoting relaxation. Simple gestures, such as setting an appealing table or including fragrant herbs and spices, transform mundane routines into meaningful rituals that celebrate nourishing the body. In these moments, the link between proper nourishment and emotional well-being becomes palpable: not only does mindful eating foster a sense of calm and gratitude, but it also reinforces a commitment to long-term wellness.

A key outcome of these dedicated efforts is the energy they create for everyday pursuits. Tasks like gardening, walking with friends, or even exploring new hobbies become more accessible and enjoyable when supported by a steady flow of nutrients and adequate hydration. Over time, the combination of smart meal planning, select supplementation, and conscious awareness of the body's signals helps maintain a state of equilibrium that gracefully supports continued growth and adaptation. In essence, this holistic approach cements the understanding that the food on one's plate acts as both sustenance and a source of empowerment, shaping the future with every bite.

Another dimension of a vital eating strategy focuses on how different foods can be combined to optimize their nutritional profiles. Certain vitamins require adequate dietary fat for proper absorption, such as vitamins A, D, E, and K. Pairing leafy greens with a drizzle of olive oil or enjoying roasted vegetables alongside avocado can amplify the value gained from each meal. On the flip side, many nutritional elements can either hinder or enhance each other's uptake. Phytates found in some grains and legumes may bind to minerals like iron, reducing their bioavailability, while vitamin C can promote more efficient iron absorption. Understanding this interplay allows individuals to refine their menus in ways that make each bite count, particularly for those who strive to meet specific health goals without over-relying on supplements.

Finding variety in one's diet is not merely an exercise in creativity; it addresses the practical need to supply the body with a wide range of macro- and micronutrients. Instead of sticking rigidly to a handful of standard meals, experimenting with seasonal produce and exploring recipes rooted in different global cuisines can enliven the daily routine. A shift from routine to discovery can reframe eating from a perfunctory task into a gratifying ritual, sustained by the knowledge that every new flavor or texture might bring added health benefits. Even simple modifications, like rotating different types of fish each week or switching between quinoa, brown rice, and barley, expand one's nutrient repertoire. Over time, these variations accumulate, weaving an invisible net of diverse vitamins, minerals, and essential fatty acids that fortify general well-being.

Dehydration remains an underappreciated hazard, especially for those who no longer experience thirst as acutely. The mildest form of fluid imbalance can sap energy, impede digestion, and compromise the body's ability to regulate temperature. Purposefully sipping water throughout the day, rather than waiting for pronounced thirst signals, keeps the kidneys functioning optimally and supports the transport of vital nutrients to cells. While it is possible to count ounces or liters to track fluid intake, many find that habitually carrying a reusable water container or setting recurring reminders offers a more natural way to stay hydrated. This straightforward approach helps circumvent the fatigue or mild confusion sometimes triggered by inadequate fluid levels.

In addition to water, clear broths, herbal teas, and even the moisture within fruits and vegetables such as cucumbers or melons all contribute to hydration. Unlike sugary drinks, which can spike blood glucose and encourage weight gain, these options align more consistently with a balanced approach to nutrition. When cravings for more flavorful options arise, water infused with slices of lemon or mixed berries can balance taste without undermining daily goals. Meanwhile, sweetened beverages can remain an occasional treat for special events rather than a habitual staple. By maintaining an awareness of liquid intake and its effects, individuals fortify not only their physical endurance but also mental acuity, a resource that becomes increasingly prized over time.

Yet perhaps one of the most profound benefits of thoughtful nutritional choices is the sense of empowerment they bring. As the body responds positively to well-chosen meals and regular hydration, a ripple effect can enrich multiple dimensions of life. Sleep often becomes more restorative, alleviating daytime fatigue and regulating mood. Skin may reflect the improved nourishment, and hair can regain fullness and luster. Small signs of vitality, observed in one's reflection or felt in an uplifted spirit, reaffirm the value of consistent self-care. This steady, incremental buildup of well-being amplifies the confidence to keep pursuing healthy patterns in other domains, like seeking new social connections or adding extra steps to an exercise regimen. In this way, every mindful swallow becomes part of a larger tapestry in which daily food choices translate into practical longevity, bridging the gap between fleeting mealtime pleasures and the enduring reward of sustained energy.

For those who seek a deeper level of personalization, consultations with nutrition experts or trusted medical professionals can shed light on individual requirements, guiding efforts to bolster energy and maintain robust health. In assessing dietary needs, factors such as metabolic rate, existing conditions, and personal preferences all come into play. Some people learn that they thrive on slightly higher protein intake, while others discover that they benefit from meticulous attention to sodium levels. Tailoring strategies in this manner recognizes that the body's relationship with nutrients is both universal and deeply unique. This duality acknowledges broad principles, like the importance of whole foods and hydration, while respecting that each person's body tells its own nuanced story.

Consistency in implementing new habits often leads to more pronounced, longer-lasting results. Rather than drastically overhauling one's entire eating pattern overnight, it can be more effective to introduce small but meaningful adjustments. For instance, replacing late-evening snacks with herbal tea or trading refined grains for complex alternatives might feel less overwhelming while still producing significant improvements over time. Such incremental shifts not only ease the transition into healthier living but also allow the body and mind to adapt at a sustainable pace. This method reduces the strain of abrupt changes and diminishes the temptation to revert to less beneficial patterns.

In this framework of gradual adaptation, meal timing can influence how nutrients are processed and how energy is distributed across the day. Some find that a hearty yet balanced breakfast lays a solid foundation for the hours that follow, particularly when it includes protein and fiber. Others prefer a lighter morning meal, favoring a more substantial lunch. Listening to internal cues, such as hunger patterns and fluctuations in alertness, can help tailor meal frequency and size. No one schedule suits everyone, and the art lies in harmonizing external obligations with internal rhythms. Over time, this alignment fosters a balanced flow of vitality, minimizing mid-afternoon slumps or late-evening restlessness.

Emotional well-being remains intimately tied to nourishing choices. Beyond providing raw materials for the physical body, food can affect neurotransmitter production and hormone regulation. Ingredients rich in omega-3 fatty acids, for instance, have been linked to improved mood stability, reflecting the brain's reliance on the quality of one's diet. Similarly, magnesium, found in foods like nuts, legumes, and whole grains, participates in many chemical reactions that help manage stress responses. In the broader sense, savoring mealtimes as a moment of calm, or a chance to connect socially, adds another layer of emotional and mental support. By prioritizing the deliberate preparation and enjoyment of food, individuals create pockets of rest and reflection that shield them from life's frantic pace.

Over the years, the body tends to be more vocal about deficiencies or imbalances, often conveying these signals through persistent fatigue, aches, or unexpected changes in appetite. Learning to distinguish these messages and respond quickly reduces the risk of compounding minor issues into major health concerns. Working hand in hand with medical professionals, one can track relevant biomarkers—such as cholesterol levels, bone density, or blood glucose—to confirm that dietary measures align with overall wellness targets. This proactive attitude frames nutrition not as a restrictive endeavor but as a dynamic, ever-evolving practice. When balanced skillfully, these efforts produce a gratifying sense of self-reliance: the conviction that every morsel can either reinforce or undermine one's quest for lasting energy and well-being.

In the pursuit of longevity, food becomes both fuel and symbol. It testifies to a respect for the body's complexity and a willingness to value self-care as an integral part of daily life. As these principles become ingrained, nourishing meals take on an element of ritual, punctuating the day with moments of awareness. Far from constraining appetites or imposing joyless menus, the ultimate goal lies in discovering, and then maintaining, the equilibrium that best matches each person's unique constitution and aspirations. Over time, this approach establishes an unshakeable foundation for graceful aging, allowing individuals to nurture not only their bodies but also the passions and relationships that bring life its greatest fulfillment.

Exploring the culinary traditions of various cultures can further inspire a sense of discovery and pleasure in day-to-day eating.

New recipes and flavor combinations often introduce beneficial ingredients that might otherwise be overlooked. One might experiment with lentil stews rich in spices known for their anti-inflammatory properties, or sample stir-fries that incorporate cruciferous vegetables and mushrooms, thereby delivering a potent blend of antioxidants. In this way, every mealtime becomes a small journey of self-education, revealing that the realm of nutrition is as vast and evolving as any subject worthy of lifelong study. By approaching the table with curiosity, people find themselves less tempted by monotony, more open to diverse nutrients, and better equipped to meet their body's changing demands.

Seasonal shifts offer an opportune moment to adapt cooking and shopping habits. Warmer months might highlight lighter, water-dense fruits and vegetables, while cooler weather lends itself to hearty soups and roasted root produce. Aligning meals with the rhythm of nature not only supports local farmers but also ensures that ingredients are at their peak freshness, carrying optimal flavor and nutritional content. As these foods rotate through the year, the palate remains stimulated, and a broad spectrum of vitamins and minerals naturally finds its way into the diet. This synergy between personal health and the environment underscores a more holistic perspective: humans, plants, and the changing seasons are interconnected, each influencing the well-being of the others in subtle yet significant ways.

Techniques for preserving nutrients in the cooking process, such as steaming or sautéing with minimal oil, can further refine the impact of one's menu. While boiling certain vegetables for extended periods may leach away essential vitamins, gentler methods help retain their natural color, taste, and nutritional density. It is not necessary to overhaul cherished culinary traditions; small adjustments, like reducing cooking times or incorporating raw salads more frequently, can suffice. Whether seeking a crunchier bite or a softer, comforting consistency, there is a strategy to respect both taste preferences and nutrient retention.

For those who face dietary restrictions, whether from allergies, intolerances, or personal convictions, it can be helpful to consult a knowledgeable dietitian to confirm that meals remain balanced. Substituting cow's milk with fortified plant-based alternatives, replacing wheat-based staples with gluten-free grains, or selecting vegetarian protein sources like tofu or tempeh demands an understanding of how each choice may alter the balance of micronutrients. While these substitutions can open new avenues of flavor, they sometimes bring the risk of overlooking certain vitamins or minerals if not carefully planned. In the end, the overarching goal is to maintain variety and balance, ensuring that any dietary plan is both nourishing and sustainable for the individual.

Over time, a pattern emerges: thoughtfully considered meals become an act of daily self-respect. Rather than succumbing to purely convenient options, prioritizing nourishment reflects the value placed on health, independence, and longevity. This mindset does not imply an aversion to occasional indulgences. Enjoying a sweet dessert or a favorite comfort dish can evoke satisfaction, especially when woven into a broader framework of conscious choices. By maintaining perspective—acknowledging that moderation in treats complements a generally nutrient-rich diet—individuals avoid the guilt or rigid rules that sometimes overshadow the pleasure of eating. Through a balanced lens, one sees that each plate holds the potential not only to satisfy hunger but also to uplift the spirit, thereby contributing to a more resilient, energized experience of life.

Though the points covered so far provide a substantial overview of why nutrition stands as a cornerstone of health and longevity, there remains value in reinforcing and expanding upon the most critical threads of this discussion. Whenever one reflects on the profound link between food intake and physical resilience, the human body emerges as a remarkable instrument—capable of adapting, healing, and flourishing when given the right care. In later phases of life, that adaptability may seem more measured, yet its potential remains extraordinary, and a wholesome eating pattern can serve as the bridge connecting present well-being with future vitality.

At the heart of this bridge is awareness. By cultivating a habit of observing how certain foods affect energy levels, digestion, and mood, individuals become better able to tailor their choices. If certain meals induce discomfort or persistent fatigue, those observations can guide subtle changes: perhaps adjusting portion sizes, incorporating gentler cooking methods, or swapping out ingredients that trigger negative reactions. Over time, this dialogue between body and mind refines culinary decisions, yielding an intuitive sense of what truly nourishes. Such fine-tuning goes beyond rote rules, allowing for an accommodating, personalized approach that can integrate traditions, preferences, and specific health considerations.

From a medical standpoint, the significance of proactive measures cannot be overstated. Factors like insulin sensitivity, cardiovascular health, and immune system robustness do not shift abruptly but develop over years of either beneficial or detrimental influences. Consistent attention to nutrient intake helps ensure that small but favorable steps accumulate into larger, sustained benefits. Aligning dietary habits with regular health screenings or blood tests further cements a systematic way to verify that the body's inner workings remain balanced. Within this framework, even modest reductions in processed sugars or an increase in leafy greens can deliver tangible improvements over time, showcasing how thoughtful restraint and timely additions forge resilience from within.

While these considerations might appear detailed or even taxing at first glance, they often form a foundation that makes the rest of life more manageable and enriching. By fueling oneself with nutrient-dense foods, one experiences steadier energy and a heightened ability to engage in the pursuits that bring meaning— be that physical activity, social events, or intellectual challenges. This quality of engagement extends beyond personal benefit, as energetic participation in community or family life fosters unity and inspiration for others. A strong mind and body can serve as a beacon for friends or loved ones who look to more experienced individuals for guidance on balanced living, further reinforcing a constructive cycle of mutual support.

None of this implies that each meal must be measured, scrutinized, or devoid of pleasure. Rather, it emphasizes that harmony, grounded in knowledge and self-awareness, consistently outperforms extreme tactics. Overly rigid diets often become unsustainable, whereas a flexible but informed strategy fosters adherence and joy. Sharing a nutritious dish that has been meticulously prepared, experimenting with new recipes for the sheer delight of discovery, and savoring fresh produce during its peak season all enrich the connection between food and life's many milestones. In these simple yet profound acts, one recognizes nourishment not as a chore but as an art and a gift.

This broader philosophy does not discount the challenges that may arise. Changing habits requires patience, openness to trial and error, and a willingness to celebrate small successes instead of fixating on any setbacks. Over time, these minor triumphs gather momentum, gently reshaping patterns until they coalesce into a lifestyle that feels less like a conscious effort and more like a natural extension of one's deepest values. Embracing nutrition as a lifelong companion—rather than a fleeting objective— validates the reality that health and longevity stem from a series of thoughtful choices made moment by moment. By honoring the body's needs and applauding its capacity to adapt, individuals light the path ahead, ensuring that future years unfold with resilience, optimism, and the buoyant energy necessary to savor every discovery.

Preventative healthcare is rooted in the principle that safeguarding one's well-being before disease takes hold offers immeasurable benefits for both individuals and society at large. By striving to catch potential concerns early, it becomes possible to address underlying risk factors that might otherwise manifest as complex medical problems. Through consistent attention to overall health, people experience improved quality of life, reduced healthcare expenses, and a more active role in their own physical and mental maintenance. Many medical professionals emphasize the benefits of regular visits to a practitioner not only for diagnosing ailments, but also for offering guidance on how to enhance everyday habits and mitigate future complications. These checkups can reveal subtle indicators that may precede the onset of conditions such as hypertension, diabetes, or other chronic diseases that silently develop over time. Even with the most conscientious efforts to maintain healthy routines, there is simply no substitute for timely examinations and personalized advice from a knowledgeable clinician.

In seeking early detection, individuals safeguard both themselves and their loved ones. By taking advantage of periodic screenings recommended by healthcare experts, it becomes easier to pinpoint shifts in bodily function, vitamin levels, and specific biomarkers that can suggest the need for targeted interventions. This vigilance fosters an environment in which medical conditions are identified promptly, often at a stage when treatments or lifestyle adjustments prove far more effective. Moreover, establishing a close relationship with healthcare providers allows for ongoing conversations about risk factors unique to each patient, enabling personalized strategies for mitigating negative outcomes. Such proactive measures translate to fewer hospital visits, decreased financial strain, and a heightened awareness that extends beyond clinical settings, ultimately creating lasting improvements in overall well-being.

When chronic conditions do arise, consistent management and attentive monitoring are essential for preventing serious complications. Rather than waiting for acute symptoms to escalate, individuals benefit from following detailed plans that incorporate medication, structured exercise, nutritional guidelines, and stress reduction techniques designed to stabilize long-term health. Effective management often requires cooperation among multiple healthcare professionals, including primary care doctors, specialists, nutritionists, and mental health counselors, ensuring that every facet of a patient's well-being is given due consideration. By addressing the emotional impact of chronic illness alongside its physical manifestations, people can develop coping strategies that transform daunting diagnoses into manageable parts of a balanced life. This holistic perspective not only boosts compliance with treatment regimens but also enhances self-esteem and motivation to maintain positive changes.

In addition to mainstream medical approaches, many have found value in exploring methods that complement conventional therapies. By incorporating practices like acupuncture, meditation, or specialized dietary choices, patients cultivate a more comprehensive strategy for sustaining overall health. Such integrative tactics acknowledge the connection between mind and body, aiming to support the individual as a unified whole rather than treating disparate symptoms in isolation. This broader scope inspires greater ownership of personal well-being, encouraging a continued commitment to nurturing the body, mind, and spirit in the quest for optimal health and longevity.

Chapter 5: Prioritizing Preventative Healthcare

These complementary methods, when thoughtfully integrated with conventional medical care, can help individuals gain a deeper appreciation of their bodies' innate capacities for healing and resilience. Patients who explore these avenues often cultivate a sense of harmony between physical and emotional well-being, reinforcing the idea that health maintenance can be a fluid, dynamic process rather than a rigid set of guidelines. At the same time, it remains vital to distinguish credible sources of holistic guidance from questionable or unverified practices. Collaborating with trained, licensed professionals and discussing all potential treatments with primary care providers can prevent misunderstandings or adverse reactions, ensuring safety while still welcoming innovative perspectives.

Beyond clinical appointments and alternative interventions, maintaining wellness depends heavily on personal responsibility and day-to-day diligence. The accessibility of technology has allowed countless individuals to track data such as heart rate, blood glucose levels, and sleep patterns, granting unprecedented insight into the body's rhythms. With the help of wearable devices and smartphone applications, people can observe subtle changes in their physiology, identify triggers that may exacerbate existing conditions, and refine lifestyle choices accordingly. Though technology alone cannot replace the expertise of healthcare professionals, it can inspire a sense of autonomy, motivating users to ask more informed questions during office visits and feel more engaged in their overall care.

Stress management, often overlooked in discussions of preventive measures, plays a crucial role in mitigating chronic disease risk and enhancing daily well-being. Pervasive stress contributes to hormonal imbalances, weakened immune responses, and a heightened vulnerability to anxiety and depression, all of which can shape a person's physical health over time. Incorporating stress-reduction techniques, such as mindfulness, deep breathing exercises, or even structured journaling, provides a constructive outlet for emotional tension. This approach works particularly well when combined with a supportive environment, whether that means professional counseling or simply an open dialogue with family and friends. Recognizing that mental and physical health are inexorably linked underscores the value of comprehensive self-care plans that address the whole person rather than individual symptoms.

Those facing chronic illnesses often discover that a multi-pronged strategy yields the greatest benefits. For instance, a patient diagnosed with diabetes might rely on medication while simultaneously embracing nutrition education to manage blood sugar levels effectively. In tandem with these interventions, stress management techniques can help stabilize hormonal fluctuations that can exacerbate metabolic disorders. This synergy illustrates why a blend of evidence-based medicine, informed lifestyle modification, and thoughtful exploration of holistic methods can yield results that may surpass those of a strictly conventional or purely alternative approach. By acknowledging the interdependence of different facets of health, individuals have a wider toolkit at their disposal, enabling them to adapt and refine their regimens as their conditions or needs evolve.

Ultimately, the unifying principle behind all preventive strategies is consistency. Lasting benefits come from steady, incremental actions that accumulate over weeks, months, and years. By observing warning signs, consulting trusted professionals, maintaining open lines of communication, and embracing a broad perspective on what constitutes health, people can fortify their defenses against disease while enjoying a fuller, more satisfying experience of life as they move forward.

Another crucial element of preventative healthcare involves fostering a supportive social network that encourages healthy behaviors and facilitates the sharing of resources and knowledge. Individuals who participate in community groups, volunteer organizations, or local fitness classes often report enhanced motivation and a stronger sense of accountability. By interacting with others who share similar goals or challenges, people gain both camaraderie and inspiration. Even brief conversations with neighbors about healthy meal ideas or exercise routines can spark renewed commitment to self-care, demonstrating that prevention is not a solitary pursuit but rather a collective effort driven by shared values and mutual encouragement. These interactions can also function as opportunities to discuss potential misconceptions, compare personal experiences, and refine one's understanding of best practices based on diverse perspectives.

Furthermore, as lifestyles become busier and more technologically reliant, it is essential to strike a balance between digital convenience and the necessity for periodic in-person evaluations. Telemedicine has ushered in new possibilities, allowing patients to consult healthcare providers remotely for routine checkups or follow-up appointments. This can be particularly beneficial for those living in remote areas or individuals with mobility challenges, ensuring that critical medical guidance is not hindered by physical distance or logistical barriers. However, there remain certain aspects of preventive care—such as hands-on examination, detailed diagnostic imaging, or specialized lab work—that are best conducted within a professional healthcare setting. By combining virtual tools with traditional visits, patients can maximize the benefits of both approaches, staying engaged with medical advice while still receiving direct, thorough assessments as needed.

In many instances, the partnership between patient and healthcare provider can be likened to a long-term collaboration in which both parties continually exchange information and adapt strategies. This collaboration may extend beyond the doctor's office to include pharmacists, physical therapists, and even family members, underscoring the interconnected nature of preventive health. A balanced approach might involve regular phone or video check-ins with a healthcare practitioner to review medication regimens and discuss improvements in daily routines. Meanwhile, face-to-face appointments can be scheduled at intervals recommended by professional guidelines or prompted by evolving symptoms. By merging convenience, practical oversight, and timely intervention, individuals gain more consistent access to the support structures that make a substantial difference in long-term health outcomes.

Incorporating mindfulness into preventative healthcare strategies also encourages a deepened connection to one's own body and emotional states. Paying close attention to physical sensations can help detect warning signs that might otherwise go unnoticed. Increased self-awareness often acts as a catalyst for immediate adjustments in routine, such as modifying meal choices, adjusting sleep schedules, or seeking professional advice at the onset of discomfort. Mindful eating, for example, encourages individuals to slow down, savor each bite, and tune into cues of fullness or indigestion, thereby preventing the habitual overconsumption that can lead to weight gain or other metabolic imbalances. Similarly, mindful exercise routines can reduce the likelihood of injury by emphasizing proper form, measured pacing, and gentle progression rather than quick, excessive exertion.

Moreover, effective preventive measures require an ongoing willingness to reevaluate and refine established habits. As individuals move through different stages of life, what worked in the past may become insufficient or inappropriate for new physiological realities. A child's active schedule might naturally support cardiovascular health and bone density, but as an adult, those benefits might wane without dedicated exercise routines. By consciously adjusting physical activities and nutritional intake to reflect changing needs, individuals can sustain a proactive mindset, ensuring that each choice aligns with evolving goals and circumstances. This continual reassessment applies equally to mental health: stressors in adolescence differ from those encountered in middle age, necessitating flexibility in coping strategies to maintain emotional equilibrium over time.

Cultivating a balanced diet is a cornerstone of preventive care, but nutritional needs can shift dramatically depending on one's stage of life, underlying medical conditions, and personal preferences. Children might benefit from diets rich in proteins and essential nutrients to support growth, while older adults often require an emphasis on calcium, vitamin D, and fiber to counteract age-related changes in bone density and digestion. For those managing chronic illnesses, certain dietary adjustments—such as reducing sodium intake for hypertension or monitoring carbohydrate consumption for diabetes—can substantially influence clinical outcomes. Working with knowledgeable professionals, including registered dietitians, ensures that individualized plans account for both medical requirements and personal tastes. This personalized approach increases the likelihood of long-term adherence, enhancing overall effectiveness in disease prevention and management.

Regular movement and exercise also figure prominently in the daily effort to stave off disease. Physical activity supports cardiovascular health, bolsters immune function, and helps maintain a healthy weight. While strenuous workouts may appeal to some, others might find equal benefit in walking, yoga, swimming, or dancing—activities that promote flexibility, endurance, and balance. The key lies in consistency and proper alignment with one's abilities, environment, and personal interests. By setting realistic goals and seeking incremental improvements rather than dramatic, short-lived efforts, individuals often discover a more enjoyable path toward sustained physical fitness. In conjunction with a well-rounded diet, this focus on daily movement forms an integral part of the foundation for long-term wellness.

Another vital dimension of preventive healthcare involves remaining informed about emerging research, as medical recommendations evolve alongside new scientific insights. Over time, the best practices for addressing certain conditions or risk factors may shift, highlighting the importance of keeping an open mind and adapting existing routines when evidence suggests it is prudent to do so. By remaining engaged with trusted health resources, individuals can glean valuable knowledge about novel screening methods, updated guidelines for immunizations, or the availability of advanced diagnostic tools. This commitment to continuous learning fosters a proactive stance that underpins effective preventative strategies at every turn.

For many people, prioritizing mental health is also essential when striving for a comprehensive approach to prevention.

Psychological well-being profoundly influences physical health, and emotional distress can manifest as fatigue, disrupted sleep, or diminished motivation to maintain healthy routines. Therapy, counseling, and support groups each serve as potential avenues for addressing emotional challenges that might otherwise impede preventive efforts. Even within social circles, frank conversations about stress, burnout, or interpersonal difficulties can help individuals navigate their lives more constructively, reducing the likelihood of prolonged isolation or overlooked warning signs. By giving mental health the same level of attention as physical health, people open themselves to meaningful growth, reduced anxiety, and improved resilience—all of which contribute to a more holistic perspective on wellbeing.

In this broader picture, holistic and alternative approaches to health can serve as valuable adjuncts. Many find that practices such as massage therapy, herbal medicine, or tai chi provide not only physical relief from tension or discomfort but also a deeper, more mindful engagement with the body's signals. Taken together with conventional medical care, these additional options supply a flexible array of choices that allow individuals to craft a strategy reflecting their unique beliefs, goals, and circumstances. Safety remains paramount, so it is advisable to conduct thorough research, seek recommendations from reputable practitioners, and keep an open dialogue with conventional healthcare providers to avoid harmful interactions. This integrative mindset underscores the principle that preventive healthcare need not be rigid or one-dimensional; rather, it can be a fluid, evolving journey that aligns with each person's specific needs and aspirations.

Family history also plays a significant role in shaping preventive healthcare strategies. Individuals with a genetic predisposition to certain illnesses, such as breast cancer or heart disease, benefit greatly from early and more frequent screenings that account for inherited risk factors. By understanding which ailments might pose a greater threat, it becomes possible to focus resources where they are most needed, whether that entails specialized testing, increased surveillance, or discussions with genetic counselors about the viability of advanced diagnostic techniques. This proactive approach empowers individuals to make informed decisions about lifestyle adjustments and medical interventions, enhancing the likelihood of catching issues in their earliest stages. Knowledge, in this sense, truly is power, transforming what could otherwise be an unknown peril into a manageable concern addressed through targeted measures and careful monitoring.

Emotional well-being remains deeply intertwined with these preventive measures, since fear or anxiety about potential diagnoses can sometimes cause people to avoid regular checkups, screenings, or other medical appointments. Encouraging open dialogue about such fears and ensuring that individuals feel supported and informed can lessen the stigma or apprehension associated with receiving healthcare. A compassionate approach from medical professionals, along with reassurance that early detection is a life-saving tool rather than a source of dread, can help patients adopt a more confident attitude toward preventative practices. Moreover, community education initiatives or local support networks can demystify complex medical processes, providing tangible examples of individuals who have navigated comparable situations. In sharing experiences and emotions, patients and their loved ones can nurture hope and resilience, diminishing the sense of isolation that often accompanies medical uncertainties.

When managing chronic conditions, adopting a mindset of prevention goes beyond simply taking prescribed medications on schedule. For instance, individuals with asthma might implement specific environmental adjustments to reduce exposure to allergens or irritants, invest in air filtration systems, or incorporate targeted breathing exercises that help fortify lung capacity over time. Those with autoimmune disorders can emphasize stress management, nutritionally balanced diets, and careful pacing of activities to minimize inflammatory flare-ups. The same principle applies to conditions like arthritis, where gentle movement and exercise, complemented by any required medication, can deter the progression of joint damage while improving daily comfort. Such a multifaceted approach places individuals in the driver's seat of their healthcare, urging them to remain vigilant for minor shifts in their symptoms and to proactively communicate any changes to their care team. This vigilant, engaged posture not only enhances the efficacy of treatments but also fosters a sense of empowerment and optimism that can positively influence the day-to-day experiences of living with chronic illness.

In tandem with mainstream preventative measures, many have found that complementary therapies instill a sense of balance and calm during otherwise taxing periods of medical intervention. This might entail journaling about symptoms, practicing restorative yoga to maintain strength and flexibility, or employing stress-relief techniques such as progressive muscle relaxation and visualization. These modalities invite individuals to take an active part in their personal journey toward improved well-being, transforming what might otherwise be a purely clinical framework into a more holistic and sustainable lifestyle. By valuing the input from various fields of knowledge—ranging from modern scientific research to centuries-old traditions—people who embrace these techniques can develop layered, effective prevention strategies that function harmoniously alongside the latest medical advancements.

An equally important dimension of maintaining a proactive stance lies in the realm of community resources and public health programs. Many local and national organizations provide free or low-cost screenings, informational workshops, and initiatives designed to raise awareness about common medical conditions. These efforts often target underserved populations or neighborhoods where access to primary care may be limited, reducing disparities in healthcare outcomes. By taking advantage of such programs, individuals broaden their support network and gain practical insights that might otherwise be overlooked, such as the significance of regular blood pressure checks or how to interpret basic lab results. Public health campaigns focusing on smoking cessation or early cancer detection can further amplify these messages, uniting society around the aim of thwarting preventable diseases before they escalate into crises.

In shaping a long-term strategy for better health, one must also acknowledge that success hinges on adapting to cultural, familial, and personal contexts. Where some traditions celebrate communal meal preparation, others might feature individually sourced diets that cater to varied schedules or geographic realities. Likewise, living arrangements and family roles can either hinder or bolster preventative efforts, depending on the level of cooperation and shared understanding among household members. Aligning health goals with cultural values—perhaps by modifying inherited recipes to include more nutrient-dense ingredients or timing medical appointments to accommodate extended family gatherings—helps integrate prevention seamlessly into daily life. When individuals can appreciate how these measures align with their own heritage and worldview, they are more likely to embrace them with enthusiasm and consistency.

While the goal of prevention is to avert illness, it is also a means of enriching life as a whole, as it highlights the importance of continual growth in self-awareness, community engagement, and purposeful decision-making. The potential benefits extend well beyond the physical, encompassing enhanced emotional stability, economic security through reduced medical costs, and the sheer peace of mind that comes from being prepared. For healthcare practitioners, prevention represents a guiding ethos that resonates with the fundamental desire to serve patients in the most effective way possible, turning every routine checkup into an opportunity for early detection, education, and empathy.

Meanwhile, for those who have already encountered significant health challenges, adopting a preventive perspective can prompt a renewed sense of hope and determination. Instead of viewing illness as merely an obstacle, it can become a catalyst for lifestyle changes that empower individuals to safeguard the health they still possess. Care teams can deliver resources to facilitate these transformations, from educational materials about nutrient composition to counseling services that address the emotional toll of chronic conditions. By framing health crises as moments for reflection and recalibration, patients often discover a resilience and clarity of purpose that carries forward long after acute treatment has concluded.

Ensuring that preventive philosophies remain grounded in reality requires continual reflection on environmental factors, technological advances, and shifts in cultural norms. In regions where pollution or water contamination poses serious threats, community-level interventions may be as critical as personal vigilance. Similarly, widespread use of mobile health applications and telemedicine requires thoughtful regulatory frameworks and training programs that help users evaluate the reliability of online information. Balancing these modern developments with age-old wisdom remains an ongoing dialogue, one fueled by curiosity, scientific rigor, and a collective aspiration to create environments where optimal health can flourish.

Striking a balance between personal accountability and external support remains a defining principle of this holistic, preventive outlook. Even the most conscientious individuals may encounter obstacles—workplace stress, sudden life changes, or economic constraints that limit access to nutritious food—and these factors can complicate efforts to maintain consistent health practices. When adversity arises, it is beneficial to remain adaptable and seek resources that can lighten the burden, such as local support groups, counseling services, or government assistance programs that provide nutritional subsidies. Each of these avenues is a reminder that prevention, while deeply personal, also flourishes in environments where communal frameworks uplift those who are vulnerable or struggling.

Moreover, genuine commitment to prevention calls for measured self-reflection and a willingness to make course corrections when necessary. At times, rigid adherence to a single approach can lead to frustration or burnout, especially if it fails to produce the anticipated results. Instead, recognizing that health is dynamic—and thereby welcoming diverse strategies—enables individuals to pivot gracefully, adopting new techniques that better suit their changing needs. This could mean modifying an exercise routine to accommodate an injury, exploring a different dietary philosophy that better aligns with cultural or ethical values, or adjusting therapeutic interventions to reflect new research findings. By approaching prevention as an ongoing, evolving endeavor, people can avoid becoming discouraged by setbacks and instead focus on the incremental gains that accrue over a lifetime of active engagement.

Collaboration and compassion extend beyond individual interests, influencing broader societal goals as well. When communities champion prevention, they often observe declines in healthcare costs, fewer missed workdays, and stronger educational outcomes for children who grow up with robust support systems. School-based initiatives that promote routine dental checkups, vision screenings, or mental health assessments can profoundly affect a child's development, fueling positive behaviors and academic achievements that carry forward into adulthood. On a larger scale, government policies that incentivize healthcare providers to prioritize preventive measures foster a healthier population overall, underscoring the interplay between individual responsibility and institutional involvement. In these instances, the synergy between personal effort and public infrastructure serves as a testament to the far-reaching power of prioritizing health at every level.

In the end, true prevention is not about rigidly checking off a list of duties or living in perpetual fear of disease, but rather about embracing a forward-thinking mindset that empowers people to remain vigilant, resourceful, and resilient. It is grounded in mutual trust between patients and practitioners, nurtured by transparent communication and honest reflection, and strengthened by open-minded curiosity about the myriad tools at our disposal—whether they originate in cutting-edge research labs or have been passed down through generations of holistic traditions. By understanding that health is an interconnected tapestry, individuals learn to take greater responsibility for themselves while acknowledging the role of the communities and systems that surround them. These cumulative efforts yield benefits that ripple outward, illuminating the path for a future in which fewer preventable conditions escalate into critical emergencies, and where more people can enjoy the freedom, confidence, and vitality that come from anticipating potential pitfalls and taking decisive action before they arrive.

Chapter 6: Mental Health and Cognitive Wellness

The human mind, in all its complexity, shapes not only how individuals perceive the world, but also how they respond to life's challenges and opportunities. Even the most resilient person can find it difficult at times to maintain clarity and poise in a society marked by relentless demands on time and energy. By cultivating a deeper understanding of mental well-being, people equip themselves with strategies to nurture cognitive function, manage psychological pressures, and explore deeper states of self-awareness. Protecting the mind's health is an integral component of a comprehensive approach to overall vitality, serving as a bridge between emotional stability, physical wellness, and the ability to navigate life's transitions with greater confidence.

Central to sustaining a sharp intellect is an appreciation for lifelong learning, which can be approached in a variety of ways. Whether one prefers in-depth academic pursuits, reading novels of different genres, or immersing themselves in creative hobbies, engaging in mental exercises challenges the brain to form new connections and adapt to evolving demands. It is often said that curiosity is the engine of intellectual stamina, and individuals who actively seek knowledge in their everyday activities help ensure that their minds remain agile as they age. This quest for mental sharpness may be woven into simple daily routines such as listening to informative podcasts while commuting, tackling puzzles designed to stretch problem-solving abilities, or learning the fundamentals of a foreign language through short, consistent study sessions. Such habits stimulate neuroplasticity—the brain's innate capacity to reorganize itself in response to novel experiences—thereby promoting cognitive resilience that can endure well into later life.

Another aspect of nurturing mental acuity is the deliberate incorporation of physical activity and balanced nutrition, both of which have profound consequences for cognitive function. When individuals engage in regular exercise, they encourage healthy blood flow to the brain, which in turn supports the growth of new neurons and the maintenance of existing neural pathways. Even moderate workouts, such as brisk walking or gentle stretching routines, can be beneficial in boosting concentration and mood. Nutrition plays a similarly vital role, as diets laden with essential vitamins, antioxidants, and omega-3 fatty acids foster optimal brain function, while excessive sugar, unhealthy fats, and ultra-processed foods have been associated with cognitive decline over time. A consistent routine of physical exercise and a diet rooted in nutrient-rich foods serve as tangible investments in preserving long-term mental acuity.

Social engagement has also been identified as a key factor in preserving cognitive vitality. Opportunities to connect with friends and family, participate in community events, or join interest-based clubs stimulate the mind in ways that solitary exercises cannot. Through these interactions, people exchange ideas, confront different perspectives, and practice conversational skills that help the brain remain attuned to the nuanced realities of human relationships. Friendships and social ties encourage empathy, which further refines mental sharpness by teaching individuals to attune themselves to emotional cues. In turn, practicing empathy fosters deeper emotional intelligence, contributing to an enhanced understanding of the self as well. By maintaining an active social life, the mind is consistently exposed to novel experiences, which supports mental flexibility and the capacity to adapt.

Despite one's best efforts to maintain a vibrant outlook and engage in stimulating activities, psychological distress remains a common experience, often influenced by the relentless pressures of modern living. Stress manifests in various ways, such as tension headaches, chronic fatigue, irritability, or disrupted sleep. Left unchecked, it can escalate and predispose individuals to more serious mental health concerns. Much like physical ailments that intensify if not promptly addressed, emotional wounds require timely attention to prevent an accumulation of unresolved burdens. People who understand this dynamic often choose to be proactive in identifying sources of stress, developing healthy coping mechanisms, and enlisting the help of professionals or supportive networks when necessary.

An important part of addressing stress lies in recognizing its root causes. Sometimes the demands of the workplace, family obligations, or an overloaded schedule can create a constant state of heightened vigilance, leaving little room for relaxation or self-care. On other occasions, stress may arise from less explicit triggers, such as perfectionistic tendencies or an ingrained fear of failure that keeps the mind in a perpetual cycle of worry. By reflecting on these underlying factors, individuals increase the likelihood of implementing meaningful, lasting changes in their daily routines. This sense of awareness may prompt them to reorganize priorities, set firmer boundaries, or even explore new career paths if it becomes apparent that certain situations are no longer sustainable.

Anxiety and depression often emerge when stress lingers unresolved, or when certain predispositions—genetic or otherwise—make individuals more susceptible to emotional dysregulation. These conditions can manifest in numerous ways, including persistent feelings of dread, intrusive worries, numbness, or pronounced feelings of despair. While anxiety is often associated with a heightened sense of caution or fear that can disrupt normal functioning, depression can bring lethargy, loss of interest in previously enjoyable activities, and pervasive hopelessness. Both are significant challenges that require comprehensive approaches to management.

Many benefit from first-line interventions such as therapy or counseling, where professional guidance fosters clearer insight into unhelpful thought patterns and emotional reactions. Over time, therapeutic sessions can highlight strategies to address specific triggers, break cyclical patterns of negative thinking, or improve interpersonal relationships that may be contributing to emotional turmoil. In addition to traditional talk therapy, options like cognitive-behavioral therapy and other specialized modalities offer structured frameworks for tackling the roots of anxiety and depression. Through these focused interventions, individuals can learn to monitor and adjust responses that lead to emotional discomfort, thereby recapturing a sense of control and positivity in daily life.

Support systems within one's community play a similarly crucial role, as they provide spaces for shared understanding and collective reassurance. Group sessions or informal gatherings of peers who have faced comparable challenges can diminish isolation by emphasizing that mental health struggles are neither rare nor insurmountable. Even in the most difficult moments, simply knowing that others have successfully navigated similar emotional terrain can kindle hope. In certain cases, medical intervention via medication is recommended alongside therapy for short- or long-term symptom relief. This combined approach can yield substantial improvements in well-being, particularly when medications are taken under the close supervision of a qualified healthcare professional who can adjust prescriptions according to patient progress.

In addition to professional help, self-guided routines are increasingly recognized as a valuable complement to formal treatment. Activities like journaling, artistic expression, or physical exercise act as constructive releases for pent-up tension, enabling people to articulate their worries, channel frustration, or find solace in more serene pursuits. Regular exercise routines, whether they involve running, dancing, or swimming, provide a physiological counterbalance to the mental weight of anxiety or depression, as endorphins released during physical activities contribute to better mood regulation. Over time, these self-care practices can bolster a person's sense of inner strength, reminding them that they possess tangible ways to influence their mental state.

A further dimension of emotional well-being emerges from cultivating mindfulness and a contemplative approach to daily experiences. Taking the time to slow down and focus on the present moment helps break habitual cycles of rumination or anticipatory dread. Rather than allowing thoughts to spiral unchecked, a mindful approach invites an attitude of patient observation, which can reveal destructive patterns that perpetuate negative emotions. Through heightened awareness, individuals learn to respond to difficulties with composure, acknowledging uncomfortable feelings without letting them undermine self-worth or drive impulsive behavior. In this way, mindfulness fosters not only tranquility, but also a sturdy resilience in the face of adversity.

Many discover that meditation offers a structured way of integrating mindfulness into everyday life. In its basic form, this practice involves selecting a point of focus—often the natural rhythm of the breath—and anchoring one's attention there. Whenever the mind drifts to intrusive thoughts or sensory distractions, the practitioner gently returns focus to the present moment, thus training the brain to be more adaptable and less reactive. This discipline can be particularly beneficial for those grappling with stress, anxiety, or the lingering aftereffects of depression. By consistently devoting time to observe the flow of thoughts without judgment, individuals gain a certain detachment from their worries, freeing mental space for clarity and constructive problem-solving.

Further variations of meditation incorporate imagery or guided instructions that promote relaxation, self-compassion, or even the cultivation of empathy toward others. Some practitioners find solace in chanting or the repetition of mantras, while others favor silent meditation under the guidance of a teacher who can offer gentle corrections and encouragement. Regardless of the chosen method, a dedicated, consistent practice yields a calmer mind, better emotional regulation, and an improved sense of perspective. Even short sessions—perhaps ten minutes in the morning and ten minutes at night—can bring measurable benefits over time, serving as an anchor in fast-paced environments.

Mindfulness can also extend beyond formal meditation. Simple tasks, such as eating a meal or taking a brief walk, become opportunities to deepen present-moment awareness. By consciously tasting every bite of food, noticing its texture and aroma, the mind refines its capacity for focused attention. Similarly, when the mind slows down enough to absorb the details of a morning stroll—the pattern of sunlight through trees, the sensation of fresh air—there is a grounding effect that helps restore equilibrium. These small daily interludes remind individuals that well-being does not only dwell in extraordinary experiences; it flourishes through the attentive appreciation of life's nuances.

Emotional resilience grows hand in hand with mindfulness. When individuals build the capacity to anchor themselves in present awareness, they also develop the skill to face difficulties without being wholly consumed by them. This ability to weather emotional storms with less turmoil and recover more rapidly from setbacks is a hallmark of robust mental health. Instead of reacting to every upset with panic or despair, emotionally resilient people establish an internal baseline of calm, preserving emotional energy for productive and constructive action. Such resilience does not shield individuals from hardships; rather, it equips them with the steady attitude needed to tackle life's uncertainties and reframe challenges as opportunities for personal growth.

At the same time, building emotional resilience goes beyond solitary practices. It demands relationships built on trust and empathy, where authenticity and open communication are welcomed. When people can share their personal struggles without fear of judgment, they strengthen their emotional support systems. Over time, communal bonds enhance resilience by offering diverse perspectives, collective wisdom, and a sense of belonging. Acts of kindness and mutual care—be it a neighbor delivering a homemade meal after a stressful week or a friend who offers an empathetic ear—reinforce the belief that no one must face psychological challenges in isolation. Cultivating a network of compassionate connections is as vital to mental health as any individual technique or coping mechanism.

As the quest to maintain cognitive sharpness unfolds, the interplay between regular mental stimulation and emotional stability becomes increasingly clear. A preoccupied mind weighed down by worry has limited bandwidth to delve into new ideas or refine existing knowledge. Conversely, an engaged intellect can lend structure and inspiration to the pursuit of well-being, fueling curiosity about innovative mental health techniques and the desire to refine coping strategies. In this sense, strategies such as learning new skills, reading diverse material, or engaging in thought-provoking discussions also serve as indirect methods of stress relief, providing alternate focal points when everyday anxieties threaten to dominate awareness.

Nature often proves to be a powerful ally in this multidimensional approach to mental health and cognitive vigor. Spending time outdoors can awaken the senses, whether through the soothing rush of a river, the crisp fragrance of pine trees, or the simple pleasure of warm sunshine on one's face. Many find that natural settings facilitate a sense of perspective, reminding them of broader cycles that dwarf daily grievances. When an individual combines this gentle immersion in nature with the mindful observation of surrounding sights and sounds, any sense of agitation tends to recede, replaced by a calmer, more balanced mindset. Such experiences can reinforce the idea that mental health flourishes most abundantly when nurtured by self-awareness, supportive relationships, intellectual stimulation, and engagement with the natural world.

Alongside conventional approaches, additional tools exist to nurture cognitive and emotional well-being. Certain breathing techniques, for example, help regulate the nervous system by modulating the body's stress response. Slow, intentional breaths signal to the brain that it is safe, dampening the rush of stress hormones like cortisol. Over time, consistent practice in breath regulation can retrain the body's default reactions to anxiety, facilitating quicker recovery from emotional agitation. When combined with structured relaxation methods, such as progressive muscle relaxation or the visualization of tranquil scenery, these techniques can foster calm even under less-than-ideal external circumstances.

Another potent option for many is the exploration of creative outlets. Artistic endeavors, whether they involve painting, creative writing, or playing a musical instrument, bridge the gap between cognitive stimulation and emotional exploration. They offer an avenue for self-expression that can reveal unconscious worries or help process painful memories, turning raw feelings into tangible, often beautiful creations. This process can be both liberating and therapeutic, igniting a sense of achievement and joy that transcends the boundaries of everyday stressors. Additionally, creativity encourages flexible thinking and breaks routine mental patterns, adding variety to daily existence in a manner that can benefit long-term mental acuity.

For those who enjoy more analytical tasks, games that challenge memory, spatial reasoning, or logical deduction can serve as potent tools to keep the mind engaged. Digital brain-training applications often incorporate puzzles that target specific cognitive functions, such as working memory or pattern recognition. While these should not be considered a standalone prescription for robust mental health, when paired with other healthy routines, they can add a playful dimension to one's overall plan for preserving mental agility. The key lies in finding balance: variety in mental exercises, in addition to well-rounded self-care, prevents monotony and maintains curiosity, which is a driving force behind lasting cognitive sharpness.

In parallel, it is important to remain attentive to the potential pitfalls of excessive digital consumption. While the internet and social media provide enormous opportunities for learning and connectivity, they can also become significant sources of stress and anxiety. Constant exposure to alarming news stories, an unending stream of social updates, and the pressure to maintain an idealized digital image may combine to erode self-esteem and disrupt focus. Exercising discernment in daily usage, setting periods of intentional disconnection, or carefully curating one's online environment can mitigate these effects. Replacing passive scrolling with more constructive online activities—such as engaging in thoughtful discussions or acquiring new skills—harnesses technology's strengths while minimizing its drawbacks.

In cultivating mental wellness, consistent and intentional daily practices gradually accumulate to form a robust framework that can withstand life's ups and downs. Small pockets of time devoted to spiritual or philosophical reflection—like reading a poem that resonates deeply or contemplating positive experiences from the day—serve as anchors for emotional stability. Journaling about one's goals and fears can transform vague anxieties into concrete objectives or tasks, clearing mental space for fresh perspectives. The act of writing itself helps organize thoughts, clarifying paths forward and giving shape to intangible concerns. It also provides a valuable record of growth, allowing individuals to revisit past reflections and recognize patterns that might inform better decisions in the future.

When stressful events inevitably occur, this foundation of daily mindful routines enables individuals to approach hardships with greater equanimity, identifying constructive steps rather than succumbing to overwhelm. This is where the value of consistent meditation practice becomes apparent, as it trains the mind to respond thoughtfully to triggers instead of reacting impulsively. Over time, the cumulative effect of such discipline is a more measured approach to uncertainty, supported by a clearer sense of priorities. Thus, while mental wellness cannot promise a life free from emotional challenges, it empowers people to navigate those challenges in a way that promotes adaptability and personal growth.

Cognitive wellness also involves recognizing when professional intervention might be beneficial. Self-awareness is crucial in distinguishing normal fluctuations in mood from the more persistent difficulties that signal a need for therapy, counseling, or medical evaluation. Sometimes, the greatest act of self-care is seeking help before a crisis spirals out of control. While societal stigmas around mental health have historically discouraged open conversation, progress has been made in normalizing therapy and psychiatric support. By confronting potential barriers head-on— such as fear of judgment or misunderstanding about what treatments entail—individuals can seize control of their well-being and foster a preventative mindset, thereby reducing the intensity and duration of mental health struggles.

This willingness to reach out for qualified help is an acknowledgment that emotional life is seldom straightforward. Genetic predispositions, traumatic experiences, and unforeseen crises can strain even the strongest coping mechanisms. During periods of heightened vulnerability, having access to specialized expertise, whether from psychologists, psychiatrists, social workers, or licensed counselors, provides an invaluable safety net. These professionals are trained to unravel complicated emotions, guide patients in exploring deeply rooted belief systems, and, when necessary, incorporate evidence-based therapies that address conditions ranging from panic disorders to severe depression. By availing oneself of expert guidance, the path to recovery and renewed cognitive clarity can be shorter, safer, and more sustainable in the long term.

Beyond one-on-one therapeutic relationships, it is essential to remember that communities themselves can play a powerful role in mental and cognitive health. Shared endeavors that encourage personal fulfillment—whether they stem from religious organizations, community gardening groups, or cultural collectives—integrate social support with purposeful activity. Engaging in meaningful communal tasks fosters a sense of belonging, sharpens mental faculties through collaboration and planning, and reduces the isolation that can exacerbate anxiety or depression. People who feel genuinely connected to those around them gain a sense of mutual responsibility that nurtures hope in even the most daunting circumstances.

Maintaining hope is at the core of emotional resilience. Although it can be elusive during dark times, hope provides a sense of direction, a reminder that the future is not solely defined by present hardships. Rituals that inspire gratitude—such as expressing thanks for small mercies or celebrating minor victories—can rekindle that flicker of optimism. Gratitude itself has been repeatedly linked to improved psychological outcomes, possibly due to its ability to shift mental focus from burdens to blessings. When grateful reflection becomes a habit rather than an occasional exercise, it gradually reconfigures one's worldview, highlighting opportunities for contentment and dissolving the grip of fear.

As people explore the interplay of emotional stability, cognitive agility, and mindful awareness, they often discover that each realm reinforces the others. A well-regulated emotional state paves the way for deeper intellectual pursuits, free from the fog of worry or self-doubt. In turn, a lively mind expands a person's problem-solving repertoire, offering alternative angles from which to confront adversity and further refine stress-management skills.

Adding mindfulness to this mix unites both spheres, concentrating attention in the present and nudging the mind away from destructive patterns that sabotage long-term growth. The result is a positive feedback loop that supports mental, emotional, and intellectual flourishing.

It is also vital to remain open to experimentation, recognizing that what works for one person may not necessarily suit someone else. Not everyone responds to meditation in the same way, and some might find solace in robust physical exercise or structured creative outlets. A key step in refining mental health strategies lies in paying close attention to personal responses, adjusting routines as circumstances change, and periodically re-evaluating what serves the mind and heart best at each life stage. This flexibility is itself a hallmark of mental adaptability, reflecting an understanding that growth occurs most fluidly when individuals remain receptive to learning and unafraid to discard practices that prove unhelpful.

A balanced approach involves merging supportive relationships, daily self-care, targeted interventions, and the freedom to explore new possibilities. When mental health deteriorates or cognitive performance wanes, it often signals the need for greater alignment, whether by seeking medical advice, reconnecting with a meaningful social circle, or carving out time for spiritual reflection. These re-alignments can be viewed not as failures but as turning points, opportunities to realign the intricate layers of well-being that modern life can disrupt so easily.

The pursuit of mental and cognitive wellness, then, is not a single destination but an evolving journey that calls for patience, compassion, and proactive engagement. On one level, it requires tending to the simple daily rituals that anchor the mind in steadiness, such as quiet reflection, conscious breathing, and deliberate acts of kindness. On another, it demands the willingness to push mental boundaries by challenging oneself to learn new skills, absorb fresh perspectives, and embrace novel experiences. This combination—of calm introspection and thoughtful outward exploration—helps fortify mental acuity while safeguarding against emotional stagnation.

In essence, safeguarding the mind and emotions is a profound testament to the interconnectedness of personal habits, social environments, and individual aspirations. Each day presents an opportunity to refine coping strategies, expand cognitive potential, and nourish one's emotional core with empathy, hope, and mindfulness. Through consistent practice and open-minded curiosity, the mind remains not just functioning, but thriving— capable of adaptation, capable of resilience, and capable of forging meaningful connections with the people and world around it. Most importantly, this investment in cognitive wellness and emotional equilibrium forms a lasting cornerstone upon which overall quality of life is built, allowing each person to navigate life's shifting tides with purpose and grace.

Ultimately, recognizing the delicate balance between challenge and rest is key to preventing burnout and maintaining a sense of vitality. Periods of focused effort, when balanced by restorative intervals of play or relaxation, keep the mind energized and ready for whatever comes next. By integrating moments of delight and lightheartedness, such as the joyous freedom of an impromptu dance in the living room or the sense of accomplishment that comes from finishing a puzzle, people safeguard their mental reserves and develop a more optimistic, engaged attitude toward each day. In weaving together these moments with purposeful self-inquiry, social cohesion, and structured mindfulness practices, a framework for holistic mental health emerges that is both flexible and robust.

This framework benefits from an enduring resolve to nurture oneself gently yet persistently. Without an ongoing commitment to reflection and self-awareness, even the most sophisticated methods can lose traction. Conversely, those who remain attuned to their emotions, regularly evaluate their coping mechanisms, and welcome new insights are more likely to sustain high levels of mental sharpness and emotional wellbeing. Over time, they experience the satisfaction of witnessing personal growth that touches every facet of life, from the ability to engage more deeply with loved ones, to the capacity for creative problem-solving in challenging professional landscapes, to the quiet confidence that arises from knowing one can handle unexpected difficulties with poise.

At the heart of this ever-evolving journey is the concept that building a vibrant mind involves not just protecting it from harm, but actively cultivating joy, curiosity, and connection. The same individual who once struggled to calm anxious thoughts may discover in themselves a gift for guiding others toward self-discovery. That spark of insight can shape entire communities, as each person who fosters self-knowledge, kindness, and emotional strength stands to contribute positively to the collective human experience. While there is no single prescription for the perfect balance between cognitive sharpness and emotional peace, the willingness to engage in honest self-exploration and strategic action remains a universal pathway to wellness.

In forging such a path, individuals often realize that true mental health is fundamentally a partnership with the self. It involves caring for the body through exercise and nutrition, caring for emotional equilibrium through mindfulness and supportive relationships, and caring for intellectual energy through continual mental stimulation. All these dimensions function as an integrated tapestry, revealing that the deeper the care invested in one dimension, the more robustly the others flourish. A mind kept active through problem-solving games or new learning endeavors also becomes more adaptable in handling emotional stress. A heart sustained by empathetic connections produces a steadier baseline for creative thought. And a spirit that knows how to remain centered amid life's upheavals channels that stability into every aspect of personal growth.

Some might embrace formal meditation as the linchpin of their well-being, while others might rely on journaling, group therapy, artistic self-expression, or a combination of many approaches. The diversity of possible methods underscores the uniqueness of each individual's journey. What unites them all is the principle that deliberate, ongoing choices matter, and that even minor daily actions—such as pausing for a few mindful breaths—can set the stage for profound transformations in how a person feels, thinks, and interacts with the world.

Taken in total, these elements form a cohesive vision of mental vitality that transcends mere survival or the absence of clinical disorders. It is an active, affirmative state that revolves around appreciating the present moment, challenging one's mind with purposeful tasks, and cultivating robust emotional scaffolding capable of supporting oneself and others. Though achieving such balance is not an effortless feat, it gradually becomes a more natural and rewarding way of living. Each day then becomes not merely something to endure, but a space in which to thrive, create meaning, and share compassion.

As people experience different stages of life, these core principles remain relevant, even if the specific practices shift to suit changing needs. Younger adults, confronted with academic pressures or career uncertainties, might benefit from adopting daily mindfulness exercises that ground them amid hectic schedules. In midlife, juggling personal ambitions with familial obligations could necessitate a blend of stress management techniques, active social engagement, and clarity on setting personal boundaries. Later in life, cognitive challenges might require more focused exercises to reinforce memory, while emotional well-being might benefit from reminiscing in healthy ways that celebrate life's triumphs and bring closure to unresolved events. In each phase, mental health is a continuum, and the choices made create ripples that affect the next chapter of a person's journey.

Ultimately, an unwavering dedication to mental well-being and cognitive excellence can yield profound, lasting rewards. When individuals commit themselves to understanding the relationship between stress and their own vulnerabilities, to honing techniques that anchor their minds in the present, and to embracing compassion for themselves and others, they build the internal resources needed to face life's turbulence with strength and hope. Out of that resolve emerges a greater harmony in one's personal relationships, an enriched sense of purpose in everyday tasks, and the ability to hold onto optimism even when confronted by uncertainty. Through intentional effort and a compassionate spirit, the mind grows more lucid, the emotional bedrock steadier, and the capacity for resilience more expansive, ensuring that each new day can be met with a renewed sense of possibility.

Part III: Staying Relevant and Socially Connected

Chapter 7: Building and Maintaining Meaningful Relationships

Relationships lie at the heart of human existence, shaping the emotional tapestry that defines each person's journey and providing channels for mutual support, understanding, and cooperation. No matter how independent one strives to be, there remains a fundamental desire to share experiences and cultivate deeper connections with those around us. In many ways, the pursuit of meaningful bonds stands as a universal endeavor, transcending cultural and socioeconomic boundaries. People seek to build families, forge friendships, and remain active members of their communities because these links empower them with a sense of belonging. Indeed, the ripple effect of authentic connections can influence everything from an individual's emotional stability to broader societal cohesion. Throughout life, the nature and function of these relationships continually evolve, highlighting the importance of consciously nurturing them as part of overall personal and communal wellbeing. At every turn, it becomes clear that sustaining these ties requires intention, empathy, and a willingness to adapt to changing circumstances.

A strong family unit provides a foundational sense of security. It offers emotional anchors that promote resilience and reassure individuals that they do not face challenges alone. Shared histories, formative memories, and the comfort of belonging to a group with deeply rooted bonds can fortify one's capacity to navigate uncertainties. Yet families are not immune to tensions or misunderstandings. Communication may falter when old hurts linger unspoken, or when new responsibilities place unforeseen pressures on each member's time and energy. In certain instances, conflicts arise from generational gaps, differing perspectives on tradition, or varied approaches to problem-solving. When individuals approach these challenges with openness, they discover that the key to strengthening these connections lies in dedicating time and effort to honest, constructive dialogue. Rather than letting harmful assumptions fester, family members benefit from patiently articulating their thoughts and feelings, setting the stage for understanding that bridges divides.

Yet speaking openly is only one step. The willingness to listen is equally, if not more, critical. In families, each member's voice resonates differently, shaped by distinct backgrounds, personalities, and worldviews. Conflict often intensifies when someone feels their perspectives are dismissed or patronized. By making space for each other's narratives—especially when they challenge one's own perceptions—families foster mutual respect and empathy. This process can be aided by setting aside structured times for discussion, like weekly gatherings or even meal-based conversations, in which each person has an opportunity to share updates or concerns. Although seemingly simple, these rituals have the power to prevent deeper rifts by ensuring that communication remains consistent. In such supportive environments, disagreements no longer loom as threats but emerge as chances to learn from one another.

Fostering a harmonious atmosphere also involves recognizing that each generation brings unique strengths. Older relatives, for instance, often possess time-tested wisdom gleaned from life experience, which can illuminate the best ways to approach challenges or crises. Younger members, on the other hand, tend to be more attuned to current social, technological, or cultural trends, and can introduce valuable adaptations for a family's continued growth. When a household embraces each generation's contributions, people feel validated for their knowledge, reinforcing intergenerational solidarity. Mutual respect paves the way for healthier relationships and a cohesive sense of identity, wherein differences no longer fragment the family but instead bolster its collective potential.

Though numerous studies underscore the positive impact of familial bonds on mental and emotional stability, the quality of these relationships tends to matter far more than the mere fact that they exist. Occasionally, well-intentioned traditions can become oppressive or stifle individual expression. Certain families struggle with unspoken expectations—perhaps around career paths, lifestyle choices, or the perpetuation of certain cultural norms—that weigh heavily on those who dare to break from the mold. Emotional maturity within the family means recognizing the difference between guiding principles that enrich each member's life and rigid dictates that generate resentment or guilt. Through patient communication, families can refine their traditions, preserving those that offer a shared sense of meaning while adapting others to respect changing realities. This willingness to evolve not only reduces friction but also keeps the familial environment conducive to genuine closeness.

Meaningful time spent together often serves as a bridge between separate experiences. In a fast-paced world, with obligations and schedules filling every minute, loved ones may unintentionally drift apart. Coordinating shared activities can rekindle connections that might otherwise fade behind the demands of daily life. Some families find renewal in simple activities, such as cooking meals together, embarking on periodic day trips, or playing recreational games that spark lighthearted competition. Others gravitate toward more organized endeavors, perhaps engaging in collective community service or creating family-wide projects that celebrate common interests. Structured or casual, the act of carving out consistent time to interact and laugh fosters the memories that bind people through life's transitions. Even when disagreements arise, the shared experiences and communal achievements form a bedrock of trust upon which reconciliation can be built.

These same principles of open communication, mutual respect, and collaborative experiences serve as the backbone for all types of close relationships, including friendships. Bonds between friends are typically rooted in shared interests or compatible personalities, yet they often extend far beyond casual pastimes or fleeting conversations. True camaraderie emerges when individuals trust one another enough to reveal their vulnerabilities, support each other through hardship, and celebrate successes with genuine joy. In this sense, a friend can become an extension of one's emotional foundation, a chosen confidant whose presence enriches life's many facets. Over time, these connections may endure changes in geography or personal circumstance, provided both parties remain deliberate about sustaining the bond.

Maintaining vibrant friendships, however, can be challenging as priorities shift and responsibilities multiply. People may move to different regions for employment opportunities, start families of their own, or devote more energy to personal endeavors. When a friend is physically distant, it is easy to lose touch, even if the underlying appreciation remains intact. For this reason, consistent communication stands out as a crucial element of lasting friendships. Whether through phone calls, online messaging, or visits when possible, investing time in one another's lives is a testament to the value placed on that connection. These small gestures of closeness—exchanging anecdotes, seeking advice, or sharing humorous stories—form a tapestry of mutual care, bridging the gaps created by distance or hectic schedules.

Friendships also flourish under conditions that allow for authenticity, empathy, and understanding. When individuals know they can express themselves without judgment, their bonds deepen, laying the groundwork for support that can be pivotal during times of difficulty. For instance, someone grappling with grief or professional setbacks may find solace in friends who gently listen without pushing for immediate solutions, and who offer subtle reassurance that the individual is not alone. Conversely, an overabundance of unsolicited critiques or insensitive remarks can quickly erode a friend's sense of safety. Friendships require a balance between honesty and compassion. While candid feedback is essential for fostering growth, its delivery must be tempered with respect, acknowledging the friend's emotional state. Overly blunt remarks may weaken trust, undermining the depth and stability of the connection.

As people mature, new friendships may blossom in settings that reflect their evolving interests. Educational courses, volunteer programs, professional seminars, or even casual interest groups create opportunities for like-minded individuals to find each other. Sometimes, a chance conversation with a neighbor or a warm exchange with a work colleague can spark a relationship that endures for years. By staying receptive to unexpected connections, the likelihood of expanding social circles grows. Rather than viewing relationships as static, individuals who remain open to forming new bonds enrich themselves with fresh perspectives. Such expansions of social networks help mitigate isolation and can introduce novel opportunities for learning and collaboration.

Yet forging new connections does not mean abandoning existing ones. People can nurture longstanding relationships while allowing new friendships to flourish. Indeed, vibrant social circles often consist of old friends whose histories are interwoven with one's identity, as well as more recent acquaintances who bring a sense of novelty. Some older bonds will inevitably fade as interests diverge or life circumstances shift drastically, but maintaining contact with those who share integral memories preserves a sense of continuity. Although it may seem easier to rely on the convenience of digital communication, in-person gatherings—or at least periodic video calls—reinforce the warmth that underlies enduring friendships. Simple gestures, such as remembering birthdays or occasionally sending thoughtful messages, affirm that these individuals still hold a cherished place in one's life.

In communities that are tightly knit, it is common for neighbors to become friends as well, forging shared experiences in local events or supporting each other in small but meaningful ways. When people look out for one another in the immediate surroundings, they create a culture of mutual care that can buffer stresses. Whether by helping a neighbor in need or organizing a local gathering, the ability to rely on the goodwill of others magnifies the sense of communal belonging. While modern societies often emphasize individuality, there is a timeless value in forging collective ties that span beyond immediate family and close companions. When multiple households unite around shared goals—like improving neighborhood safety, cleaning up common areas, or celebrating seasonal festivities—they strengthen a local network where friendships can develop organically.

Over the years, technological advancements have dramatically altered how people maintain relationships, often blurring the lines between geographical and social distance. Platforms that facilitate instant messaging, voice and video calls, and social networking sites have made it possible to reach others in real time, no matter how far away. In many respects, these tools counter the practical challenges of distance. A relative living overseas can stay updated on familial milestones in real time, while friends scattered across multiple time zones can organize group calls or collaborative projects. Technology thus broadens the scope of connection, enabling individuals to nurture bonds that might otherwise wither due to a lack of face-to-face contact.

Yet the convenience of digital communication also poses its own set of hurdles. People may find themselves bombarded by constant notifications, from trivial updates to urgent messages, creating a sense of relentless connectivity that can be overwhelming. Paradoxically, this abundance of digital contact can diminish genuine interaction if individuals fall into passive modes of scrolling through curated content rather than engaging in meaningful conversation. Substantive dialogue and shared experiences risk being replaced by superficial clicks and impersonal "likes," diluting the essence of authentic human connection. While technology offers remarkable tools for keeping relationships alive, it demands conscious effort to ensure that genuine empathy and direct dialogue remain at the forefront of online interactions.

Striking the right balance between online and offline communication can significantly enrich relationships. Virtual gatherings, for instance, can bring family members scattered across continents into a shared moment—perhaps a digital celebration of a loved one's accomplishment or a weekly ritual in which all log in to chat about daily life. These e-gatherings can become emotional lifelines for those who feel disconnected by distance or constrained by circumstances that limit travel. Similarly, organized online communities or forums can serve as a means of finding like-minded individuals with similar interests, leading to friendships that might later extend into the real world. However, it is prudent to recognize that not all digital encounters encapsulate the same emotional depth as time spent in person.

The intimacy of a face-to-face discussion, accompanied by eye contact, subtle gestures, and the warmth of human presence, frequently fosters a stronger bond and leaves a more lasting memory.

When used thoughtfully, social media platforms function as spaces for sharing important life updates, personal reflections, or creative endeavors, granting friends and relatives the chance to participate in moments they might otherwise miss. A major part of strengthening relationships in the digital age involves learning to communicate intentions clearly, setting boundaries for healthy online engagement, and appreciating that nuanced or difficult subjects may be better addressed through direct interaction rather than brief text-based exchanges. Misinterpretations abound when typed words lack context or the reassuring tone of a loved one's voice. To prevent misunderstandings, many families and friends opt for voice notes or video calls, which retain vocal inflections, facial expressions, and gestures that convey more than words alone. This more personal form of online interaction can be a valuable compromise in bridging physical separations.

Another factor to keep in mind is the risk that technology can sometimes project an idealized image of other people's lives, leading to harmful comparisons or unrealistic standards for success, happiness, or relationship dynamics. It can be disheartening, for instance, to see a constant stream of celebratory posts while one is experiencing personal difficulties. In this environment, envy or self-criticism may eclipse gratitude for what one does have. Healthy engagement with technology thus entails being mindful of the emotional impact that digital content can exert, reminding oneself that social media rarely captures the full complexity of any person's reality. True intimacy is nurtured through authenticity, a quality that can be more challenging to express and perceive in online platforms prone to emphasis on highlights over ordinary or vulnerable moments.

Yet even acknowledging these pitfalls, the capacity of technology to keep loved ones connected in modern society is undeniable. Whether through group chats for immediate family, shared calendars that track significant events, or playful online collaborations that let cousins or friends brainstorm ideas together from distant places, these tools can amplify the sense that individuals are part of something larger than themselves. People can quickly coordinate real-world get-togethers or surprise parties by messaging each other across multiple platforms. Parents with busy schedules might set up family reminders so that everyone remembers important deadlines, school events, or seasonal traditions. When harnessed responsibly, these digital resources serve as powerful aids for reducing friction and ensuring that ties remain active and meaningful, rather than slipping away under the weight of life's practicalities.

In some cases, technology opens the door to forging entirely new forms of community, especially for those who feel marginalized or find it difficult to connect in traditional settings. Online forums and support groups can offer comfort to people facing health challenges, identity-based discrimination, or other specialized issues. Members can exchange coping strategies, share personal stories, and develop friendships that transcend geographic barriers. For many, these virtual alliances prove vital, combatting isolation and offering inspiration or empathy that can significantly bolster emotional wellbeing. By bridging physical distance and connecting individuals who share similar life experiences, online networks can spark connections that blossom into close friendships, displaying the power of technology to create inclusive spaces where people feel understood.

At the same time, moving these connections beyond the screen can further enrich the bond. Face-to-face meetings—if feasible—provide a dimension of mutual presence that digital text and images cannot replicate. For those who initially meet online, deciding to meet in person often marks a meaningful transition, transforming what might have been a purely virtual exchange into a multi-layered relationship supported by direct interaction. The laughter, shared meals, or collaborative projects that take place in physical proximity help humanize online interactions, turning digital acquaintances into tangible friends. Such experiences highlight the complementary nature of technology and in-person contact, showcasing how both can combine to form relationships that are strongly woven into daily life.

Meaningful connection demands attentive nurturance, and this truth remains consistent across family ties, friendships, and casual acquaintances that might one day evolve into deeper bonds. Because each relationship involves a complex interplay of emotions, habits, and expectations, conscious reflection plays a significant role in sustaining harmony. When people take time to consider the emotional needs and communication styles of others, as well as their own, they heighten the quality of interaction. This might mean pausing before responding to a tense message, reminding oneself that the other person might be stressed or pressed for time. Or it might entail adopting a more considerate approach to scheduling, ensuring that each person's obligations and individual preferences are respected. These small acts of thoughtfulness have cumulative impact, building an environment where trust and goodwill can flourish.

In families, empathic consideration might emerge through offering practical assistance—like helping a sibling move houses or preparing meals for a parent recovering from surgery. In friendships, it can take the form of emotional availability: listening without distraction, celebrating triumphs as if they were one's own, and offering consolation or gentle advice when sorrow or doubt loom large. By giving energy to these supportive gestures, the deeper essence of care becomes palpable. Time and again, life's unpredictable nature tests the resilience of relationships. Illness, career changes, and financial hardship, among other challenges, disrupt equilibrium. In these moments, the strength of one's bonds can either provide a sustaining cushion of compassion or erode under the weight of frustration and misunderstanding. Intention, mutual respect, and empathy can transform these crises into catalysts for greater unity, as shared adversity reveals the power of standing together.

Even casual relationships or acquaintanceship networks are worth tending, as they can grow into major sources of support or joy over time. Speaking kindly to neighbors or colleagues may spark a sense of friendliness that blossoms into lasting camaraderie, forging new circles of trust and reciprocity. In some circumstances, these connections might even become stepping stones to new experiences, such as joining a local sports team, discovering an appealing volunteer opportunity, or introducing acquaintances with common interests. By treating every interaction as an opportunity to practice respect and understanding, people expand their social horizons, weaving a broader net of compassion and fellowship.

Another dimension of meaningful relationships lies in acknowledging when certain ties are harmful or no longer conducive to individual growth. Instances of manipulation, repeated disrespect, or sustained negativity can corrode self-esteem and mental health. Although reconciling with those who cause harm is sometimes possible through open dialogue, professional mediation, or counseling, there are cases where preserving one's wellbeing means limiting contact or disengaging altogether. This decision can be painful, particularly if the bond once held significance. Yet it is also a testament to the importance of upholding personal boundaries in the quest for healthier, mutually beneficial connections. Thus, building and maintaining relationships is not merely about adding new ties but also about carefully evaluating the quality of existing ones, prizing reciprocity and respect over mere obligation.

In navigating the delicate balance between closeness and personal identity, many discover that a thriving relationship fosters growth for all involved. It encourages self-expression and respects individuality while cherishing shared moments of unity. Loved ones provide encouragement for new endeavors, offer constructive feedback, and act as mirrors that reflect not only each person's strengths but also areas for development. Such camaraderie can spur transformative changes: a friend's suggestion to join a creative workshop might awaken dormant passions, or a parent's guidance might help a child navigate moral dilemmas more effectively. In each scenario, the reciprocal flow of positive influence underscores the idea that relationships are a powerful mechanism for collective enrichment.

However, for any relationship to evolve in a healthy manner, it must adapt to the inevitable changes and shifts that accompany passing time. Life events—a new career path, the birth of a child, relocation to a different country—alter how individuals relate to one another. Old routines that once sustained a bond may no longer be feasible, requiring fresh approaches to maintain closeness. Successful adaptation often involves proactive problem-solving and collaboration, rather than passively hoping that the bond will withstand these shifts on its own. For instance, if a best friend moves across the globe, both parties can commit to regular online chats, occasional visits, or joint social media projects that help them remain part of each other's daily narratives. A family that is scattered across different time zones might implement a rotating schedule for group calls, ensuring that no one person bears the entire logistical burden. These creative solutions flourish when individuals remain committed, flexible, and willing to learn from trial and error.

For those seeking to expand their circle of connections, a degree of courage is often required. Reaching out to new people can feel daunting, particularly if one has experienced rejection or shyness in the past. Yet with openness and a willingness to risk vulnerability, individuals can cultivate fresh bonds that enrich their lives. Whether by initiating a conversation with a coworker during a break, attending a community event without a companion, or volunteering at a local shelter, people can position themselves in spaces that naturally foster connection. Overcoming initial trepidations frequently yields rewards: new viewpoints, friendships born out of shared passion, and the thrill of discovering unexpected commonalities. In this sense, expanding social circles is an act of optimism, a tangible expression of belief in the possibility of forging meaningful links at every stage of life.

Naturally, balancing these extended ties with preexisting relationships can be challenging. Maintaining an active social life sometimes strains family routines, especially when there are household obligations or caregiving responsibilities to consider. Rather than seeing these demands as mutually exclusive, thoughtful scheduling and communication can ensure that one's time is fairly distributed among personal pursuits, family commitments, and friendships. People who communicate their plans clearly and remain sensitive to the needs of others can often integrate various spheres of their lives harmoniously. Partners, children, and siblings might also share in new social activities, fostering cross-pollination of relationships that fortifies both family bonds and external connections. This synergy can create a robust community of interconnected people, all linked through shared acquaintances who become catalysts for deeper understanding and cross-cultural appreciation.

When reflecting on the profound role that relationships play, it becomes apparent that human interdependence shapes not just our emotional landscapes, but our understanding of self and place in the world. The emotional nourishment that arises from supportive families, steadfast friendships, and kind-hearted communities can alleviate loneliness, foster confidence, and encourage individuals to pursue meaningful ambitions. Relationships built on trust and sincerity create psychological safety, a valuable resource that enhances resilience during times of crisis or uncertainty. By integrating positive influences from loved ones and colleagues into daily life, a person can more readily navigate obstacles, standing firm in the assurance that they are not solitary in their endeavors.

Part of maintaining long-term relationships involves adopting an adaptable mindset, wherein growth is welcomed and recognized as a natural process. A friend who once shared every interest may diverge onto a distinct path, while a family member's perspective might shift after traveling abroad or encountering life-altering events. Harboring flexibility instead of rigid expectations creates space for relationships to evolve. When people celebrate each other's personal development rather than resist it, they forge a mutual understanding that the bonds between them can remain meaningful even if they change form. By treating these shifts as opportunities to learn, individuals transcend the fear that growth inevitably leads to disconnection, and instead perceive transformation as part of an ongoing narrative of closeness and shared empathy.

Empathy itself remains integral to the fabric of all human bonds. The effort to place oneself in another's position, to grasp their emotional states and contexts, builds a foundation of kindness. Gestures of empathy extend beyond simple acts of politeness, delving into the willingness to confront difficult truths, resolve conflicts with understanding rather than judgment, and remain patient when those we care about stumble. Families that cultivate empathy witness improved communication among members, while friendships rooted in empathy weather misunderstandings more effectively and recover from disagreements with less acrimony. Each empathic response paves the way for a culture of openness, in which people dare to express themselves without fear and listen with an intent to understand rather than retort.

When carefully integrated into relationship-building, technology can bolster empathic engagements by providing rapid avenues for comfort and reassurance. In times of crisis, quick messages or calls can deliver crucial support, while group chats may function as virtual circles of empathy, allowing many voices to unite around someone in need. Even so, empathy is most potent when accompanied by consistent action. If a friend is suffering from burnout, simply acknowledging their distress online is beneficial, but offering practical help—such as running an errand or offering a calm ear for a deeper conversation—represents a fuller expression of care. By melding the immediacy of digital contact with the tangible impact of real-world support, relationships gain a dimension of authenticity that extends beyond fleeting digital interactions.

As individuals seek to preserve and expand their network of meaningful relationships, they come to recognize that relationships are, in essence, living entities. They require nourishment, deliberate attention, and periodic renewal to maintain their vitality. Efforts spent on communicating more transparently, embracing new experiences together, or stepping outside comfort zones to meet new people are investments that yield returns in the form of companionship, understanding, and shared purpose. This dynamic also necessitates acknowledging one's own fallibility. Misunderstandings can occur, and pride can obstruct effective resolution. Yet if both parties approach these moments with humility—a readiness to accept responsibility for missteps and a desire to reconcile—damage can be repaired, and trust restored. Indeed, relationships often emerge stronger for having survived such trials, a testament to the profound capacity for forgiveness and learning that underscores human connection.

Over time, these principles unite the various threads of familial, platonic, and community ties into a tapestry of harmonious co-existence. The overlapping spheres of one's life—home, workplace, friendship groups, and broader society—allow for the emergence of supportive networks that stand by individuals during both adversity and celebration. Through the years, the knowledge that a listening ear or comforting presence is but a call or visit away grants people the courage to explore life's possibilities, secure in the knowledge that they belong to a supportive web of relationships. Technology amplifies this sense of potential reach, yet it takes careful discernment to wield its power in a manner that fosters closeness rather than shallow interactions. When harnessed thoughtfully, it upholds the best features of relationships, ensuring that neither distance nor time constraints erode the essence of care and understanding.

Even in environments where cultural differences or language barriers might initially complicate communication, the universal human desire for companionship transcends these obstacles. People eventually find common ground in shared laughter, creative collaborations, or joint problem-solving tasks. This adaptability is evident in multicultural families or friendships, where celebrating multiple traditions and acknowledging varied perspectives can unite rather than separate. Food, music, and art often serve as conduits for cross-cultural communion, enabling participants to explore each other's worlds with curiosity and respect. Bonds thus formed defy simplistic labels, existing as a reflection of humanity's remarkable capacity to connect through mutual recognition of core values and hopes. In such settings, technology provides a window into distant customs, enabling people to learn and communicate across languages, bridging cultural gaps in ways unimaginable just a few decades prior.

At the heart of these reflections lies the understanding that strong relationships do not materialize by accident. They require genuine care, patient work, and continuous recommitment. The process of building or mending a bond can be arduous, but its rewards resonate in countless aspects of life. Through healthy family attachments, individuals trace their origins and establish a framework of belonging, potentially passing on a legacy of warmth and unity to the next generation. Through friendships, people discover the joys of mutual discovery and acceptance, expanding their horizons beyond immediate experience and tapping into a mosaic of viewpoints that enhance self-awareness. Through technology, these relationships weave across vast distances, forging ties that can endure separation and changes in circumstance, provided that people remain attentive to the nuances of communication.

Furthermore, these connections ripen over time, like well-cared-for gardens. The seeds of camaraderie and shared purpose need fertile ground—moments of honesty, empathy, and self-disclosure—to flourish. Just as a gardener waters and prunes plants, careful attention to emotional dynamics, respect for individual boundaries, and celebration of collective strengths ensures that relationships flourish, yielding blossoms of trust and laughter. When misunderstandings arise, they must be tended to with the same diligence, lest they spread and choke the relationship at its roots. In families, this can mean clarifying longstanding resentments that have been swept under the rug. Among friends, it may require confronting perceived slights before they develop into lasting bitterness. Despite the discomfort, these acts of resolution reflect the underlying assumption that the relationship itself is worth preserving.

It is through this lens—valuing the connection and holding faith in its capacity for growth—that people often find the courage to be vulnerable. Indeed, the power of vulnerability, expressed in a safe environment, transforms relationships from cordial acquaintanceships into meaningful alliances. By sharing doubts, insecurities, and hopes, individuals forge deeper links. Friends become intimate confidants, relatives grow into a reliable safety net, and digital contacts blossom into genuine companions. Therein lies the alchemy of human closeness: it transforms solitary struggles into communal journeys, forging bonds that transcend superficial encounters. These same bonds can serve as stepping stones for collective endeavors that reinforce not only individual well-being but the welfare of broader communities. Shared volunteer projects, efforts to uplift marginalized neighbors, or creative collaborations for social good all arise from the synergy of human connection.

Taken together, these insights underscore that relationships are vital influences on health, fulfillment, and personal growth. By strengthening family ties through open dialogue, empathy, and shared experiences, individuals create lasting anchors that bolster confidence and sense of identity. By cultivating friendships and expanding social circles with authenticity and kindness, people discover fresh perspectives, new opportunities, and sources of encouragement that accompany them through life's undulations. Technology stands as both an enabler and a challenge in this process, capable of bridging enormous distances while also tempting individuals to replace authentic connection with passive scrolling or superficial exchanges. The thoughtful integration of digital tools, combined with the warmth of genuine interaction, can fortify the networks that sustain each person emotionally and psychologically.

Though no single approach guarantees perfect harmony, the collective efforts of individuals who prioritize emotional well-being, empathy, and constructive communication yield environments where strong connections thrive. Whether these environments exist within the home, the workplace, or the digital sphere, they reflect a shared ethos of compassion and inclusion. This ethos perpetuates itself, as children and newcomers learn from the examples set before them. A family that gently navigates disagreements without resorting to hurtful tactics teaches younger members how to engage in healthy conflict resolution. A group of friends that embraces diversity—welcoming different viewpoints, cultural backgrounds, or life paths—inspires confidence and fosters lifelong curiosity. An online forum that fosters respectful discussion and genuine care stands as a model of what digital communities can achieve.

In the end, meaningful bonds emerge from a mosaic of personal choices: the decision to pick up the phone and offer a kind word, to attend a gathering despite the temptation of solitude, to stand beside someone in times of turbulence, and to celebrate wholeheartedly when fortune smiles upon them. These choices reflect an underlying belief that life is enriched not by dwelling in isolation but by embracing the vast web of connections that unite people across age, culture, and geography. The synergy that arises from collective strength, mutual respect, and heartfelt appreciation underscores why relationships—whether formed through blood ties, shared interests, or serendipitous online encounters—remain an enduring cornerstone of human existence.

Chapter 8: Finding Purpose and Giving Back

A sense of purpose compels people to look beyond their immediate desires, encouraging them to seek deeper forms of fulfillment that extend past personal gain. For many, this endeavor translates into serving others through volunteering, community engagement, guiding younger generations, or supporting organizations whose missions resonate with their core values. The impulse to give back arises from a recognition that every individual, regardless of background or resources, has the power to effect positive change. Engaging in these acts of service often yields benefits not just for recipients, but also for those who offer their time, knowledge, and material assistance. While social and cultural contexts vary widely, the underlying aspiration to leave a lasting impact and forge connections that enrich both self and society remains universal. Whether one devotes a single weekend to helping in a local shelter or commits lifelong efforts to a charitable initiative, each action contributes to a broader tapestry of shared growth.

Communities thrive on the principle that individual contributions, when united, can generate far greater results than isolated acts of personal ambition. Volunteering is one such avenue through which these contributions often manifest. It represents a form of service that transcends transactional relationships and cultivates empathy. From local community centers to global humanitarian projects, volunteer initiatives have the capacity to address pressing societal needs while nurturing personal development for those who participate. The choice to volunteer might emerge from various motivations: a desire to overcome personal hardships by helping others, a conviction to uphold social justice, or a wish to partake in something bigger than oneself. Regardless of the initial impetus, consistent volunteer work tends to foster a sense of belonging and purpose. Through these commitments, people observe how their efforts, though sometimes modest in scale, can be instrumental in uplifting entire communities. Many volunteers describe a palpable sense of connection that arises when they stand shoulder to shoulder with others, working toward a shared objective.

Such endeavors can range from environmental conservation, like planting trees and cleaning up waterways, to organizing after-school tutoring programs for at-risk youth. In each scenario, direct engagement brings volunteers face to face with the tangible outcomes of their labor. For instance, an individual who helps to serve meals at a soup kitchen may witness firsthand how the simple act of offering nourishment instills dignity and gratitude in those who receive it. This kind of experiential learning not only underscores the immediate impacts of altruism but can also motivate volunteers to pursue additional avenues of social involvement. Repeated exposure to these environments heightens awareness of systemic inequalities and inspires people to advocate for reforms that could alleviate suffering on a larger scale. Instead of remaining passive observers, they become active participants in solutions, addressing root causes in addition to meeting immediate needs.

Furthermore, the relationships forged within volunteer settings often prove enduring, marked by a deep camaraderie that arises from shared commitment. Working side by side in challenging or emotionally charged situations fosters genuine empathy and respect. Those who might otherwise never cross paths—perhaps due to differences in profession, age, or socioeconomic status— find common ground in their pursuit of a service-oriented goal. Over time, these interactions can alter perceptions, dismantling stereotypes and widening one's understanding of diverse life experiences. A college student volunteering at a senior center, for example, might discover profound lessons by listening to stories from older adults who have navigated decades of societal transformation. Conversely, older volunteers may gain fresh perspectives by engaging with the hopes and ideas of younger counterparts. This intergenerational exchange often revitalizes community structures, breathing new ideas and fresh energy into initiatives that might otherwise stagnate.

The commitment to sustained volunteering can further evolve into specialized community leadership roles. Some individuals assume responsibility for coordinating entire projects, whether fundraising for a medical clinic, spearheading literacy campaigns, or initiating vocational training workshops in underserved areas. Leadership of this nature demands organizational skills, communication abilities, and the willingness to navigate challenges—from securing resources to recruiting other volunteers—yet the rewards are significant. People who lead volunteer-based projects witness the direct fruits of their labor: new facilities that support education, cleaner public spaces, or even transformations in local attitudes toward environmental stewardship. Such achievements reinforce the possibility that seemingly insurmountable challenges can be met through collective will and action. Those who step into these leadership capacities often find that serving the community shapes their identity more profoundly than they ever anticipated.

The satisfaction that arises from volunteering stems not solely from visible community improvements, but also from personal enrichment. By regularly giving time and effort without monetary compensation, individuals refine character traits like humility, patience, and resilience. Volunteering can stand as a profound lesson in gratitude, reminding participants that their own blessings or achievements do not exist in a vacuum but are often the product of favorable circumstances. Seeing others' hardships up close can evoke compassion, catalyzing ongoing service and heightening awareness of structural changes necessary to address deeper issues. This awakening can pave the way toward broader endeavors such as policy advocacy or grassroots organizing, enabling people to translate empathy into systemic reform. While volunteering focuses on direct, hands-on involvement, community work exists on a spectrum of engagement that eventually converges with more formal efforts to shape civic landscapes.

Another sphere of purpose-driven action involves guiding younger generations. Mentorship is one of the most direct ways to influence the future, ensuring that hard-earned wisdom and experience are passed along rather than lost. Mentors come from various backgrounds: some are professionals sharing insights with novices in their field, others are community members who feel compelled to support youth in navigating academic or personal challenges. The core principle remains the same: knowledge, when shared generously, can ignite the spark of confidence in those who stand at the threshold of discovery. A teenager on the cusp of finishing secondary education may benefit from hearing how an adult overcame financial obstacles or managed work-life balance in pursuit of a dream. Within professional contexts, young employees can glean invaluable lessons from senior colleagues on how best to innovate or tackle ethical dilemmas in the workplace. Through these interactions, mentors instill a sense of possibility and direction.

Mentorship is inherently reciprocal. While the mentor imparts lessons, the protégé's enthusiasm, curiosity, and fresh perspectives often reinvigorate the mentor's own passion for their chosen field or cause. In a climate where technology and cultural norms shift rapidly, experienced individuals remain updated as they engage with younger minds who embody contemporary concerns and novel solutions. Both sides benefit from open-ended dialogues about emerging trends, moral questions, and personal dilemmas. Mutual trust develops when mentors demonstrate genuine empathy, taking the time to understand the complexities of the mentee's experiences. Rather than imposing their own vision, successful mentors approach each relationship as a collaborative process that affirms the potential of the person they guide. They offer direction but also respect individuality, understanding that growth flourishes most when rooted in autonomy.

In educational settings, mentorship can bolster academic performance, encourage critical thinking, and reduce dropout rates. Students who receive encouragement and clear advice about managing coursework and extracurricular pursuits often develop the resilience needed to complete programs that once felt out of reach. Younger learners who might doubt their own abilities may discover in their mentors living examples that demonstrate how perseverance and creativity can surmount challenges. These lessons transcend school halls, shaping the mindset that young people carry into adulthood. The mentor's role is not merely to improve test scores or help compile a standout résumé, but to instill values of integrity, compassion, and adaptability that endure in the long term. Even brief mentorship encounters can profoundly redirect a person's life trajectory if they reveal possibilities that were previously unseen.

Beyond formal structures, mentorship frequently unfolds in more casual contexts: an older neighbor offering guidance to a teenager on small home repairs or finances, a local artisan teaching a dedicated apprentice the secrets of a craft, or an artist patiently critiquing the work of a budding illustrator. In these settings, the knowledge transfer is often deeply personal, interwoven with stories of hardship and triumph that give weight to the lessons imparted. The underlying principle of sharing wisdom so the next generation can thrive remains constant, whether the mentor is a high-level executive or a grandparent passing along family traditions. Over time, the tradition of mentorship weaves communities together, forging bonds across generations, professions, and cultural identities. People realize that the knowledge they glean in their own lives gains further value when used to uplift others.

When seen through a broader lens, mentorship is a tangible step in shaping society's future. Individuals who are guided early on to harness their strengths and uphold ethical standards often become leaders who carry forward inclusive, responsible ideas. They, in turn, may become mentors themselves, perpetuating a cycle of shared support that mitigates generational divides. This recursive phenomenon illustrates how one thoughtful gesture can catalyze a chain reaction of empowerment. Rather than confining knowledge to a single career or geographical area, mentorship broadens the scope of influence, linking minds and hearts across distances. Community mentorship programs, whether organized by schools, nonprofits, or civic associations, often rely on these principles. They pair experienced volunteers with younger participants in need of guidance, cultivating dialogues that help reduce the risk of negative outcomes—such as delinquency or academic failure—and foster a mindset of inclusivity and respect for diversity.

Beyond volunteering and mentorship lies another avenue for individuals seeking to align their lives with a sense of purpose: supporting causes that resonate with personal convictions through philanthropy. While the term philanthropy may conjure images of billionaires endowing universities or funding large-scale research, the concept extends to charitable giving at any scale. It encapsulates the decision to dedicate financial resources, goods, or services to effect positive change in areas that individuals care about, whether related to healthcare, environmental protection, social equity, or the arts. This realm of contributing typically occupies a space between direct service and advocacy work, as donations can sustain initiatives run by seasoned professionals who understand the complexities of their respective fields.

Philanthropic contributions empower organizations that often rely on external support to implement solutions. Hospitals, shelters, educational institutions, and cultural institutions all benefit from the generosity of donors who believe in their missions. A single donation might provide scholarships that transform a student's future prospects or bankroll research for life-saving medications. At the same time, consistent philanthropic engagement places the donor in a role that goes beyond writing checks. By following the progress of the chosen cause, asking questions, and sometimes volunteering alongside financial contributions, donors forge deeper connections with the mission they support. This alignment of values and resources carries significant motivational weight, reminding people that tangible changes can be enacted when conscious effort pairs with thoughtful funding.

Philanthropy does not necessitate vast wealth. Many individuals make small, regular contributions to local charities, faith-based initiatives, or online crowdfunding campaigns. Even modest gifts, when combined with those from others, can gather momentum, enabling nonprofits to expand their scope, adopt new technologies, or reach neglected communities. The principle rests on a collective ethos: if numerous participants share a common goal, their combined support can produce large-scale impact. Some philanthropic models emphasize recurring micro-donations to sustain day-to-day operational costs, while others center on one-time sponsorships of capital-intensive projects. In either scenario, the sense of responsibility that accompanies philanthropic involvement underscores that money is not an end in itself, but a means of fueling solutions for pressing social, environmental, or educational issues.

Yet the pursuit of philanthropic engagement also demands due diligence. Many donors research the track records, transparency, and ethical standards of the organizations they intend to support, ensuring that funds are utilized effectively and in accordance with the stated mission. Some explore philanthropic advisement or join philanthropic circles that bring together like-minded contributors, allowing them to pool resources and knowledge, thus amplifying their combined influence. In such circles, members share strategies and collaborate on identifying the most pressing local or global challenges. By exchanging insights, they optimize their efforts and prevent duplication of initiatives. This collective form of giving reflects the same spirit behind volunteering and mentorship: pooling strengths to multiply the chance of success.

One particularly meaningful dimension of philanthropic activity emerges when individuals align their giving with personal experiences or passions. For instance, someone who has overcome a severe illness might direct their resources toward medical research or patient support programs in that area. Another individual inspired by wildlife conservation may channel donations into projects preserving endangered habitats. Tailoring philanthropy to personal narratives adds emotional depth to the act of giving, transforming it from an abstract duty into a heartfelt endeavor. The sense of purpose multiplies when donors witness the real-world outcomes their contributions facilitate, whether the opening of a new healthcare wing, the restoration of wetlands, or a public campaign that raises awareness for a neglected cause. This tangible confirmation of impact often fuels ongoing involvement, prompting donors to expand their contributions or become ambassadors for the cause among their family and friends.

In many instances, the synergy between volunteering, mentorship, and philanthropy emerges as individuals find ways to blend all three dimensions of service. A philanthropist with a passion for education might also volunteer as a tutor or provide mentorship to promising students, thereby creating a comprehensive support ecosystem. In this model, time, knowledge, and financial resources intersect to enact holistic change. Students not only benefit from improved funding that supplies textbooks, equipment, or scholarships, but also gain direct guidance and moral support from the same person or group providing the resources. This integrated approach can engender a sense of continuity and trust, which might encourage young recipients to stay the course until they achieve their educational objectives. Over time, these students may emulate their benefactors, offering the same combination of support to others.

At every stage, a unifying thread underlies such efforts: the awareness that giving back in any form fulfills a deeper human aspiration to leave the world improved in some measure. People who find purpose in these endeavors often express a sense of harmony with their values, feeling that their daily actions contribute to a broader moral tapestry. This alignment of personal conviction with outward engagement offers a reprieve from the fragmentation and self-focus that modern life sometimes fosters. Rather than solely measuring success by career milestones or financial wealth, these individuals gauge their achievements by the positive transformations witnessed in the communities they serve, the gratitude of those who benefit, or the hope sparked in the eyes of mentees. These moments of affirmation inspire continued dedication, sustaining motivation even in the face of setbacks.

Nevertheless, pursuing a path of service can present emotional and practical challenges. Volunteers sometimes grapple with compassion fatigue when confronted with never-ending crises or systemic injustices that feel daunting. Mentors may encounter disillusionment if the individuals they guide become disengaged or face hardships that mentorship alone cannot alleviate. Philanthropists might feel overwhelmed by the magnitude of global or local problems, particularly if large-scale projects do not deliver expected results or succumb to bureaucratic difficulties.

Recognizing and respecting these challenges allows participants to adapt strategies, collaborate with others for support, and maintain a balanced perspective. There is no single formula for effectively giving back, and each person must navigate a personal learning curve. Engaging in these community-oriented endeavors often involves periods of re-evaluation and recalibration to ensure one's sense of purpose remains intact.

Those who continue regardless of obstacles cultivate resilience and humility, qualities that empower them to refine their approach. A volunteer might channel renewed energy into seeking better resources or partnering with organizations that have the infrastructure to broaden impact. A mentor, having learned from a mentee's setback, may revise their guidance strategy, focusing more on emotional support than purely academic or professional advice. A philanthropist may reassess donations and shift them to a more transparent or effective organization, or fund new pilot programs aimed at filling identified gaps. In each case, setbacks function not as definitive failures but as signposts for improvement, reminding people that genuine change is rarely swift or straightforward, and that perseverance, allied with wisdom, ultimately yields the greatest outcomes.

The intangible rewards of persevering in these efforts are immense. People often describe feeling part of a broader, benevolent movement, in which each individual's contributions are woven together to create collective progress. This notion counters the isolation that can plague a world increasingly dependent on digital interactions and personal achievement. The volunteer's sense of warmth when seeing a once-struggling neighborhood flourish, or the mentor's delight in watching a former protégé blossom into a leader, highlights that a legacy of compassion extends well beyond the self. Likewise, the philanthropist's realization that a grassroots organization can expand to serve thousands, thanks to carefully allocated resources, underscores the fundamental idea that caring about the welfare of others is not merely a sentimental impulse but a strategic act that advances human potential.

Connections formed through service efforts also often evolve into deeper relationships. Those who regularly volunteer together or meet at fundraising events build social networks bonded by shared ideals. Such communities sometimes transcend the immediate project and extend into spheres of personal life, forging lasting friendships or collaborations in other areas. Similarly, mentors often keep in touch with their mentees, celebrating milestones and providing advice long after the formal mentorship period ends. Over time, these ties can accumulate, resulting in a web of like-minded individuals spanning regions and cultures, all united by a desire to uplift. This extended network can amplify impact, as coordinated endeavors and the free exchange of ideas spur further innovations in service methodologies.

People who engage passionately in volunteering, mentorship, and philanthropy also influence societal perceptions. Their stories, if shared, can motivate others to take steps that once seemed daunting. A single narrative of a professional who sacrificed spare hours each week to mentor struggling adolescents, or an entrepreneur who donated a portion of profits to a literacy nonprofit, may spark a chain reaction of emulation. Community members witness that altruism and success are not mutually exclusive, that by weaving service into daily or professional life, one's sense of accomplishment is magnified rather than compromised. Such role models bolster the belief that giving back is not a chore to be fulfilled grudgingly, but a meaningful way to integrate personal goals with a larger vision for humanity.

The ripple effects of this mind-set stretch far beyond immediate recipients. Younger generations, raised in households or communities where service is normalized, are more likely to internalize values of generosity, empathy, and collective responsibility. Rather than waiting until adulthood to discover the importance of giving back, children can learn from early examples, participating in age-appropriate volunteer tasks or witnessing philanthropic gestures at family gatherings. They observe their elders, adopt attitudes of compassion, and eventually become leaders and contributors themselves. This generational continuity cements the idea that each person has a place in the cycle of support, at times receiving help and at other times offering it to others. The cyclical nature of giving back ensures that resources, knowledge, and encouragement are continually replenished in the community.

The concept of giving back inevitably intersects with personal reflection. Many people find clarity about their passions and values only once they invest in community or philanthropic endeavors. These activities reveal where their deepest sympathies lie, whether it be child welfare, environmental preservation, healthcare outreach, or artistic endeavors that promote cultural understanding. In discovering where the heart naturally aligns, individuals experience a grounding sense of authenticity, as if their actions echo their true aspirations. The impetus to give expands into an enriched self-awareness that can inform career decisions, relationships, and the overall approach to living. A finance professional might realize that their true calling lies in supporting microfinance institutions that empower small businesses in underserved areas, prompting a career shift or a redirection of philanthropic focus.

Engaging in volunteering, mentorship, or philanthropy can also serve as a buffer against the monotony or disenchantment that sometimes shadows adult life. The routine of daily obligations may lose its luster over time, leaving a gap that personal hobbies cannot always fill. Undertaking service-oriented projects disrupts this stagnation, fueling a renewed sense of urgency and purpose. Instead of feeling trapped in cycles of consumption or passive entertainment, individuals invest their energy in tasks that cultivate hope and foster tangible improvements in the lives of others. This mindset extends beyond altruistic pursuits, permeating other facets of life and inspiring a positive outlook. Encountering community members who show gratitude, or watching an under-resourced student flourish, can transform cynicism into renewed faith in humanity's capacity for solidarity.

Moreover, in regions shaped by intense social disparities or deep cultural rifts, the presence of volunteers, mentors, and philanthropic efforts can mend divides that politicians or institutions struggle to address. Service initiatives that welcome people of diverse backgrounds create dialogues that highlight common challenges and shared hopes. Rather than focusing on identity-based differences, participants unite around collective goals: better education, safer neighborhoods, cleaner air, or improved healthcare. Over time, these points of mutual effort can moderate tensions and encourage a culture of collaborative problem-solving. A volunteer-based cleanup project, for example, might attract residents from opposing ethnicities or faiths, forging friendships as they pick up litter side by side. Through acts of communal labor, individuals find empathy for those they once viewed with suspicion. The philanthropic extension of building wells or sponsoring medical drives in less advantaged regions similarly binds donor and beneficiary communities in a narrative of common humanity.

Such interactions enrich the concept of giving back by illustrating its capacity to transcend personal satisfaction. It becomes a tool for societal harmony, bridging gaps and fostering understanding. In a world often fraught with polarization, acts of collective service and generosity serve as reminders that human beings, regardless of background, share many core values: dignity, peace, education, and the desire to provide for future generations. When people see each other participating in philanthropic activities or wholeheartedly mentoring youth, they glimpse the possibility of cohesive progress. Institutions, governments, and businesses sometimes build partnerships with grassroots volunteers, mentors, and donors in these contexts, merging bottom-up enthusiasm with top-down support to create lasting transformations.

Amid these wide-ranging possibilities, personal reflection remains invaluable. Individuals seeking to determine which approach aligns with their passions might ask what causes or communities have touched their lives most profoundly. Volunteering at a local community center could be a first step toward discovering an aptitude for teaching, leading someone to formal mentorship roles. A small but consistent philanthropic effort might ignite a desire to expand charitable giving, culminating in larger-scale campaigns or collaborations with established nonprofit organizations.

Through such iterative exploration, people refine their sense of purpose, discovering the forms of engagement that resonate most powerfully and produce the greatest sense of fulfillment. The deliberate combination of introspection and real-world experimentation underlies many a successful journey of community involvement.

To sustain momentum, participants might benefit from forming or joining networks where like-minded individuals share best practices, offer moral support, and collectively celebrate successes. Local meetups and online forums dedicated to volunteer work, youth mentorship, or philanthropic endeavors provide a platform to discuss challenges and brainstorm creative solutions. Mentors who encounter difficulties connecting with a new mentee, for instance, can learn from others' experiences, possibly uncovering fresh techniques for communication. Volunteers who sense burnout might glean tips from those who have established self-care routines, ensuring that the impulse to help does not come at the expense of personal well-being. Philanthropists seeking greater impact can connect with philanthropic advisors or peer donors, gaining insights on how best to evaluate prospective projects or measure the effectiveness of past initiatives.

Ultimately, the synergy of volunteering, mentorship, and philanthropy transforms communities by interweaving practical aid with inspiration and tangible resources. These gestures form a triad of service, addressing immediate needs (through volunteering), shaping the future through education and guidance (mentorship), and providing the financial support required to fortify programs and institutions (philanthropy). Taken as a whole, they represent a multidimensional way to give back, reinforcing the conviction that the pursuit of individual goals can be harmonized with the pursuit of collective betterment. By channeling time, expertise, and wealth into the service of others, people broaden the scope of what they themselves can achieve, adding depth and authenticity to their personal narratives.

The resonance of these efforts endures across time. Volunteers who begin at a local level, assisting in grassroots movements or neighborhood coalitions, may discover leadership abilities that propel them to champion larger initiatives. A single act of mentorship can spark a lifelong transformation for a child or young adult, who then grows to fulfill their dreams and may choose to mentor others in turn. Strategic philanthropic endeavors leave legacies in the form of community centers, well-funded research, or scholarship programs that benefit multiple generations. Through perseverance and collaboration, the sum of these positive influences shapes a world where mutual support becomes the norm, rather than the exception.

These developments reflect an underlying principle: meaningful acts of service reveal and expand the best facets of humanity. By observing the real impact on those who receive help, participants deepen their empathy, while those who witness such endeavors may be inspired to initiate their own. The cycle becomes self-sustaining, with each success story fueling further engagement. Even when challenges appear discouraging, the knowledge that others are working together to surmount them provides powerful motivation. The idea that personal talent, money, and time can be harnessed to address societal imbalances adds an invigorating sense of agency to daily life. It fosters hope that individuals are not powerless in shaping the narratives of their communities or the destinies of those who have yet to realize their full potential.

For those still searching for their unique path in this tapestry, experimentation is often the best starting point. One might volunteer in several different capacities—working in an animal shelter, tutoring in a local school, or participating in a community garden—to see which environment resonates. Another person might explore multiple mentorship opportunities, such as guiding a niece or nephew through college applications, then offering professional advice to a newcomer in the same industry. The philanthropic realm, too, is ripe with options: donations to local art collectives, microloans to entrepreneurs in developing regions, or contributions to healthcare programs in distant countries. By sampling diverse opportunities, individuals refine their sense of purpose, zeroing in on where they can be most effective and satisfied. With each new venture, they glean insights that not only clarify personal calling but also strengthen the broader networks of compassion and generosity.

As these networks grow and interconnect, the potential for collective impact magnifies. Volunteers from one region might share success stories with counterparts across the globe, exchanging strategies on disaster relief or social entrepreneurship. Mentorship programs that prove efficacious in rural communities can adapt to urban contexts, spreading knowledge that bridges seemingly disparate populations. A philanthropic endeavor in one sphere of social justice may link with allied organizations, forming a coalition that tackles issues through a multifaceted lens. These collaborations mirror the complexity of real-world problems, suggesting that solutions, too, must be multidimensional. The interplay of hearts and minds in service underscores the human inclination toward cooperation.

When people reflect on the course of their lives, they may attribute a significant measure of fulfillment not just to personal achievements, but to the ways in which they contributed to something larger. This perspective offers solace and meaning, especially in moments of hardship or uncertainty. A parent might feel pride in having consistently volunteered, setting an example for their child. A professional might find renewed vigor in their job, knowing that part of their earnings nurtures philanthropic initiatives. An elder might pass on a legacy of mentorship, recalling past protégés who have since blossomed into compassionate, inventive leaders. These reflections emphasize that giving back acts as a powerful anchor, rooting individuals in a vision of humanity's shared destiny and diminishing the sense of isolation that can otherwise hinder personal growth.

In truth, finding purpose through volunteering, mentorship, or philanthropy offers a reciprocal benefit: by helping others, one also helps oneself. Psychologically, acts of service can alleviate stress, imbue a sense of gratitude, and inspire optimism. Socially, they knit individuals into supportive communities, while intellectually, they facilitate learning from diverse perspectives. Philosophically, they raise deeper questions of responsibility and ethical stewardship, urging participants to ponder the broader implications of their choices. Over time, these layers of enrichment craft a life story that is both personally rewarding and outwardly impactful. Even a seemingly small gesture can set off a chain reaction that ripples far beyond what the giver initially imagined.

The substance of this journey ultimately rests on an ethic of shared humanity. It recognizes that behind the barriers of wealth, geography, or education, there remains a fundamental capacity for empathy and cooperation. Service endeavors—whether framed by volunteerism, mentorship, or philanthropic giving— emphasize that people do not exist in insular bubbles. Instead, they inhabit an interconnected world where each person's progress is tethered to the well-being of others. Thus, the call to give back resonates with those who yearn for meaningful belonging, who believe that compassion extended outward circles back to strengthen the giver's spirit. In contributing to the broader welfare, individuals find a renewed sense of confidence in human resilience and ingenuity.

Every step taken on this path, from the initial willingness to volunteer an afternoon to the more ambitious pursuit of systemic reform through large-scale funding or mentorship programs, embodies a statement of hope. It asserts that people are not powerless in the face of social and environmental challenges, nor must they cede their agency to distant authorities. Rather, they can become active protagonists in shaping the narratives of their own lives and the lives of those around them. By embracing the manifold approaches to giving back, each person can illuminate the corners of the world within their reach, dispelling cynicism and creating avenues for dialogue, healing, and growth. Ultimately, this approach to life—rooted in service, guidance, and compassion—transcends temporal gratification, forging a legacy that resonates through families, communities, and the generations that follow.

Chapter 9: Lifelong Learning and Personal Development

Curiosity is woven into the fabric of human nature, driving people to question, discover, and expand their understanding of the world around them. This innate impulse to learn persists throughout life, though its form can evolve in response to shifting responsibilities and changing environments. Over time, some come to recognize learning as an endeavor that reaches far beyond the classroom, a lifelong pursuit that offers not just knowledge, but personal growth and a reinvigorated sense of possibility. By embracing this ongoing process, individuals open themselves to the richness of new ideas, practical skills, and creative expression that continually reshapes the way they live. The value of such constant learning extends beyond the professional realm, influencing well-being, interpersonal relationships, and one's overall perspective on life. Each discovery—whether gleaned from formal courses, informal online communities, or immersive experiences—adds depth to a person's worldview, yielding resilience and adaptability in an ever-transforming landscape.

While many acquire early education through traditional schooling, learning does not end with graduation. The capacity to grow intellectually persists throughout every stage of adulthood. Indeed, adults may find it particularly beneficial to engage in formal or informal study once they have accumulated experiences that allow them to contextualize newly acquired insights. This phenomenon can manifest in various ways: a professional might seek an additional degree or certification to advance in their field, a retiree could indulge in an online seminar about a subject that once seemed remote, or a mid-career individual might discover emerging fields of technology that pique their curiosity. In each instance, the process underscores that academic environments, even virtual ones, remain open to learners of all ages. The intellectual stimulation derived from coursework, peer discussions, and instructor feedback can revive a sense of wonder, reminding participants that there is always more to explore. Such enthusiasm often rekindles the excitement of childhood discovery, but grounded in the maturity that comes from a lifetime of lived experience.

Continuing education has become increasingly accessible. Many colleges and universities offer flexible programs designed for working professionals or older adults. These can range from evening classes held on campus to entirely remote options where participants engage with lectures, readings, and discussions at their own pace. This adaptability means that even individuals managing full-time jobs, family commitments, or health concerns can integrate further learning into their schedules. For some, the motivation stems from a desire to pivot into a fresh career path, requiring formal certifications that signal expertise in a new domain. Others seek to enhance existing skills, hoping to keep abreast of industry developments and remain competitive in an evolving market. Regardless of the precise objective, the opportunity to interact with knowledgeable instructors and fellow students who share similar ambitions can spark deep engagement. Many find that the camaraderie formed in these learning communities offers encouragement during challenging assignments and fosters networking opportunities that extend well beyond the confines of the virtual or physical classroom.

Online learning platforms have also contributed significantly to the proliferation of continuing education. In recent years, the digital domain has witnessed a surge in platforms designed to make high-quality instruction accessible to anyone with an internet connection. These options span diverse disciplines, from technical fields like computer programming and data analytics to creative pursuits such as watercolor painting or photography. The asynchronous structure of most online modules allows participants to learn at any time, even if they live in different time zones or juggle inconsistent schedules. Through recorded lectures, interactive quizzes, and digital discussion boards, learners can engage with new material at a pace that suits their abilities. Many platforms supplement these core materials with optional group projects or real-time video conferences, ensuring that distance does not equate to isolation. In fact, some online communities develop strong bonds, as students around the world discover shared passions and collaborate on projects that reflect their collective curiosity.

While formal credentials obtained through these platforms can bolster career prospects, not all learners pursue continuing education solely for professional advancement. Some enroll in courses that promise no immediate economic reward, following intellectual inclinations or personal passions that might have been neglected for years. Perhaps it is a fascination with ancient philosophy, an interest in early astronomy, or a desire to study comparative religion. Nurturing these areas of curiosity invites people to understand past civilizations, global cultural exchanges, and the human journey through the ages. Engaging with such content fosters a broader view of the world, reinforcing empathy by illuminating perspectives far removed from everyday routines. Even when knowledge gained in these fields does not translate directly into income, it enriches inner life in ways that can influence moral decision-making, interpersonal communication, and self-awareness. Often, the true reward is the joy that arises from intellectual discovery itself, a reminder that the human mind thrives when challenged.

Beyond structured programs, the digital revolution has also spawned an array of informal learning opportunities, including podcasts, webinars, blogs, and forums dedicated to exchanging ideas on virtually any subject. A casual interest in gardening can evolve into expertise by following knowledgeable horticulturists online, replicating their methods, and consulting fellow enthusiasts about troubleshooting pests or optimizing soil conditions. In much the same way, novices dabbling in photography can glean advanced techniques from seasoned professionals who post tutorials or critique images in virtual communities. This interactivity democratizes knowledge: a new learner can pose questions, share experiments, and receive varied feedback, all without the restrictions of geography or time. In many respects, these spaces approximate the collaborative spirit of a traditional workshop but are more convenient and open-ended. Some learners thrive in the absence of a rigid schedule, preferring the organic process of exploring an unfamiliar topic step by step, guided by serendipitous connections among people united by shared enthusiasm.

For those seeking a more hands-on approach, exploring new hobbies and skills can be a route to discovery and self-improvement. Unlike formal classes, personal interests often begin as fleeting curiosities that, when nurtured, grow into meaningful pursuits. A busy professional might come across a video demonstrating bread-making and decide to try it, initially as a stress-relieving diversion, only to find solace and creativity in the process. A retiree who once dreamed of learning to play the violin can finally invest time in music lessons, delighting in small improvements that come from daily practice. These endeavors, whether leisurely or skill-intensive, function as forms of mental exercise, requiring focus, problem-solving, and sustained attention. Through trial and error, hobbyists gradually develop confidence in their abilities, discovering new facets of themselves that might remain hidden in everyday routines.

Artistic and craft-based activities often play a role in these explorations, providing avenues for creativity that can release emotional tensions and invigorate a sense of accomplishment. A person may begin painting watercolors without ever intending to produce a masterpiece, finding contentment in the gentle brushstrokes and the interplay of color. Another might experiment with pottery, delighting in the tactile sensation of clay and the satisfaction of shaping it into a functional piece. Hobbies that fuse mindfulness with dexterity—like knitting, origami, or sketching—offer the dual benefit of relaxation and mental stimulation, a rare combination in a world often geared toward rapid consumption. Participants in these activities gradually refine their techniques while nurturing patience and resilience. Mistakes in the creative process are typically not failures but stepping stones to deeper understanding, reinforcing the notion that growth emerges from a willingness to confront personal limitations and persevere.

It is not only traditionally "artistic" endeavors that open doors to new skills. Hobbies such as woodworking, metalworking, or digital design also combine invention with practicality, leading to outcomes that blend form and function. Some might choose to assemble or repair computers, discovering the joys and frustrations of troubleshooting hardware or optimizing software configurations. Others may pour energy into developing a green thumb, experimenting with hydroponic gardens in compact spaces or tending entire vegetable plots that supply fresh produce. Each of these efforts demands incremental learning, whether through reading manuals, watching tutorials, consulting local experts, or simply practicing relentlessly. In many cases, individuals who begin with modest ambitions end up producing work that surprises even themselves, reminding them that aptitude can blossom unexpectedly when nurtured with patience.

Beyond hands-on crafts, new skills can span the realms of interpersonal communication, technology, and personal organization. A person might learn a new language to broaden career prospects or to converse with relatives who speak different dialects. Someone else might delve into financial literacy, discovering how to balance budgets or invest responsibly, an endeavor that can have transformative impacts on personal stability and confidence. Others may become interested in mindfulness techniques or therapeutic practices that help them manage stress effectively. Whatever the focus, the process of learning something new fosters self-awareness. It reveals not just knowledge gaps but hidden strengths, whether it is a knack for detail-oriented tasks, an unexpected aptitude for empathy-based communication, or an aptitude for quick adaptation.

These reflections on learning new skills naturally extend to intellectual and creative pursuits that stimulate the mind in holistic ways. Many find that reading—whether fiction, history, science, or poetry—provides an accessible gateway for broadening intellectual horizons. Books, and the discussions they inspire, can spark curiosity about cultures, moral philosophies, or scientific paradigms. Engaging with a novel full of nuanced characters challenges readers to envision diverse perspectives, building empathy in the process. Delving into historical accounts fosters an understanding of how past events shape present circumstances. Scientific literature broadens comprehension of the natural world, prompting questions about how human civilization can align more harmoniously with ecological processes. By dedicating time to reading thoughtfully, individuals cultivate reflective habits that reach well beyond the text, influencing conversations and daily decisions.

Group activities that emphasize collaboration can also prove instrumental in intellectual growth. Book clubs, study groups, or even volunteer organizations that incorporate educational elements create a space for the exchange of ideas among people with varied backgrounds. Hearing alternative viewpoints compels participants to reconsider preconceived notions, refine arguments, and challenge biases. By voicing opinions or summarizing learning experiences in front of others, individuals sharpen communication skills, articulating complex ideas in accessible language. This process fortifies critical thinking, highlighting how every issue can be understood from multiple angles. Over time, the mental dexterity that emerges from such group interactions translates into heightened awareness in daily life, as individuals become more adept at analyzing problems, identifying hidden assumptions, and evaluating potential courses of action.

In addition to collaborative reading or discussions, structured intellectual activities can push the mind toward greater agility. Some enjoy puzzle-solving, approaching crosswords, sudoku, or brainteasers as daily mental workouts that refine logical thinking. Others might enroll in clubs dedicated to chess, go, or other strategy games, savoring the thrill of strategic depth and the sense of accomplishment that comes from each incremental improvement. Such pursuits keep the mind flexible and receptive to novel approaches, given that many strategy games demand constant adaptation to the opponent's moves. These mental exercises build patterns of thinking that can prove advantageous in real-world problem-solving, whether it is navigating workplace projects, sorting out personal dilemmas, or planning future goals.

Creative expression, meanwhile, cultivates imagination and emotional intelligence. Musical activities, such as composing, playing instruments, or singing, integrate fine motor skills with an acute awareness of timing, pitch, and tone. Individuals who involve themselves in these fields can experience a sort of meditative focus, where everyday concerns fall away and are replaced by the intricacies of harmonic progression or melodic improvisation. Theater, dance, and acting foster self-expression and empathy, challenging performers to step into roles that convey various facets of the human experience. Visual arts, including painting, sculpture, or digital graphics, harness observation, interpretation, and whimsy. Even writing—whether fiction, poetry, personal reflections, or academic analysis—draws deeply on one's internal landscape, making intangible emotions and thoughts accessible to others through language. Each of these creative outlets generates an environment where curiosity, discipline, and passion coalesce, spurring personal development.

Establishing a deliberate routine for intellectual and creative pursuits fortifies commitment, especially when everyday obligations threaten to consume energy and time. By carving out regular intervals for study, practice, or creative exploration, individuals reinforce the understanding that learning is neither a luxury nor an afterthought, but a cornerstone of mental and emotional health. A consistent schedule, even if modest in frequency or duration, provides structure that sustains motivation. Over the long term, these small efforts compound, leading to surprising leaps in skill level and conceptual understanding. It helps to remember that the essence of lifelong learning lies not in speed but in steady progress, shaped by curiosity and perseverance rather than external pressure.

When the mind is engaged in this manner, self-confidence tends to grow. Possessing a repertoire of knowledge or refined abilities instills a sense of capability that can positively affect one's broader life. Facing difficulties—be they professional hurdles or personal trials—becomes less intimidating when individuals trust in their capacity to adapt and learn. The realization that they can acquire new knowledge, master unfamiliar tools, or uncover hidden aptitudes empowers them to persevere through unforeseen challenges. Moreover, the pursuit of learning can mitigate stress, providing an absorbing focus that temporarily distances the mind from day-to-day anxieties. This phenomenon resonates with the concept of "flow," a mental state in which people become so wholly immersed in an activity that they lose awareness of external distractions, emerging later with renewed clarity.

Connecting learning experiences with social networks can further amplify their impact. Participating in a local writing club, for instance, encourages accountability, as members anticipate sharing progress with peers. People enrolled in online or offline courses might find study partners who enrich their perspective by offering different insights. Hobbies that demand teamwork—like forming a band, co-authoring an article, or organizing a community event—foster the negotiation of roles and the blending of strengths, forging relationships based on shared goals. This collective dimension of learning underscores how personal development can coincide with communal ties. By uniting, participants lend moral support and celebrate each other's milestones, transforming individual pursuits into shared victories.

Naturally, obstacles can impede the process of lifelong learning. Time constraints, financial limitations, or uncertainty about where to begin can deter those who yearn to explore new intellectual or creative avenues. Addressing these issues often requires planning, resourcefulness, and realistic goal-setting. Someone constrained by a demanding work schedule may choose shorter but more frequent study sessions in lieu of extended blocks of study. Another individual who lacks tuition funds for a formal degree might rely on free online resources, public libraries, or community workshops to assemble a do-it-yourself curriculum. For those unsure of their direction, experimenting with varied topics or techniques can clarify interests. Sampling free online lectures, reading about emerging fields, or simply conversing with others about their passions can illuminate paths previously overlooked. The key lies in approaching potential barriers not as insurmountable walls, but as prompts to seek creative solutions.

As individuals accumulate knowledge and proficiency, they often discover reciprocal benefits to the broader community. Parents who learn about nutrition might incorporate wholesome meals into the family routine, positively influencing children's habits. A person who gains fluency in a new language can become a cultural bridge in their neighborhood or workplace, supporting meaningful interactions with those who speak that language natively. An amateur photographer with refined skills might volunteer to capture community events, preserving local memories. A self-taught programmer could design an app that simplifies processes for a local nonprofit. In each case, personal development merges with social engagement, weaving an ecosystem where shared expertise uplifts collective welfare.

Over time, this ethos of lifelong learning cultivates an outlook that prizes adaptability, open-mindedness, and continuous self-evaluation. The dynamic world of technology and ideas ensures that no knowledge base remains static. People who embrace ongoing education can better respond to disruptions such as market fluctuations, technological breakthroughs, or unexpected personal changes. Rather than feeling threatened by these shifts, they sense an opportunity to grow. This resilient mindset perceives challenges as stimuli for further learning. Viewed in this light, stumbling blocks become catalysts, urging exploration of new fields or methods. The ability to retool quickly can prove invaluable in a rapidly evolving professional climate, but it also enriches one's private life, preventing stagnation and invigorating daily routines with fresh perspectives.

Individuals who engage in wide-ranging studies—one year learning a new instrument, the next exploring a coding language—often report heightened creativity. By crossing conceptual boundaries, they form novel connections that might not emerge if they confined themselves to a single domain. Insights gleaned from one discipline can spark innovative solutions in another, culminating in a multidisciplinary synthesis. This phenomenon echoes the way historical inventors and thinkers, from Leonardo da Vinci to Ada Lovelace, often combined interests in science, art, and philosophy to generate groundbreaking ideas. In modern times, the interplay between technical prowess and artistic vision is visible in fields like user-interface design, where coding skill and aesthetic sensitivity must converge, or in projects that merge environmental science with community activism. Through ongoing cross-pollination of ideas, individuals feed their inner spark, maintaining a sense of excitement in their pursuits.

At the same time, the path of lifelong learning can be humbling. Mastering a new skill or diving into complex subjects frequently reveals just how little one knows. Beginners may become frustrated by slow progress or an inundation of unfamiliar terminology. Facing these difficulties requires a willingness to persist, to accept moments of awkwardness or confusion as necessary stages of growth. Seen from another angle, humility fuels curiosity, for those who assume they have all the answers leave no room for fresh insights. By acknowledging areas of ignorance and confronting them head-on, people cultivate intellectual honesty and a growth-oriented mindset. This shift in attitude can carry over to relationships and problem-solving, as learners become more receptive to feedback, more patient with others' shortcomings, and more confident in navigating uncertainty.

In building a foundation for lifelong learning, the role of mentorship and peer support should not be underestimated. Mentors provide invaluable guidance, clarifying complex concepts and offering constructive critique. They act as role models, demonstrating that proficiency in a subject or skill often emerges from repeated effort rather than inborn genius. Meanwhile, learning alongside peers encourages collaboration and healthy competition, spurring each participant to advance further. Groups or forums dedicated to a shared pursuit sometimes evolve into tight-knit communities bound by trust and mutual admiration. Individuals discover that the sum of collective knowledge often exceeds what each could achieve in isolation, revealing an expansive landscape of discussion and experimentation. Such environments become crucibles for shared achievements, in which each success resonates for everyone involved.

An important dimension of personal development emerges when learners transfer lessons from one sphere of life to another. A person who has mastered the discipline to practice a musical instrument regularly might apply that same perseverance to exercise regimens or financial management. An amateur astronomer who meticulously analyzes stellar data can draw upon that analytical thoroughness when tackling everyday challenges at work. These parallels underscore how the process of acquiring knowledge or skills transcends the immediate subject matter, permeating broader thought patterns and behavioral habits. Through regular, intentional engagement in activities that exercise the brain, learners accumulate intangible assets—focus, problem-solving ability, adaptability—that become invaluable in countless situations.

As adults continue to explore new avenues of education and creativity, they may also reflect on the idea that learning is not an end, but a gateway to deeper understanding. Each discovery reveals more questions, prompting a continuous spiral of inquiry. Those who approach this journey with a sense of wonder rather than chasing finite "endpoints" are often rewarded with a sustained passion. While some goals—earning a certificate or mastering a particular technique—can be celebrated upon completion, the deeper essence of learning lies in the momentum it imparts. It reshapes a person's worldview, fosters humility, and encourages an agile mindset that welcomes future endeavors. In a sense, personal development flourishes most vibrantly when it is recognized as an ongoing narrative rather than a static destination.

To maintain enthusiasm over the long term, learners can diversify their methods. Formal education, such as university courses or professional certifications, provides structured rigor but can sometimes be intense and time-consuming. Supplementing these experiences with low-pressure, self-directed hobbies or intermittent short courses helps prevent burnout. The satisfaction gleaned from quickly creating a small handicraft or grasping a simple concept can serve as fuel during more demanding stints of concentrated study. Additionally, switching between different subjects at intervals can rekindle curiosity. A person might spend a few months exploring digital illustration, then pivot to reading about marine biology. This alternation prevents monotony and helps form cognitive bridges between seemingly unrelated fields. The habit of lifelong learning becomes a series of mini-adventures, each chapter offering fresh discoveries that collectively enrich the tapestry of personal knowledge.

Encounters with novel material or new skills frequently provoke a reevaluation of older beliefs, refining one's sense of identity. Perhaps someone who spent decades in a linear career path, rarely straying from an established expertise, discovers an inherent talent for creative writing and eventually redefines themselves as both a strategist and a storyteller. Another individual might have once dismissed art as impractical, only to find compelling meaning in sculpting or collage that resonates with emotional depth. These transformations highlight how learning can drive self-discovery, releasing people from assumptions they formed when their experiences were narrower. Embracing change on this intimate level fosters resilience, confirming that identity is not fixed but open to reinvention through continued exploration.

In some cases, intellectual or creative pursuits can turn into a secondary vocation, generating supplementary income or even transitioning into a new primary career path. The expansion of the digital marketplace, combined with global connectivity, allows individuals to monetize specialized skills or crafts more readily than in previous generations. A dedicated hobbyist who refines their talents in baking, illustration, or jewelry-making may open an online store to share creations with a broader audience. Another might use the technical knowledge gained from online courses to freelance in web development or data analysis. These ventures can be deeply gratifying, merging passion with practical benefits. Nevertheless, the decision to commercialize a beloved pastime should be approached with caution, ensuring that the original joy of learning remains intact rather than becoming overshadowed by financial or performance pressures. Some find that monetizing a hobby distances them from the intrinsic rewards, while others thrive on the balance of creativity and entrepreneurship. Ultimately, the choice to convert a personal interest into an economic pursuit depends on individual preferences, with no universal formula that fits everyone.

On the other side of the spectrum are those who prefer to keep creative and intellectual pursuits purely non-commercial, treasuring them as sanctuaries from the demands of professional life. Even if the works produced never reach a wide audience or the scientific discoveries remain modest in scope, the personal significance can be profound. In a hectic world, the mere act of dedicating time to introspection, imagination, and skill-building can foster mental clarity. Engaging in these endeavors purely for one's own fulfillment cultivates intrinsic motivation, affirming that self-worth does not hinge on external validation. People who preserve these private realms of creativity often find them a source of solace, a reminder that learning and personal expression hold intrinsic value beyond recognition or profit.

Over a lifetime, the accumulation of these experiences—formal study, online exploration, casual hobbies, or deeper artistic and intellectual quests—shapes a legacy of continuous self-improvement. In families, children who observe adults passionately learning are more inclined to adopt a similar mindset. They absorb the notion that education transcends age and that curiosity can be nurtured as a lifelong companion. Friends and colleagues witnessing a loved one's progress may feel inspired to confront their own fears about trying something new. Over time, entire communities benefit from the collective energy of individuals who remain open to fresh discoveries, combining what they learn into innovative solutions, social progress, or cultural richness.

The metamorphosis that occurs when people view life as an unending classroom is subtle yet powerful. It may manifest in nuanced behaviors, such as adopting more measured opinions, asking thought-provoking questions, or displaying greater empathy toward those who hold different viewpoints. The impetus to learn fosters humility—an understanding that personal knowledge is finite but can perpetually expand. This humility softens rigid boundaries, paving the way for new collaborations and bridging divides that arise from ignorance or preconceived prejudice. By engaging in diverse learning experiences, individuals accumulate context that helps them see how others' backgrounds and insights can fill the gaps in their own perspective. This open-mindedness, nurtured by ongoing learning, serves as a balm against insularity, breeding a sense of interconnectedness across cultural, generational, and professional divides.

An additional benefit of lifelong learning is improved psychological well-being. Researchers have long pointed to the correlation between mental engagement and cognitive function. Continual intellectual challenge helps maintain neural plasticity, potentially reducing the risk of cognitive decline. The mind, much like any muscle, thrives when it is exercised. A routine that includes reading, puzzles, skill acquisition, and creative activities can contribute to a more alert, resilient intellect, even as the body ages. The emotional satisfaction gleaned from these activities extends well beyond mental acuity, as the feeling of mastery or progress can spark delight and pride. It also provides a constructive outlet for energy and emotion, sometimes offsetting the pressures that accumulate from professional or familial responsibilities.

While the benefits are manifold, the ultimate gift of ongoing education, exploration, and creative pursuit lies in the discovery that no stage of life is too late for reinvention or deeper engagement with the world. Over the decades, countless stories highlight individuals who found their calling or honed a remarkable skill only in their later years. There is no deadline for curiosity. With each new endeavor, people reaffirm their vitality and agency, warding off the stagnation that can emerge when life settles into an unchanging routine. On a broader level, the collective effect of people continually learning fosters a society more capable of grappling with complex issues, innovating across disciplines, and empathizing with myriad viewpoints.

Ultimately, the notion that learning is ever-present underscores a guiding principle of human development: the mind's growth is not restricted by time or circumstance, but by the limits of one's resolve and imagination. Embracing that recognition invites a sense of adventure, turning each day into a potential gateway for discovery. Formal courses, informal online resources, new hobbies, and creative undertakings all form elements of a mosaic that can be reshuffled in infinite ways to yield fresh patterns. The challenge is to remain receptive, to channel the sense of childlike wonder into adult responsibilities, and to remember that personal evolution is a privilege that continues for as long as one is willing to pursue it.

By weaving consistent effort into a broader tapestry of curiosity, individuals gain more than a roster of skills or a diverse knowledge base. They integrate a mindset that perceives the world in vivid detail, recognizing hidden opportunities and forging connections that spark insights. The interplay between structured, credentialed learning and spontaneous exploration fosters both discipline and liberty. It affirms that while objective metrics like grades or certifications have their place, they cannot fully capture the subtler transformations at the heart of human growth: the softening of judgment, the expansion of empathy, the acquisition of resilience in the face of repeated mistakes, and the enduring sense of fulfillment that arises from mastery—even if that mastery remains personal and unseen.

In forging new pathways of lifelong learning and personal development, a person repeatedly affirms their autonomy. Instead of confining personal worth to a fixed identity shaped by early education or societal expectations, they choose an ongoing refinement of self. Regardless of whether the impetus is to stay competitive in a chosen profession, to expand social connections, or to chase a burning curiosity in the arts or sciences, each lesson learned contributes to an enriched internal landscape. It is this ever-expanding understanding that ultimately breathes vitality into day-to-day life, enabling people to adapt to rapid changes with composure and to find meaning in moments that others might overlook. The ultimate invitation is to see learning not as an isolated task, but as an integral dimension of being human, unbounded by time or circumstance.

Part IV: Productivity, Financial Independence, and Security

Chapter 10: Financial Well-Being in Retirement

Financial well-being in the years following a primary career represents a delicate interplay between disciplined stewardship and a willingness to adapt to changing circumstances. Many individuals enter this phase of life with visions of peaceful days unburdened by workplace obligations. Yet realities soon emerge that underscore the need for careful planning and open-mindedness about new possibilities. The concerns that shape financial security during these later years hinge on managing day-to-day expenses, securing income streams that do not demand constant oversight, and protecting assets against the uncertainties of health issues, market fluctuations, and unexpected life events. Viewed in a broader context, these endeavors form a cohesive framework in which prudent budgeting, thoughtful investment strategies, and consistent vigilance define the difference between financial precariousness and sustained well-being.

Some people transition into retirement having saved methodically throughout their careers, confident they can now rely on accumulated funds. Others enter this life stage wishing they had begun earlier or contributed more to pensions and accounts. Regardless of starting point, what unites all those stepping away from a main occupation is the need to assess living costs and discern whether resources align with desired lifestyles. This assessment is rarely a one-time effort. Although initial calculations may indicate whether one can maintain certain habits, emerging factors—ranging from shifting economic trends to escalating healthcare expenses—require ongoing attention. The notion that retirement is a static, predictable era belongs to a time when life expectancies were shorter and labor markets simpler. In today's environment, financial well-being demands the same degree of vigilance and adaptability that individuals once devoted to their full-time careers.

Budgeting stands at the heart of this vigilance. For many, constructing an orderly view of household finances brings clarity to what can otherwise be a nebulous task. The act of setting pen to paper, or using digital tools to track each expense, transforms worry into concrete awareness. Instead of vague notions about what might or might not be affordable, a structured budget illuminates areas that may need refinement. Some retirees discover that certain costs—insurance premiums, taxes, or specialized services—occupy a larger slice of the pie than anticipated. Others find that smaller, seemingly inconsequential purchases accumulate to create a more sizable monthly outlay. By examining every expense, individuals gain the insight needed to direct funds more effectively, potentially reducing superfluous categories so that money can be better channeled toward personal goals, healthcare, or improved investment opportunities.

Budgeting is often associated with a feeling of limitation, yet a balanced view frames it as a means of empowerment. Rather than focusing on restrictions, many find it more helpful to regard budgeting as a compass that guides spending. It clarifies how much can be devoted to leisure, family gifts, or philanthropic pursuits without jeopardizing essential obligations. This mindset shift elevates budgeting from a punitive exercise to a thoughtful practice that reveals the interplay between priorities and available resources. Within this framework, every purchase or payment can be measured against its capacity to foster well-being. An individual who recognizes that the greatest joy arises from shared experiences might reduce nonessential subscriptions or memberships and redirect funds toward travel with friends or family gatherings. The discipline inherent in budgeting, therefore, functions as a way to shape finances in alignment with deeper values.

Technology has accelerated the capacity to budget with precision. Whereas older generations may remember scanning paper bank statements and updating handwritten ledgers, retirees today can leverage apps and software to sync transactions in real time. This shift not only saves time but also reduces errors. Tools that categorize spending automatically can highlight patterns that might otherwise remain concealed. Some apps allow the user to create alerts when certain categories exceed predefined thresholds, triggering a timely reminder that facilitates corrective measures before overspending becomes an issue. In many cases, these digital solutions also provide forecasts based on historical data, predicting where fluctuations might occur based on previous months or annual cycles. As with any tool, the key is consistent use. No software can replace the human element of interpreting data and making informed decisions that align with personal objectives.

A practical outgrowth of systematic budgeting is the ability to set or adjust financial goals. Among retirees, these goals often include setting aside emergency funds to cover short-term needs, planning for possible long-term care expenses, or ensuring that grown children and grandchildren receive meaningful support without undermining one's own security. Establishing contingency funds becomes essential in later life because unexpected medical issues or home repairs can place significant strain on a fixed or semi-fixed income. Though these emergency reserves may resemble the "rainy day" funds maintained during working years, they take on particular importance when one's earning power has decreased. Similarly, structured goals around travel, hobbies, or charitable giving can only be realistically pursued once household necessities are accounted for and protected.

In addition to budgeting, planning for retirement success often involves looking for ways to generate income that does not require a return to a full-time occupation. This pursuit of supplementary income often leads retirees toward passive or semi-passive streams of revenue, especially if they prefer to preserve the freedom and leisure they have worked so hard to achieve. Passive income can arrive from diverse sources, including dividends on stocks, rental income from real estate, royalties from creative endeavors, or interest from bond holdings. Each of these streams carries unique risks and rewards. Dividends and interest earnings fluctuate with market conditions, while real estate investments entail upkeep costs, taxes, and tenant management. Nonetheless, these avenues have become increasingly popular among retirees looking to preserve capital and benefit from long-term appreciation.

One of the foundational elements in establishing successful passive income streams is understanding personal risk tolerance. Individuals accustomed to the ups and downs of the stock market may be more comfortable allocating funds toward higher-yield, albeit more volatile, instruments. Those who are new to investing might consider more conservative vehicles, such as bonds or balanced funds, in pursuit of predictable, albeit more modest, returns. Carefully balancing volatility and stability becomes vital at a stage in life when one's runway to recoup large losses is diminished. The concept of diversification, often touted in earlier life stages, does not lose relevance in retirement. Instead, the significance of maintaining a well-rounded portfolio grows, as retirees typically need some level of growth to combat inflation, particularly when retirement could span several decades. Balancing short-term accessibility with long-term appreciation can help ensure that monthly expenses and future healthcare costs are met without depleting the principal assets prematurely.

Besides the conventional array of stocks, bonds, and mutual funds, alternative investments sometimes appeal to those seeking more creative paths to passive income. Real estate stands out as a favored choice, whether through the traditional purchase of rental properties, involvement in real estate investment trusts, or participation in crowdfunding platforms that pool investor resources to acquire or develop properties. While real estate can yield stable returns and serve as a hedge against inflation, it demands a degree of diligence. Repairs, property taxes, and market fluctuations can affect profitability, so many retirees opt for more hands-off models such as real estate investment trusts. These permit investors to enjoy regular dividend distributions without the complexities of being a landlord. Still, the decision to enter or expand in real estate should be weighed against one's broader financial picture, factoring in local market trends, mortgage options, and the desire for liquidity.

Beyond real estate, some retirees explore digital platforms that allow them to invest in peer-to-peer lending ventures, purchase royalties from music or written content, or even become silent partners in emerging businesses. These endeavors can be intriguing, though they often involve greater risk due to less regulatory oversight or a lack of an established track record. Vigilance becomes imperative here, as do thorough background checks and research. While it might be tempting to chase higher yields, retirees must remember that capital preservation remains a top concern. Consequently, starting small or consulting advisors with specialized knowledge in these fields can provide a buffer against missteps. The allure of passive income should never overshadow due diligence, particularly for those whose resources are primarily needed to sustain day-to-day living.

Cultivating multiple streams of passive income allows retirees to hedge against economic fluctuations in one sector. When dividend-paying stocks lag, real estate might perform well, or vice versa. This patchwork approach can reduce the likelihood of being overly exposed to a single downturn. Yet managing multiple income sources can become complex, requiring an integrated view of each investment's performance and tax implications. Although some choose to rely on financial planners, others prefer to remain hands-on, especially if they find investment management both intellectually stimulating and personally rewarding. Keeping track of each income stream's timing— quarterly dividends, monthly rental checks, annual payouts from certain funds—enables more accurate forecasting of cash flow and the timing of reinvestments.

An often-overlooked but critical aspect of successful passive income generation is understanding taxation. In certain jurisdictions, different forms of investment yields, such as dividends and capital gains, are taxed at varying rates. Rental property owners face potential property taxes and may need to navigate depreciation rules. Bond interest can push individuals into higher income brackets, influencing overall liability. At times, the strategic use of tax-advantaged accounts, if available, or well-timed trades can greatly influence net gains. Although it may seem complex, gaining at least a foundational grasp of tax strategies can protect hard-earned capital. This proficiency can also inform whether it makes sense to shift holdings from one asset class to another or to restructure them in more suitable vehicles. Tax efficiency, particularly over the span of a lengthy retirement, can mean the difference between maintaining an adequate lifestyle and facing budgetary squeezes.

Strategic planning for long-term financial security ties all these threads together. While budgeting addresses short-term cash flow and passive income streams help sustain day-to-day living, a clear vision for the future underpins the overarching plan. For some, this vision might include downsizing a residence to free up equity and reduce upkeep. Others might decide to relocate for reasons related to climate, healthcare accessibility, or cost of living. Each of these choices carries monetary ramifications that can shift the trajectory of retirement. Carefully evaluating the pros and cons before making significant moves can prevent unanticipated burdens, such as relocation expenses that outstrip the benefits of a lower cost of living, or real estate markets that do not appreciate as hoped.

Ensuring comprehensive insurance coverage forms another pillar of long-term security. Health conditions can evolve unpredictably, and even the most robust budget can be severely tested by extended treatments or specialized care facilities. Some individuals opt for long-term care insurance to shield themselves and their families from catastrophic costs. Others choose to self-insure by building an investment portfolio large enough to handle potential healthcare burdens without exhausting essential assets. The decision rests on personal preference, health status, and risk tolerance, but ignoring the possibility of significant medical costs can leave a retirement plan perilously exposed. In addition, life insurance policies still play a role for retirees who wish to provide for dependents or ensure that estate taxes do not consume a significant portion of the inheritance. Maintaining an updated view of all insurance policies, from health to property to life coverage, helps align them with changing circumstances, ensuring that monthly premiums serve a beneficial and practical function.

Some retirees come to realize that legacy planning is central to the sense of stability they wish to maintain. The desire to leave assets or cherished heirlooms to children and grandchildren often guides how money is allocated in the later phases of life. Trusts, wills, and beneficiary designations become more than mere legal documents; they are instruments for expressing priorities and values. A properly constructed estate plan can mitigate uncertainties and avoid conflicts among family members. Just as important, it can protect assets from unintended encroachments, ensuring resources benefit the intended recipients. For those with philanthropic inclinations, charitable trusts or donor-advised funds might offer a way to merge personal financial security with giving back to the community. The blending of these legal and financial tools, accompanied by periodic reviews to account for changes in the law, fosters a sense of calm, as individuals know their legacy reflects both prudent planning and personal convictions.

Although the structure of a well-devised plan might seem straightforward on paper, life rarely unfolds in accordance with neat tables and forecasts. Economic realities shift, family members face unexpected hardships, and personal passions can emerge that require rethinking assumptions about how to spend and invest. Planning for long-term financial security involves not just laying out goals but practicing an openness to reevaluating them at regular intervals. Some retirees schedule an annual or semiannual review, revisiting each aspect of their budget, investments, insurance coverage, and estate plan to confirm they remain aligned with shifting circumstances. This periodic assessment also encourages objective reflection on any mistakes or oversights that have surfaced, turning them into lessons for future improvements.

Beyond income and expenses, planning for a truly secure and fulfilling later life calls for attention to overall mental and emotional well-being. Financial stress can take a toll on one's sense of purpose, especially if it leads to constant anxiety or second-guessing. Conversely, ignoring finances in an attempt to avoid stress can produce equally harmful results when overlooked expenses or unwise investments lead to more severe problems later. Striking a balance between these extremes begins with recognizing that money is the means to a broader sense of fulfillment rather than an end in itself. Engaging in community activities, pursuing hobbies, or even mentoring younger individuals in financial or professional domains can bring about a sense of relevance and achievement. These ventures do not always generate extra income, yet the intangible returns—social connections, intellectual stimulation, emotional grounding—often feed back into improved financial decision-making.

Cultivating a mindset of lifelong learning also supports the planning process. The economic landscape may be riddled with new technologies, investment vehicles, or regulatory changes that did not exist when many retirees began their working lives. Making the effort to stay informed, whether by reading reputable sources, watching expert discussions, or attending webinars, can illuminate new strategies for stretching retirement dollars further. It may reveal emerging sectors that offer compelling opportunities for passive income or outline changing legislation that warrants adjustments to estate plans. Some retirees find it inspiring to approach these studies with curiosity, viewing them not as burdens but as a chance to maintain a mental edge while preserving assets. This constant updating of knowledge acts as a defense against complacency and helps ensure that retirement finances retain the flexibility to adapt.

At the same time, being well-informed can guard against reckless speculation. Sudden excitement around novel asset classes sometimes tempts investors of all ages, but retirees have less margin for high-stakes gambles. Maintaining a disciplined approach means measuring potential gains against the risk of principal loss, especially for those already reliant on investment returns for everyday living. By combining knowledge with prudence, one can embrace promising developments without jeopardizing core stability. Emphasizing thorough research and, where appropriate, professional advice fosters decisions based on reason rather than fear or hype. This measured approach can help safeguard even the most adventurous retiree from falling victim to market bubbles or unscrupulous schemes that often prey on those eager to maximize gains in a limited timeframe.

Long-term security rests not only on assets but also on a retiree's capacity to adapt physically and mentally. As the years progress, declining mobility or shifting family circumstances can prompt the need for different living arrangements, perhaps a smaller, easier-to-maintain home or a setting closer to loved ones who can provide support. Financial planning interlocks with these considerations by setting aside funds that can cover such transitions without eroding an established portfolio. In some instances, retirees contemplate moving to regions with lower living costs, hoping to stretch their resources. While this can be beneficial, it pays to consider other variables: the availability of quality healthcare, a sense of community, and proximity to relatives or close friends. These less tangible factors can exert a significant impact on quality of life, making them worthy of inclusion in a detailed financial blueprint.

Another dimension of long-term security arises from the interplay between finances and health-related routines. Chronic conditions might require adjustments to diet, exercise, or daily care. Expenses for specialized foods, prescriptions, or therapy sessions can accumulate rapidly. For some, these costs can be partially offset by insurance, but co-pays, deductibles, and coverage gaps still factor in. A robust plan acknowledges these scenarios early, so resources are not unexpectedly strained. In certain cases, a reevaluation of how much is allocated to other pursuits might be required to maintain overall stability. Balancing health-related needs with discretionary spending can be difficult, but awareness of how each choice affects overall well-being ensures that finances support, rather than obstruct, a retiree's desired lifestyle.

Alongside these pragmatic considerations, emotional undercurrents run strong in later life. The emotional significance of leaving behind one's professional identity can prompt impulses to spend as a means of reclaiming purpose or reward. On the flip side, fear of outliving funds may spark excessive frugality that undermines enjoyment or stokes anxiety. Finding the middle ground between these extremes is an ongoing process that intertwines with each financial decision, from daily purchases to major portfolio shifts. Some find comfort in creating small rituals to reaffirm that money is under control, such as reviewing account balances at consistent intervals or planning modest indulgences that do not disrupt broader goals. This steady hand on the tiller, guided by calm self-awareness, enables retirees to relish their newfound freedom without jeopardizing long-term security.

Married or partnered retirees also face the need to coordinate finances in ways that reflect shared objectives. When one partner has different spending habits or investment philosophies, balancing personal preferences becomes a delicate endeavor. Early, honest discussions about expectations can avert conflict later, as can the alignment of retirement timelines and lifestyle aspirations. Jointly prepared budgets help clarify what standard of living is realistic, and how each partner's resources can combine. In some cases, blending funds might simplify tracking and decision-making, while in others, retaining separate accounts fosters autonomy while still contributing to common needs. Recognizing each partner's comfort with risk also aids in structuring investments so that neither person feels unreasonably vulnerable. Communication serves as the lubricant for these arrangements, ensuring that minor disagreements do not escalate into major financial rifts.

For singles or widowed individuals, financial planning can pose additional complexities, especially if they relied on a spouse's expertise in certain areas. Transitioning to a solo approach may mean shouldering responsibilities such as managing rental properties, analyzing complex investments, or updating estate documents. Establishing a supportive network of professionals and peers becomes vital in this scenario. Financial advisors, accountants, or specialized attorneys can offer guidance tailored to individual needs. Trusted friends might step in as sounding boards for key decisions. The capacity to navigate these tasks independently fosters empowerment while preserving resources for personal priorities.

As retirees strive to protect and enhance their portfolios, the specter of market volatility emerges. Economic cycles can bring about downturns that erode equity values, property prices, or bond yields. Though impossible to eliminate risk completely, consistent strategies lessen the blows that might otherwise derail a retirement plan. Maintaining a cushion of easily accessible cash or liquid investments helps manage immediate expenses if markets are particularly unfavorable, preventing the need to sell assets at reduced prices. Diversification, a principle that may have been emphasized earlier in life, remains indispensable. Allocating funds across asset classes, geographic regions, and industries offers resilience. This balanced approach ensures that if one portion of the portfolio declines, others might stabilize or even rise, mitigating the overall impact on daily finances.

Taking a dynamic view of retirement allows for a broader horizon of possibilities. Some discover that part-time or project-based work provides not only added income but also intellectual engagement. Even a few hours a week of consulting, teaching, or freelance writing can offset leisure costs or other outlays while preserving valuable professional skills. For those averse to working for others, small-scale entrepreneurship can be an avenue to explore. Whether by leveraging a long-standing hobby or tapping into specialized knowledge accumulated over a career, these efforts can yield fresh streams of revenue. Though not as entirely "passive" as traditional investment income, these undertakings can combine personal passion with financial gain. If pursued judiciously, they do not necessarily infringe on the sense of freedom that characterizes retirement but rather enhance it by introducing new avenues for creativity and challenge.

The drive to plan effectively for the future also brings attention to inevitable changes in technology that might affect the administration of finances. As digital platforms evolve, banks and brokerages continually refine their processes. Embracing these changes, at least to a certain extent, can streamline managing accounts, paying bills, and monitoring investments. Secure online portals often provide analysis tools that can help retirees visualize how different withdrawal rates, investment allocations, or annual expenses might shape long-term outcomes. While some are cautious about cybersecurity threats, taking basic precautions, such as using secure passwords and multi-factor authentication, can mitigate the majority of risks. In many cases, these digital solutions reduce the paperwork once associated with retirement finances, freeing up time for activities that bring personal satisfaction.

Solid planning can do more than ward off financial risk; it can also improve family relationships by reducing uncertainty about responsibilities and expectations. Children may wonder if they are expected to provide financial support or if they will eventually inherit certain assets. Meanwhile, retirees might feel anxious about becoming a financial burden or losing autonomy. Having open, thoughtful conversations about estate arrangements and any contingencies—such as health events that could necessitate long-term care—can reduce the stigma or fear surrounding these issues. If family members are aware of a person's preferences and have some insight into resources, they can better collaborate if problems arise. Although not every detail needs to be shared publicly, especially if privacy is paramount, a shared understanding of broad strategies promotes unity, ensures that help is available if needed, and respects everyone's boundaries.

In cases where serious health challenges occur, the financial ramifications can multiply. The loss of mobility or cognitive functions might require specialized accommodations at home or the need to hire caregivers. These conditions can deplete funds if not adequately addressed in the planning phase. For example, some may opt to modify their homes preemptively to prevent falls or to install features that support assisted living should that be necessary. Others purchase insurance specifically for potential in-home care or opt to move to a community that offers graduated levels of care under one campus. While these scenarios evoke emotional hurdles, addressing them with foresight preserves the quality of life that retirees desire, rather than leaving important decisions to be made amidst crisis. The peace of mind afforded by such preparation often justifies the expenditure, as it frames healthcare costs not as an unpredictable wave but as a foreseeable consideration that can be budgeted for, insured against, or otherwise mitigated.

Retirement may also be the period when people feel drawn to philanthropic or community engagement in ways that transcend financial donations. Sharing time, expertise, or leadership within nonprofit boards can yield profound personal satisfaction. Although such commitments might not translate into direct income, they can lead to valuable connections and foster a sense of belonging. Paradoxically, volunteering and community service can sometimes open doors to part-time roles or consulting opportunities, which might bolster income streams or at least defray expenses. By staying engaged, retirees maintain ties to social circles that can be important for emotional well-being, and these networks frequently serve as conduits for useful information about grants, scholarships for grandchildren, or community resources that can reduce living costs.

Preserving autonomy remains a central theme in financial well-being for older adults. Sizable accounts or an array of assets do not guarantee independence if individuals lack an underlying structure to manage them prudently. The balance of autonomy and support can be delicate if diminishing physical or cognitive capabilities emerge. Some preemptively designate powers of attorney or establish trusts that place routine matters in the hands of professionals or trusted family members, while retaining personal control over significant decisions. Such arrangements can ease administrative burdens, especially if the complexities of multiple investments, rental properties, or philanthropic commitments become overwhelming. Though it requires an initial leap of faith to delegate responsibilities, it can prove liberating, freeing up time for creative pursuits or community roles that add flavor and meaning to daily life.

Periodic reviews of financial plans are not only prudent but also affirming. Each review session can highlight progress made, clarifying how close one is to achieving specific goals, such as funding a grandchild's education or securing a legacy gift to an institution. These benchmarks can instill a sense of accomplishment that enhances well-being. If a shortfall is discovered or new challenges emerge, the discovery phase allows for timely recalibration. Perhaps expenses have risen in one area while investments have underperformed in another, prompting a shift toward more conservative instruments or a temporary reduction in discretionary spending. Adapting early typically costs less emotional turmoil than postponing action until the situation worsens. There is an inherent power in knowing that a plan is a living entity, shaped by changing markets, shifting family needs, and individual growth.

Sound monetary decisions in later years benefit from perspective acquired through decades of personal and professional experiences. Retirees often possess the wisdom to weigh opportunities and analyze consequences with the composure that comes from seeing economic cycles rise and fall. This vantage point can be valuable not only for personal gain but also when guiding others who may lack equivalent life experience. Younger family members or friends might turn to a retiree for advice, especially around budgeting, debt management, or setting up foundational investments. Although disclaimers are warranted—since every individual's circumstances differ—offering insights can reinforce the retiree's sense of purpose and sharpen their own financial acuity. By articulating lessons learned, many clarify latent truths about their own finances, ensuring that they remain proactive rather than passive observers of their economic well-being.

Change, though sometimes disconcerting, represents the vital force that reshapes retirement finances in beneficial ways. As new investment platforms emerge, healthcare solutions advance, and personal aspirations shift, the capacity to pivot can define success. Regularly revisiting strategies, possibly with the guidance of a trusted financial advisor or through independent research, transforms retirement from a static stage to a vibrant period of recalibration and evolution. It can also inject a sense of novelty, moving beyond the stereotype that retirement heralds an end to personal development. Instead, individuals can embrace it as the stage that ushers in a fresh chapter of autonomy, intellectual discovery, and even targeted entrepreneurship.

Whatever choices are made—whether it is a renewed focus on budgeting, the pursuit of passive income through strategic real estate purchases, or an expansion of philanthropic commitments—the unifying principle remains one of intentional stewardship. Retirees become the architects of their lifestyles, sculpting daily routines and financial pathways in alignment with the priorities that bring meaning to their days. This perspective can transform tasks like monitoring accounts or planning withdrawals into expressions of self-determination rather than chores. Each decision reinforces the sense of independence and security that prudent financial management is meant to protect.

The continuum between short-term satisfaction and long-term planning needs continual refinement. Some might be tempted to budget in the strictest sense early in retirement, then allow more spending freedom as they gain confidence in their resources. Others may adopt the reverse: enjoying a travel- and experience-heavy first few years, then dialing back expenditures later to preserve funds. Neither approach is inherently superior; the key lies in the coherence between personal values and financial moves. If traveling the world to learn about different cultures holds immeasurable significance, that choice might be worth minor compromises in other areas. Conversely, if quiet stability near extended family resonates more strongly, then safeguarding funds for healthcare and community activities might take precedence. The point is less about replicating someone else's path and more about forging an individualized route consistent with personal aspirations.

In formulating these routes, many find peace in the subtle synergy between acceptance of life's inevitable contingencies and determination to shape outcomes as much as possible. Nothing can eliminate the unknown; even the best-prepared retiree can face unforeseen events. Yet the ability to adapt calmly often flows from the assurance provided by a thoughtful financial framework. This framework comprises meticulous budgeting, deliberate cultivation of passive income streams, and the establishment of safeguards for long-term security. In essence, these elements intertwine to form a resilient tapestry that can withstand strains without unraveling. They also leave room for spontaneity, creativity, and communal engagement, affirming that personal growth is neither inhibited nor overshadowed by financial imperatives.

Throughout this unfolding process, confidence and clarity often grow in parallel. A retiree who once felt adrift might discover that systematically evaluating expenses not only eases stress but also reveals unexpected capacities for enjoyment or generosity. The step-by-step exploration of investments may awaken an intellectual curiosity about global markets or economic history, leading to deeper discussions with peers and family. Confronting the reality of mortality through estate planning might sound somber, yet many find it serves as a poignant reminder to live each day more fully, aware that resources can be directed toward experiences or causes that reflect their core values. Each facet of prudent money management resonates beyond spreadsheets and account balances, shaping outlooks on how to inhabit the years that remain.

This holistic approach anchors itself in the recognition that financial well-being is a fluid state, not an endpoint. Just as career ambitions can morph over time, retirement objectives evolve. Life does not halt at a certain age, nor does it simplify in a linear fashion. Some transitions may be smooth, while others demand radical rethinking of established practices. Embracing this fluidity liberates retirees from the belief that all decisions must be finalized at the moment they step away from work. They can grant themselves permission to continue experimenting, learning new skills, relocating, adjusting budgets, or trying fresh investment strategies when circumstances call for it. These experiments gain a measure of safety from the presence of a well-maintained core plan that accounts for anticipated costs and risks.

In cultivating these qualities of awareness, flexibility, and accountability, retirees rarely walk alone. Modern resources, from online communities to specialized financial advisors, stand ready to provide guidance. The choice to seek help, whether for clarifying tax codes or fine-tuning a portfolio, reflects wisdom rather than an admission of ignorance. Indeed, collaborating with professionals or knowledgeable peers can streamline complex tasks and save time. Those who remain open to such collaborations often find that new perspectives spark innovative solutions. An advisor might highlight a little-known investment or a tax optimization strategy, while a fellow retiree might share personal anecdotes about downsizing or traveling that shed light on hidden costs or unexpected benefits. In these shared explorations, individuals strengthen each other's capacity to navigate retirement finances with confidence and creativity.

Ultimately, maintaining financial well-being during these years is less about reaching a static plateau than about perpetuating a pattern of informed choices. By systematically budgeting, retirees gain an intimate understanding of their cash flow. By harnessing passive income and investment strategies, they establish a reliable means of supporting day-to-day living while preserving the possibility of capital growth. By engaging in long-term planning, they anchor themselves against potential upheavals, whether from health complications, market downturns, or family transitions. Together, these efforts form a network of security that supports a meaningful existence, allowing one to relish the freedoms and opportunities that come with stepping away from a career.

Such is the subtle art of financial independence in later life. Each new morning offers a reminder that discipline in money matters can serve as a conduit to deeper satisfaction. A prudent yet adaptive plan alleviates the nagging anxiety that might otherwise erode the joys of retirement, and it safeguards the future without strangling the present. There is no absolute formula to guarantee a worry-free experience in these years. However, by embracing steady self-reflection, thoughtful resource allocation, and a willingness to adjust when necessary, a retiree can cultivate an environment in which financial stability and personal fulfillment coexist harmoniously. This environment, shaped by conscious effort and enriched by continuing exploration, represents the essence of thriving in retirement: an existence marked by security, meaning, and the calm knowledge that one's resources are responsibly stewarded for whatever may come.

Chapter 11: Staying Professionally Engaged

Remaining active in one's chosen field, or branching out into new territories of professional engagement, can be a source of immense satisfaction and added financial stability later in life. Many find that once the traditional obligations of full-time employment recede, fresh opportunities for part-time arrangements, entrepreneurial ventures, or advisory roles emerge with surprising clarity. These paths do not necessarily demand the same intensity of commitment required during the peak years of a career. Instead, they offer a chance to deploy accumulated expertise in ways that are both profitable and personally meaningful. For some, the allure lies in flexible schedules and a gentler pace; for others, it is the challenge of building a new enterprise or contributing wisdom to younger professionals. Whatever the motivation, maintaining professional engagement can enrich daily life, expand social networks, and foster a continued sense of identity and purpose. In an age where definitions of work and retirement are changing rapidly, exploring such avenues provides not only material rewards but also a sense of fulfillment that transcends mere economic gain.

A major draw for many who step back from full-time roles is the option to scale down rather than retire entirely. Part-time arrangements or consulting engagements cater to those who value the stimulation of work but crave a more balanced lifestyle. Shifting from a demanding schedule to a more measured approach can accommodate personal interests, family obligations, or the simple desire to savor each day without the frenetic tempo that often accompanies a full-time career. In these scenarios, individuals may choose to retain their established connections—colleagues, industry networks, or clients—while lessening the burden on time and energy. This approach can be especially attractive for those in fields where interpersonal relationships carry significant weight, such as legal services, healthcare, or creative industries. Instead of relinquishing a lifetime of cultivated expertise, part-time practitioners can continue to deliver value to clients or organizations, reinforcing a sense of relevance and continuity.

At the practical level, the benefits of part-time work often include a steadier transition into retirement rather than an abrupt cessation of professional activity. By continuing to earn income while simultaneously drawing on savings or pensions, many discover greater peace of mind regarding their personal finances. This approach can lessen the strain on retirement accounts or investment portfolios, potentially prolonging the sustainability of existing assets. In addition, part-time commitments allow individuals to maintain active skill sets, keeping them sharp and ready should new opportunities arise. Skills honed over decades of consistent practice—problem-solving, client relations, strategic thinking—can remain in use through scaled-back engagements, offering the dual reward of income and a sense of mastery. Freed from the relentless pace of previous decades, people may also find more room to refine their abilities, focusing on areas of professional practice they find most rewarding or that clients value most highly.

Consulting arrangements follow a similar trajectory but often revolve around project-based collaborations rather than day-to-day work. In such cases, a person might coordinate with a firm, nonprofit, or public agency to tackle specific challenges within a set timeframe. For instance, a retiree with deep knowledge in architectural design might be contracted to advise on the development of a new civic space, or an IT specialist might be called upon to streamline a company's digital infrastructure. In each scenario, the consultant's primary responsibility is to offer insight, craft solutions, and occasionally guide teams toward implementation. The ephemeral nature of consulting projects can be enticing. A consultant can accept a few engagements each year, leaving ample room for personal travel, leisure activities, or family responsibilities. The projects themselves may span weeks or months, culminating in final deliverables that benefit from the consultant's specialized knowledge. For many, this cyclical rhythm of intense involvement followed by downtime aligns well with later-life priorities.

Beyond finances, part-time or project-based work also contributes to intellectual engagement. When individuals stay involved in their fields, they are exposed to emerging trends, new technologies, and the evolving demands of clients or end-users. This continuous contact with the pulse of an industry can invigorate the mind, fueling the same curiosity and problem-solving capabilities cultivated over a long career. Instead of letting those capacities atrophy, professionals in part-time roles refine them further in the face of modern developments. The result is often a gratifying sense of still being "in the mix," influencing real-world outcomes and exchanging ideas with peers. Such stimulation can stave off the boredom or disconnection that some experience when they withdraw from professional life entirely. Whether consulting for a startup, serving as an occasional instructor in a community college, or freelancing in design or writing, part-timers preserve channels of collaboration and remain abreast of innovations that shape the trajectory of their industry.

These flexible pathways can also meld seamlessly with the pursuit of fresh passions, especially when part-time roles align with newly discovered interests. An individual whose career revolved around corporate finance might decide to focus on consulting for mission-driven organizations or nonprofits, translating financial acumen into strategic guidance that benefits a cause. Another might leverage public relations skills to advise local charities on fundraising campaigns, uniting personal values with professional strengths. In such contexts, the fulfillment comes not just from an income stream but also from seeing how one's labor effects tangible improvements in the community. The effect can be deeply motivating, reminding retirees that their talents retain immense power to catalyze positive change, even if they are no longer working full-time.

For those with a thirst for challenge, exploring entrepreneurship or founding a small business may resonate more strongly. Indeed, many discover a latent entrepreneurial spirit only in later adulthood, once they have more control over their time and have accumulated a wealth of domain knowledge. Starting a business can be both thrilling and daunting. On one hand, it offers unparalleled creative freedom: the founder can shape the enterprise's mission, culture, and products or services without having to conform to a larger corporate structure. On the other hand, entrepreneurship involves risk, financial investment, and the potential for stress as the fledgling endeavor finds its footing in a competitive marketplace. Nevertheless, older entrepreneurs often bring significant advantages to the table. A lifetime of professional and personal experiences can translate into strong networks, seasoned judgment, and a nuanced grasp of industry intricacies. These qualities can help them sidestep common pitfalls that plague less experienced business owners.

Technological advances have further lowered the barriers to establishing a new venture. Digital platforms, crowdfunding sites, and social media make it feasible to reach large audiences without incurring the overhead costs that once deterred small-scale entrepreneurs. Anyone with a compelling idea and a willingness to learn can attempt to launch an online shop, consult on a digital platform, or develop an application, even if they have minimal programming experience. Many retirees have used this approach to share specialized skills, from culinary knowledge to niche arts and crafts. Such enterprises can be scaled according to personal preference. Some prefer a modest side venture that occupies a few hours each week, while others plunge into the venture wholeheartedly, replicating the drive of their earlier careers but retaining autonomy over pace and direction.

For example, a retired teacher might harness decades of expertise to create an online tutoring and educational resource hub, offering sessions to students worldwide and employing other qualified instructors to diversify offerings. A mechanical engineer could develop prototypes for sustainable household tools, leveraging mechanical know-how and forging partnerships with local artisans to expand production. Alternatively, an individual with a deep love of travel might establish a curated travel advice service, drawing on personal journeys and organizational skills to craft customized itineraries for clients. In each instance, launching such an enterprise underscores that retirement need not spell the end of professional ambition. Instead, it can open new chapters grounded in creativity, autonomy, and purposeful engagement.

Starting a business in later life also dovetails with the notion of bridging generational knowledge. Partnerships between older founders and younger, tech-savvy collaborators can yield a powerful blend of experience, contemporary perspective, and digital competence. Such intergenerational collaboration often thrives on mutual respect, where each party acknowledges the other's strengths. Experienced partners bring market insight, leadership acumen, and strategic vision derived from decades of management or client-facing roles. Younger collaborators may contribute a grasp of cutting-edge technologies, social media marketing strategies, and fresh consumer trends. This synergy fosters an environment where a business concept can flourish, guided by time-tested wisdom but dynamic enough to adapt to a rapidly shifting marketplace. The result is often a robust structure that accommodates growth, whether the venture remains a localized offering or scales to national or international significance.

As with any entrepreneurial endeavor, thorough planning and risk assessment remain crucial. While passion and a sense of mission can drive a venture, practicality and research serve as its backbone. Conducting feasibility studies, drafting clear business plans, and evaluating financial projections are time-honored steps that reduce the likelihood of unpleasant surprises. Entrepreneurs must also consider how much of their personal savings they feel comfortable allocating to the new project, weighing potential returns against the security of a retirement nest egg. Some mitigate risk by seeking external funding, exploring grants, loans, or small investor contributions that limit personal exposure. Others prefer to remain fully self-funded, relying on modest initial outlays, a methodical growth approach, and the confidence derived from controlling every aspect of the enterprise. Regardless of the chosen financial model, being systematic and seeking professional advice when needed helps ensure that the joys of business creation do not devolve into financial strain.

In parallel, an understated but significant source of opportunity lies in advisory roles. Over the course of long careers, many individuals attain a perspective rich in leadership, conflict resolution, strategic planning, or technical expertise. These insights can prove invaluable to companies, non-profit organizations, or governmental agencies looking to tackle complex projects or refine their policies. Serving on advisory boards or committees often satisfies the desire to remain influential while freeing the advisor from the daily responsibilities of operational management. Instead of orchestrating every detail, advisors act as sounding boards for executives or team leaders, offering pointed guidance, constructive critique, and the kind of institutional memory that can avert repeating historical mistakes.

Advisory roles can manifest in various forms. Some organizations establish formal boards comprising people from diverse disciplines, trusting that collective expertise fosters well-rounded decision-making. Others prefer more ad hoc arrangements, convening expert panels to evaluate new initiatives or public policy proposals. In the corporate sector, established companies may enlist the help of retirees with sterling reputations to shape expansions into unfamiliar markets or to coach rising managers. In the world of philanthropy, large foundations can benefit from advisors versed in community outreach or program design, ensuring that grant-making strategies align with real community needs. In each context, seasoned professionals wield not only subject-area mastery but also an understanding of how to navigate interpersonal dynamics. This ability to unify and guide teams can be a decisive asset in shaping outcomes.

For individuals seeking a flexible schedule and a direct line to impactful discussions, these advisory positions often deliver precisely that. Meetings may take place quarterly or semi-annually, interspersed with electronic updates or occasional site visits. This pacing allows a retiree to pursue other passions—travel, hobbies, part-time consulting—while remaining a recognized authority whose voice resonates in pivotal conversations. The moral and intellectual satisfaction can be profound: each suggestion or critique has the potential to influence real-world policies, products, or philanthropic endeavors. Financial compensation for these roles varies widely;

some are paid positions, others provide stipends or honoraria, and still others are purely voluntary. Depending on the advisor's personal objectives, each arrangement can be a conduit for continued growth, both monetarily and in terms of self-fulfillment.

In many instances, individuals combine multiple approaches, weaving together part-time consulting, entrepreneurial ventures, and advisory responsibilities in a tapestry of professional engagement that suits their preferences. One might accept a handful of consulting gigs each year, support a startup co-founded with a friend, and offer expertise pro bono to a civic board or philanthropic organization, all while maintaining ample time for personal interests. The capacity to shape this blend of activities emerges partly from a sense of self-knowledge: an understanding of which aspects of work bring genuine satisfaction and how best to pace one's commitments. By structuring professional endeavors around personal strengths and values, retirees mitigate stress and preserve the enthusiasm that inspired them to remain active in the first place.

Not to be overlooked is the effect of these engagements on mental and emotional well-being. Many who transition away from full-time employment describe a feeling of loss if they completely disengage from the working world. For decades, a professional identity can form an integral part of how an individual sees themselves, how they interact socially, and what sense of accomplishment they derive from daily life. While retirement opens space for rest and reinvention, it can also spark uncertainty about one's ongoing contribution to society. Choosing to remain professionally involved, whether through part-time work, launching a venture, or serving as an advisor, can ease these doubts. By regularly applying their knowledge and skill, individuals affirm that their experiences remain pertinent, that their insights can still benefit others, and that they can find new ways to achieve personal growth.

Furthermore, staying active in work-like activities encourages continuous learning, a facet that complements other forms of personal development. Entrepreneurs, for instance, rapidly discover that founding a new business demands embracing emerging technologies, marketing methods, and consumer behavior insights that may be alien to them. Advisors are often compelled to research new policy frameworks, alternative organizational models, and changing economic climates before proffering guidance. Similarly, part-time consultants find themselves grappling with updated industry regulations or fresh client expectations that require them to rethink entrenched approaches. These endeavors ensure that intellectual capacities remain vibrant and flexible, providing a bulwark against the monotony or mental stagnation that occasionally accompanies full withdrawal from the working sphere.

An equally valuable benefit is the influence on future generations. Seasoned individuals who become mentors or role models through their professional engagements often leave a lasting imprint. Younger employees, entrepreneurs, or community leaders glean from the depth of an experienced professional's perspective, inheriting best practices and moral lessons that can steer them away from avoidable missteps. This passing of the torch strengthens the overall ecosystem of an industry or organization, preserving knowledge that might otherwise fade. Such mentorship can occur naturally as part of advisory board service or consulting projects, but it can also be formalized. Some people choose to establish professional development programs or workshops aimed at up-and-coming talents. The pride and sense of legacy that derive from nurturing capable successors can be a deeply rewarding dimension of continued professional participation.

Nevertheless, balancing multiple professional endeavors in later life requires deliberate consideration of personal limits. While it can be tempting to take on a flurry of interesting projects or to remain in high demand, one must remember that the hallmark of this stage is the liberty to choose how time is allocated. Overextending can quickly erode the sense of freedom that partial retirement promises. Maintaining a realistic assessment of one's energy, availability, and desire is key to preserving well-being. It is entirely acceptable to decline certain engagements, especially if they threaten to consume excessive bandwidth or conflict with personal objectives. Taking on fewer but more carefully aligned opportunities often results in higher-quality outcomes and a more sustainable pace, ensuring that each project receives the full measure of attention and expertise it deserves.

Boundaries are central in this calculus. At times, old colleagues or industry partners might press for heavier involvement, especially if they are eager to capitalize on the retiree's wealth of experience. Being able to politely but firmly define one's limits—be it a maximum number of hours per week or limiting the scope of responsibilities—helps maintain harmony. Clear communication of these constraints allows those seeking assistance to respect them without harboring unrealistic expectations. To this end, drafting a concise service agreement or terms of reference for consulting or advisory roles can forestall misunderstandings. It might stipulate the frequency of meetings, the scope of advisory input, or the nature of deliverables. Such clarity fosters mutual respect, allowing the retiree to remain engaged on comfortable terms and the client or organization to plan effectively.

Likewise, for older entrepreneurs, the unpredictability of business growth underscores the importance of safeguarding personal health and finances. A brilliant concept might gain traction quickly, demanding round-the-clock focus reminiscent of earlier career phases. Setting up robust organizational structures, delegating responsibilities to competent partners, and scheduling regular periods of rest or recreation can forestall burnout. Entrepreneurs in this stage of life can also consider succession planning from the outset, identifying who might eventually manage or inherit the business. This foresight not only protects the founder's retirement but also assures any employees or customers of stable continuity. Building an entity that outlives the founder can be a poignant exercise in legacy-building, offering a tangible demonstration of how lifelong expertise can impact communities or industries well into the future.

From a financial standpoint, caution must guide the integration of these professional pursuits with broader retirement goals. While part-time income, consulting fees, or business profits can strengthen financial stability, they should ideally complement, rather than substitute, thorough retirement planning. If a new venture proves unprofitable or a contract fails to materialize, the retiree should still remain secure. Regularly revisiting one's overall financial strategy—in conjunction with advisors or wealth managers—guards against placing undue pressure on uncertain earnings. It ensures that the margin for error remains tolerable. By clarifying how much risk is acceptable in entrepreneurial initiatives, how much time can be dedicated to paid advisory work, and how all these variables intersect with personal savings, individuals lay the groundwork for a stable, gratifying mixture of professional engagement and leisure.

Equally crucial is emotional readiness. Some relish the excitement of forging ahead in new professional directions, whereas others prefer a gentler involvement or even a short sabbatical before deciding on the next chapter. The transition away from a longstanding position can prompt reflection on priorities, revealing a desire to invest more heavily in family, personal health, or community service. In such cases, smaller-scale professional roles—like occasional consulting or participating in a single advisory board—may suffice. Conversely, people who discover an unquenched entrepreneurial zeal may choose to channel their vigor into launching an enterprise, employing the business sense accumulated over decades. Each choice shapes a different experience of later life, and there is no universal path. What matters is aligning these decisions with genuine aspirations and the real constraints of personal well-being.

Over time, a pattern of engaging in part-time, advisory, or entrepreneurial activities can deepen a sense of belonging in broader networks. Former peers who took diverse paths after formal retirement may become collaborators or mentors themselves, forging a community of professionals who continue to evolve together. Peer groups can exchange ideas, critique business models, or even co-author educational materials that preserve industry knowledge. The synergy among such experienced individuals often produces innovations with potential ripple effects that benefit entire fields. Even those who do not set out to be innovators may inadvertently refine best practices or spark breakthroughs, simply because their backgrounds allow for critical perspectives that younger professionals have yet to develop. Seeing real transformations emerge from collective wisdom adds immeasurable meaning to post-career engagement.

At a personal level, staying professionally active can also counteract stereotypes that cast older adults as disengaged or technologically inept. By adapting to new work environments, mastering emerging tools, or leading cutting-edge initiatives, older professionals defy assumptions about age-based limitations. Their successes stand as examples that competence and creativity remain robust throughout the lifespan, challenging narrow views of retirement as a passive decline. Rather than receding into the background, those who persist in meaningful work remind society that diverse voices and experiences enrich the workforce, fueling intergenerational dialogue that is crucial for sustainable progress.

Notably, many glean unexpected inspiration from the synergy between professional endeavors and other facets of life. A part-time consultant might discover that the organizational skills required in business sharpen their approach to personal hobbies or philanthropic projects. An entrepreneur who dips into new realms of technology might parlay those insights into more effective home management or sharper analytical thinking. Advisors who steer organizations toward ethical decision-making often find themselves mulling over deeper questions of legacy and community involvement in their own time. Far from compartmentalizing life into discrete segments, continued professional engagement can inform how retirees conduct themselves in family interactions, volunteer roles, or creative pursuits. This holistic integration underscores that intellectual vigor and moral clarity can be ongoing sources of growth, not traits fixed by the end of a conventional career.

Examining the broader cultural impact, a willingness among retirees to keep their hands in the professional realm can help ease labor shortages in specialized industries. In some sectors— particularly healthcare, engineering, or education—a wave of retirements could otherwise leave critical skill gaps. Tapping into this reservoir of experienced talent, albeit in more flexible forms, can alleviate workforce pressures while helping novices transition into leadership roles. Formalized "returnship" programs or senior talent pools, supported by professional organizations, can match retirees with employers seeking seasoned expertise. Such initiatives reduce friction on both sides: older professionals gain structured channels to find meaningful assignments, while employers access knowledge capital that might otherwise vanish.

Throughout all these possibilities, it is worth emphasizing the importance of authentic interest. The prime advantage of this stage is the freedom to pursue tasks that resonate on a deeper level rather than merely fulfilling financial obligations or external expectations. If a certain venture or advisory role ceases to spark enthusiasm, pivoting away is far simpler for someone who has already built a stable personal foundation. This freedom forms the essence of a truly fulfilling post-career life: the capacity to align daily actions with deeper convictions about purpose, enjoyment, and contribution. By selecting activities that echo personal values and aptitudes, individuals ensure that their professional involvement remains a source of satisfaction, not a burden.

In sum, those navigating the transition from full-time employment have at their disposal a rich spectrum of ways to stay professionally engaged. Part-time or consulting roles deliver a flexible rhythm that can supplement finances, maintain cognitive agility, and preserve professional networks. Entrepreneurial ventures invite creativity, forging new enterprises that might weave together passion and profit. Advisory positions harness the gravitas of extensive experience, enabling retirees to shape decisions in fields they care about, without resuming the rigors of an operational role. Each route is adaptable, permitting individuals to modulate their commitment as life circumstances evolve. By blending these options, older adults can continue exercising their talents, bridging the gap between the achievements of the past and the unforeseen potential of the future. Taken as a whole, professional engagement in later life stands not merely as a postscript to a career well lived, but as a vibrant, relevant chapter that affirms the lasting value of wisdom, adaptability, and a spirit of perpetual growth.

Chapter 12: Travel and Adventure in Retirement

Travel represents a gateway to new perspectives and opportunities, especially for individuals who have spent many years focusing on careers, family responsibilities, and day-to-day routines. The period following a primary occupation offers a chance to explore unfamiliar landscapes, forge connections with different cultures, and step out of the comfort zone in ways that reinvigorate the spirit. While some may initially hesitate to embark on extended journeys out of concern for expense, safety, or personal convenience, many discover that thoughtful planning and a mindset geared toward discovery unlock experiences that enrich the later stages of life. The pursuit of affordable travel does not mean surrendering quality or comfort; instead, it involves a willingness to adapt, research, and embrace creative approaches to journeying. Over time, such expeditions can merge seamlessly into the broader tapestry of life beyond a main career, becoming as integral to personal fulfillment as any financial or familial endeavor.

For those contemplating travel during this stage, the first step is often a meticulous assessment of available resources, timelines, and motivations. Although it might be easy to feel intimidated by airfare prices or the cost of accommodations in popular tourist hubs, a strategic approach can yield far more accessible options. Identifying destinations during off-peak seasons, for instance, can substantially reduce expenses related to both transportation and lodging. Because many retirees are no longer bound by the rigid constraints of work schedules or school calendars, they can opt to travel when the majority of tourists stay home. This flexibility often translates into more competitive flight prices, discounted hotel rates, and a calmer experience overall. The calmness that results from reduced crowds not only benefits the budget but also allows for a deeper appreciation of local culture, as it is easier to engage with residents, explore attractions without long lines, and savor the rhythm of daily life in each place.

Just as important as selecting the right travel window is choosing accommodations suited to personal interests and comfort levels. While luxurious resorts may appeal to some, others find that homestays, apartment rentals, or small guesthouses create a more intimate connection with the surrounding area. These alternatives can also be more cost-effective than traditional hotels. Some individuals discover that renting an apartment in a well-connected neighborhood encourages immersion in community life, whether through buying ingredients at a local market, conversing with neighbors, or attending nearby social events. Moreover, with the rise of reputable online platforms, it has become simpler to locate and arrange these temporary residences, often in places that remain off the mainstream tourism radar. Taking time to compare different types of lodgings can pay dividends, as each style comes with its own advantages and trade-offs. A guesthouse might include freshly prepared breakfasts and attentive staff, whereas a rented home might offer more privacy and the freedom to cook one's own meals.

Those who wish to delve deeper into the heart of a destination sometimes opt for homestay programs that allow them to live with a local family. Although this arrangement can feel daunting, especially to travelers unaccustomed to communal living, the benefits can be profound. Whether over shared meals or group outings, guests gain insights into the host culture that would remain invisible in standard tourist settings. This immersive style often ignites lasting friendships and fosters a broader understanding of local traditions, values, and social norms. Such emotional connections transcend the typical tourist experience, offering stories and lessons that enrich the traveler long after the suitcase is unpacked. On a practical level, homestays can also be budget-friendly, making them a smart choice for those who prioritize meaningful interactions over luxury amenities.

Affordability can be enhanced further by exploring new methods of transportation. Although commercial flights remain a mainstay for intercontinental travel, trains and buses within a region can be surprisingly comfortable and cost-effective, especially for retirees with flexible itineraries. Overnight sleeper trains, for instance, offer the dual advantage of saving on a night's accommodation while providing a leisurely ride through diverse landscapes. Traveling by train often reduces stress associated with airports and layovers, and fosters opportunities for spontaneous conversations with fellow passengers. Similarly, well-established bus networks in many parts of the world feature roomy seats, on-board amenities, and scenic routes that connect travelers to rural areas seldom frequented by tourists. These journeys, albeit slower than flying, encourage a different kind of exploration that reveals local color through stops in small towns and regional food stalls, painting a vivid tableau of daily life.

For those concerned about health or comfort, careful research ensures that slower or alternative modes of transport do not compromise safety. Reputable transportation providers maintain high standards for cleanliness, punctuality, and reliability, making it possible to explore remote destinations without undue worry. It can help to pay attention to reviews from others who have recently used the service, as these firsthand accounts often highlight the nuances of any given route or mode of travel. If health considerations demand extra caution, planning shorter segments or opting for daytime travel can alleviate anxiety. An extended itinerary, broken into manageable chunks, allows travelers to pace themselves, savoring each site rather than rushing through an oversized agenda. This gradual approach blends seamlessly with the notion of retirement as a period when time becomes more flexible. Rather than feeling pressured to experience everything at once, individuals can tailor each journey to personal preferences and stamina levels.

Comfort and safety encompass more than just modes of transportation. Even in well-developed destinations, careful packing and a proactive mindset can make a significant difference in mitigating risks. Checking travel advisories, ensuring that travel insurance covers medical emergencies, and scheduling routine doctor visits before departure are all prudent measures. These steps foster peace of mind, allowing individuals to engage more fully with the surroundings instead of worrying about contingencies. In many cases, local healthcare systems may be robust, but language barriers or unfamiliar customs can complicate getting assistance should a problem arise. Documenting relevant medical information, including prescriptions, allergies, and blood type, ensures that help can be administered swiftly if needed. Simple acts like carrying a compact first-aid kit, staying hydrated, and wearing appropriate footwear for prolonged walks can prevent minor issues from escalating into major disruptions.

Local cuisine often stands out as one of the greatest pleasures of travel, but dietary shifts can pose some challenges, particularly for older travelers with specific nutritional concerns. While part of the enjoyment lies in savoring dishes unique to each region, it remains crucial to exercise moderation and vigilance. Sampling street food can be an exhilarating aspect of the experience, yet paying attention to hygiene and cleanliness is essential. Observing whether vendors use fresh ingredients, keep their stalls tidy, and store food at safe temperatures can help avoid common gastrointestinal issues. In areas where tap water is not potable, opting for sealed bottled water or carrying a reusable filtered water container prevents the discomfort of unexpected illness. These small precautions rarely diminish enjoyment. Instead, they empower travelers to indulge in local delicacies with minimal risk of compromising comfort.

Many individuals who venture into new countries or unfamiliar regions find themselves drawn to cultural and experiential pursuits that transcend passive sightseeing. Cultural immersion can take various forms, from enrolling in a short-term language course to participating in cooking classes, dance workshops, or guided historical tours. Engaging directly with local traditions opens doors to insights about social structures, spiritual beliefs, and generational knowledge that define each destination's character. Retirees often arrive with an extensive repertoire of life experiences, and they discover a renewed sense of purpose by exchanging perspectives with those from different backgrounds. This cross-cultural dialogue can spark creativity, empathy, or even personal growth, reinforcing the notion that travel in later life can be transformative rather than merely leisurely. By devoting time and resources to immersive experiences, travelers can forge memories that linger more vividly than a quick pass through a famous monument.

Experiential travel is not limited to formal programs. Sometimes the most profound interactions occur spontaneously, perhaps through a chance meeting at a local café or an invitation to a community festival. A willingness to be curious, patient, and polite often transcends language barriers, smoothing the path for meaningful encounters. Trying to learn basic greetings or phrases in the local tongue can earn respect from residents and pave the way for deeper conversations. Whether purchasing groceries at a neighborhood market, attending a crafts fair, or exploring a regional museum, curiosity rooted in genuine interest fosters bonds that are hard to replicate in purely tourist-oriented environments. These small gestures of cultural appreciation create a mutually enriching exchange, as locals frequently take pride in showcasing their heritage. Retirees who cultivate these interactions may discover that the friendships they forge abroad remain enduring and even prompt return visits in the future.

One of the joys of retirement travel lies in the opportunity to approach adventures at a deliberate, unhurried pace. Instead of arriving in a country determined to check off every landmark in record time, individuals can spend extended periods in a single city or region, delving into subtleties that short-term visitors miss. This approach suits retirees who prefer not to rush from one attraction to another, given that slower travel reduces fatigue and enriches each encounter. By renting a modest apartment for several weeks, for instance, travelers gain the luxury of exploring local life day by day. They might frequent the same bakery, striking up conversations with staff and returning customers, or become regulars at a cozy restaurant whose proprietors welcome them as part of the community. These experiences reaffirm that traveling is not merely about collecting photos; it is about forging relationships, deepening perspectives, and weaving new threads into the fabric of one's personal journey.

Budgeting for these sustained stays can be managed with creativity, particularly for those who spent earlier decades practicing prudent financial habits. The funds that might have gone toward more hurried excursions can be redirected toward extended lodging in a centrally located but not necessarily luxurious space. Traveling outside prime holiday seasons can stretch those resources further, making it possible to enjoy a comfortable environment without incurring premium rates. Additional strategies include signing up for loyalty programs associated with airlines or hotel chains, which may accumulate points that reduce overall costs. Credit cards designed for travelers sometimes provide mileage bonuses, insurance coverage for lost luggage, or waived foreign transaction fees, all of which can ease concerns about unforeseen expenditures. Throughout these efforts, a measured sense of adaptation prevails, underscoring that thoughtful planning and a flexible approach can merge affordability with depth of experience.

Volunteering abroad provides a different yet equally meaningful entry point for cultural and experiential engagement. Many retirees discover that offering their time to schools, libraries, conservation projects, or health clinics fosters a deeper sense of connection than simple tourism can achieve. While volunteer programs vary in scope and legitimacy, reputable organizations connect participants to community-driven initiatives that respect local expertise and address actual needs. Alongside the satisfaction of contributing to worthwhile causes, individuals gain a window into community life that is often unavailable to transient visitors. This type of travel can be particularly rewarding for those who want to remain active, apply professional or life skills in a fresh context, and pass along knowledge to younger generations. Additionally, living and working alongside local residents dispels stereotypes, builds empathy, and leaves a positive footprint in the places that host travelers.

For travelers inclined toward the arts, cultural festivals highlight another dimension of immersive exploration. Throughout the year, numerous cities around the world stage events that celebrate everything from music, dance, and theater to religious observances and historical commemorations. Participating in a spirited festival can be transformative, as it invites travelers to join the heart of local celebrations. Whether watching a centuries-old parade, observing traditional ceremonies, or tapping one's foot to the rhythms of regional music, the experience can kindle a revitalized sense of wonder. Some festivals have existed for generations, passing customs and folklore from elders to young people. Others reflect modern artistic fusions that bring diverse subcultures together. This interplay of past and present resonates deeply, reminding visitors that culture is not static but evolves with each generation.

Travel can also extend beyond traditional boundaries for those with a spirit of adventure and a taste for active pursuits. Some retirees seize the opportunity to go trekking in mountain regions, cycle along scenic coastal roads, or pursue aquatic sports in vibrant coral reefs. Careful preparation ensures that physical challenges match one's abilities, which might include consulting with a physician to confirm that health conditions permit moderate to strenuous activity. For many older adults, however, the sense of accomplishment after completing a challenging trek or a long cycling trip can be immense, reinforcing the belief that age need not be an impediment to exploration. By choosing routes designed for a spectrum of fitness levels, travelers can strike a balance between pushing limits and maintaining personal safety. In these pursuits, the support of qualified local guides adds reassurance, providing expertise on weather conditions, trail routes, and safe practices in remote locations.

The desire for safety also plays an integral role in shaping travel decisions. After decades of working and saving diligently, many retirees wish to savor new places without undue risks. Thorough planning includes becoming aware of local customs, laws, and potential scams that might target out-of-town visitors. Maintaining vigilance in crowded areas, such as markets or public transportation hubs, can prevent theft or misunderstandings. At the same time, courtesy and respect toward local residents go a long way in fostering a positive environment. Learning a few polite phrases in the local language can dispel tension, and a friendly smile or patient attitude often clears up minor mishaps before they escalate. Should any misfortune occur, travel insurance that provides coverage for theft, cancellation, or health-related emergencies can mitigate financial loss. This buffer allows individuals to focus on enjoyment rather than worrying incessantly about potential pitfalls.

Traveling companions matter just as much as destinations. Some prefer going solo, delighting in the freedom to shape itineraries independently, while others find that teaming up with friends or family adds depth and shared memories to the experience. Group travel can split costs on accommodations, transportation, or guided tours, making it more budget-friendly in certain contexts. Close companions also offer emotional and logistical support, which can be reassuring if language barriers or unexpected detours arise. For retirees who appreciate meeting new people, organized tours and cultural exchange programs unite travelers with similar interests. The friendships formed during such group experiences sometimes last for years, with participants planning future reunions or joint vacations. Whether traveling alone or in company, the key is recognizing personal preferences and establishing boundaries or guidelines to ensure everyone's comfort.

Unexpected events invariably occur, no matter how well an itinerary is structured. Flights might be delayed, luggage might go astray, or local political situations might prompt changes in plans. Travelers who approach these moments with patience and an open mind often find that obstacles become catalysts for unexpected discovery. A missed bus can spark a spontaneous conversation in a roadside café; a delayed flight may allow for a stroll through a previously unexplored area of an airport city. Over time, such occurrences become part of a traveler's repertoire of anecdotes and reflections, highlighting the beauty and unpredictability of the human experience. While these mishaps can be frustrating in the moment, they also underscore the resilient mindset that many develop through decades of life experience. By embracing flexibility and calm, travelers can view each hiccup as an integral component of the journey itself.

Modern technology has redefined how people prepare for and document travel. Before setting foot outside their homes, retirees can explore virtual tours, read in-depth reviews, compare prices across numerous platforms, and even preview local cultural events via streaming platforms. This level of preparation significantly lowers the risk of misinformation and ensures that travelers arrive equipped with realistic expectations. Armed with smartphones or tablets, visitors can navigate unfamiliar streets using satellite maps, manage translations through language apps, and capture high-resolution photos of their adventures. Sharing these images in real time with loved ones can nurture a sense of connection, enabling friends and family to follow along from afar. However, striking a balance remains crucial. Constantly checking devices or striving for social media perfection can detract from the sense of immediacy that is the hallmark of an enriching travel experience. Mindfully stepping away from screens when possible helps reinforce presence, ensuring that the sights, sounds, and scents of a destination imprint themselves more indelibly in memory.

Culinary exploration stands as a highlight for many who seek a rich travel experience, and this may extend beyond sampling local fare in restaurants. Cooking classes taught by talented chefs or homemakers present an authentic introduction to regional dishes. These sessions go beyond mere tastings, illustrating how flavors, ingredients, and traditions converge in a tangible expression of cultural identity. Participants often shop for produce at local markets alongside instructors, gaining knowledge of seasonal foods and specialized cooking techniques. Such hands-on experiences can lead to fresh insights into how geography and history shape a region's gastronomic heritage. Those who return home with newly acquired recipes and skills can share these culinary delights with friends and family, effectively carrying a piece of their journey into future gatherings. This form of cultural exchange underscores the ongoing impact of each trip, reminding individuals that traveling is not limited to the moment of exploration but resonates through subsequent acts of creativity and sharing.

Decisions about how to spend time in new places frequently pivot on personal passions. Some retirees have long held dreams of exploring museums that house the masterpieces of classical or modern art, while others yearn to witness the breathtaking landscapes chronicled in travel magazines. From carefully restored historical sites to natural wonders like waterfalls, deserts, or coral reefs, there is a wealth of possibilities that cater to diverse interests. This customization fosters a sense of agency, as one's itinerary becomes an expression of personal taste rather than a rushed tour designed for the masses. Those who thrive on intellectual stimulation may delve into curated exhibits, guided walks through architectural marvels, or lectures by local experts. Nature enthusiasts might opt for ecotourism experiences, seeking out wildlife reserves, pristine coastlines, or mountain trails where biodiversity abounds. Each day's discoveries enrich the traveler's understanding of the planet's complexity and serve as a reminder that wonder is not confined to youthful eyes.

To keep track of expenses and ensure that travel remains financially comfortable, some retirees maintain a dedicated travel fund distinct from other savings or monthly budgets. Contributing a consistent amount over time can offset the cost of airline tickets, guided tours, or special activities that might otherwise be unaffordable in a single lump sum. Meticulous note-taking during the trip helps identify any unexpected expenditures, which can inform adjustments for future plans. This approach treats each journey as an evolving learning experience, refining budgeting strategies and clarifying personal priorities. If an unplanned excursion unexpectedly proves transformative, an updated travel fund might earmark more resources for similar opportunities down the line. By integrating financial diligence with an open attitude toward serendipity, travelers can maintain stability while also allowing space for spontaneous indulgences that breathe life into each trip.

Another option for traveling affordably in later life involves the practice of house-sitting or home exchanges. These arrangements serve as a mutually beneficial system, where travelers watch over someone else's residence and pets while their hosts are away, or trade living spaces with individuals from other regions. These exchanges substantially reduce lodging expenses and often provide more comfortable, lived-in environments than typical rentals. They also immerse travelers in local neighborhoods that are not oriented toward tourism, enabling them to absorb the rhythms of everyday life and socialize with neighbors. Participants in house-sitting programs are screened through reputable online platforms, offering a measure of security for both parties. Though such arrangements require planning and clear communication about expectations, the result can be a distinctive, budget-friendly way to see the world while maintaining the warmth and familiarity of a real home.

A sense of humility and respect when navigating different cultures forms the cornerstone of a positive experience. Even well-intentioned travelers can inadvertently offend local customs if unaware of specific codes of behavior. Small courtesies, such as dressing modestly when visiting religious sites, removing shoes upon entering a household, or allowing extra personal space in crowded venues, can demonstrate cultural sensitivity. These acts invite reciprocal understanding and goodwill, paving the way for open dialogues and deeper engagements. For retirees who have spent many years in culturally diverse workplaces or communities, these lessons might come intuitively. Still, there is always more to learn, as each culture has subtle facets shaped by historical contexts, geographical influences, and longstanding traditions. Embracing these nuances reflects a traveler's genuine desire to learn rather than just observe.

Active listening also plays a crucial role in fostering genuine connections. People in many parts of the world are eager to share their stories, discuss their aspirations, and exchange perspectives on global events. When travelers approach these interactions with sincerity and open-ended questions, they invite honest, heartfelt exchanges. Listening attentively, without rushing to offer personal opinions, allows for a broader understanding of local experiences that might otherwise remain hidden. For retirees who have cultivated empathy and communication skills throughout their careers, this capacity to engage in meaningful dialogue can elevate a simple conversation into a formative connection. It is in these moments that travel transcends mere physical relocation, blossoming into an opportunity for shared humanity and mutual recognition.

Physical well-being on the road deserves consistent attention, especially for older adults who may face mobility restrictions or specific medical conditions. Stretching or light exercise upon waking can alleviate stiffness resulting from lengthy flights or bus rides. Staying hydrated, wearing supportive footwear, and allocating breaks during walking tours help maintain energy levels and reduce the risk of injuries. Some travelers find it helpful to schedule a day of rest after a long journey before diving into rigorous sightseeing. Others incorporate low-impact activities such as yoga, swimming, or tai chi into their travel routine, recognizing that mental relaxation is just as important as seeing landmarks. Accessibility concerns can be addressed by verifying whether sites offer ramps, elevators, or guided assistance. In many destinations, official tourism bureaus publish resource guides for visitors with limited mobility. Being proactive about these considerations ensures that each day is approached with readiness and comfort.

For those who relish a sense of spontaneity, it can be tempting to leave an itinerary open-ended, deciding destinations on a whim. This approach can work well in regions known for reliable transportation networks and traveler-friendly infrastructure. However, a measure of planning still remains wise, particularly regarding lodging reservations, critical transition points, or anticipated peak travel periods. Striking a balance between structure and freedom allows for unplanned delights—perhaps discovering an enchanting seaside village or stumbling upon a local festival—while avoiding the stress of being stranded without a place to stay. Approaches vary based on personal style, with some retirees reveling in the thrill of last-minute decisions, while others prefer mapping out each location well in advance. Both can be fulfilling if approached thoughtfully, respecting any physical or logistical limits.

Throughout these excursions, budgeting time for reflection can deepen the overall impact. Writing in a journal, recording voice memos, or posting thoughtful observations in a private online space help solidify impressions and prevent vivid experiences from fading too quickly. These reflections build a personal record that can be revisited or shared with loved ones, offering a timeless snapshot of how each journey influenced perspective. Reflective practices also encourage gratitude, as travelers become more attuned to the privilege of witnessing diverse ways of life. Each note or photograph can spark future memories, perhaps guiding the planning of subsequent trips or reinforcing newly awakened aspirations.

Cultural immersion often leads to serendipitous educational moments. Learning about local history while standing in the very places where events unfolded imprints that knowledge in a way no textbook can match. Observing traditional artisans at work, whether weaving textiles or crafting pottery, renders history tangible, as these skills are passed down through generations. Attending folk music performances, witnessing folk dances, or hearing local legends can bring new layers of understanding about a community's soul. These experiential insights resonate with many retirees, who often have the time and desire to delve deeper into a culture's roots. In doing so, they expand their own horizons and may discover unexpected parallels with their own histories, bridging perceived distances and underlining shared elements of humanity.

Some travelers expand their adventure to include multiple countries within a single journey, designing carefully orchestrated itineraries that balance variety with feasibility. This option can be exciting, though it necessitates added coordination: ensuring valid visas, tracking currency exchange rates, and staying aware of border crossing requirements. Setting realistic expectations— such as devoting enough days to each location to truly absorb its essence—helps avoid the burnout of endless transit. Scheduling periodic breaks, whether in calm rural retreats or smaller towns, provides mental and physical relief from the constant stimulus of major cities. As always, it is not the sheer number of places visited that defines the value of a trip, but rather the depth of engagement and reflection that accompanies each stop.

Those who prefer to keep their itineraries more contained might decide to revisit a favorite destination multiple times, gradually peeling back layers they missed on the initial trip. In these repeat visits, travelers can see how communities evolve with shifting politics, economic conditions, or cultural trends. Returning to a place where one feels at home and recognized by local acquaintances can be deeply comforting, merging the novelty of travel with the familiarity of a second home. In such scenarios, personal ties often strengthen, and travelers might witness how new buildings change the skyline or how festivals take on different themes each year. Over time, a second sense of belonging can form, turning a distant corner of the world into a cherished sanctuary.

Reflection on the broader significance of these journeys can be particularly profound in retirement. Travel presents an avenue for personal growth that transcends leisure or entertainment. It can reignite interests that were once set aside, provoke a reevaluation of assumptions, or clarify how global interconnectedness shapes daily life. Encounters with new climates, languages, and customs stimulate the mind, fostering mental agility that sharpens problem-solving skills and adaptability. For retirees who once worried that advancing years might narrow their horizons, travel stands as a testament to ongoing potential, showcasing that curiosity and discovery remain lifelong companions. These experiences resonate across other areas of life, inspiring an openness that might influence everything from culinary experiments at home to fresh hobbies and community engagement.

Social media and online communities dedicated to mature travelers facilitate the exchange of tips, itineraries, and success stories. This digital support network helps individuals learn from others who have navigated similar journeys, whether that involves traveling with mobility aids, bridging language gaps, or minimizing jet lag. Reading about how peers overcame unexpected obstacles fosters confidence and dispels common fears. Individuals can reciprocate, sharing insights gleaned from their own explorations, thereby contributing to a culture of collaboration. Although everyone's circumstances differ, discovering that others have taken comparable steps can motivate even the most hesitant retiree to take the plunge. The shared narrative reminds travelers that they are not alone in facing challenges and that countless people continue to seek adventure well into their later years.

Emphasizing sustainability reflects a growing awareness that travel, while enriching, can have environmental and social repercussions. Some retirees choose eco-friendly routes by favoring train travel over short-haul flights, supporting local businesses, or volunteering in conservation efforts. These decisions reduce the ecological footprint of each trip, reflecting a broader commitment to protecting the very places that provide such awe and wonder. Many communities rely on tourism income for development; traveling responsibly ensures that economic benefits are fairly distributed while cultural heritage is safeguarded. Supporting ethical wildlife experiences, avoiding single-use plastics, and participating in beach cleanups are small ways to leave a positive mark. Retirees often find meaningful fulfillment in aligning their travels with a sense of stewardship, passing forward lessons of respect to younger generations they may encounter along the way.

In reflecting on the transformative nature of these journeys, it becomes apparent that travel in this stage of life is about more than transient pleasure. It is an extension of the personal and intellectual independence that underpins a fulfilling retirement. By stepping beyond familiar borders, retirees reaffirm their vitality, curiosity, and willingness to absorb life's lessons. Each experience contributes to a mosaic of insights that can shape broader philosophical perspectives, spark creative endeavors, or inspire deeper community involvement back home. Whether the journey unfolds in a neighboring region or on a distant continent, the essence remains the same: exploration fosters growth, and meaningful encounters remind individuals of their shared humanity.

Whenever the urge to explore arises, embracing even small jaunts or weekend getaways can reinvigorate routines that may otherwise become predictable over time. A short train ride to a regional art exhibition, a day spent strolling through a quaint historical district, or a simple retreat to a peaceful lakeside cabin can restore the spirit just as effectively as an intercontinental excursion. The overarching theme is that each trip, large or small, forms part of a broader tapestry of experiences, reflecting a commitment to staying engaged with a world that continues to evolve. Retirees who wholeheartedly embody this approach often find that each journey imparts lessons in humility, resilience, and gratitude, qualities that resonate through all facets of life.

A balanced blend of anticipation and acceptance defines a well-prepared traveler in later life. It is normal to feel excitement mixed with apprehension before embarking on an overseas adventure or even a local excursion. Channeling this blend of emotions into productive planning can ease concerns, ensuring that details such as medication, insurance, local norms, and currency exchanges are well handled. Once these bases are covered, there remains ample space for spontaneity and awe. Travel then becomes a testament to the possibility of reinvention. In stepping away from the routines of one's hometown, horizons expand and a renewed sense of joy awakens. This same joy often permeates the experiences that follow, whether that means returning to supportive friends and family, venturing into more complex itineraries, or sharing knowledge through storytelling and mentorship.

Ultimately, the pursuit of travel during these later years aligns with the broader goal of cultivating a life rich in discovery and connection. Far from existing solely as a recreational pursuit, it resonates as a purposeful undertaking that enriches personal development, fosters cultural understanding, and invigorates the body and mind. Each destination holds its own tapestry of wonders, from architectural feats to natural landscapes shaped by geological and climatic forces over millennia. Encountering these marvels awakens reverence for the diversity and adaptability of life on Earth. Meanwhile, forging genuine relationships with local communities and fellow travelers underscores how deeply people can connect despite language differences or disparate backgrounds. This interplay between personal growth and communal exchange cements the integral role of travel in making the later years not just restful, but profoundly rewarding.

When the journey ends and the traveler returns to the familiar contours of home, the experiences gathered abroad continue to ripple outward. Photographs rekindle memories of mesmerizing sunrises or vibrant gatherings in bustling squares. Souvenirs, whether handcrafted textiles or locally produced spices, serve as tangible reminders that anchor intangible reflections. Conversations with neighbors or friends can spark curiosity in others, persuading them to embark on their own adventures. Meanwhile, the traveler carries forward a refreshed perspective on life's fragility and wonder, possibly even developing a renewed sense of mission or a desire to champion intercultural understanding. In these ripple effects lies the true grandeur of traveling in later life: a single trip plants seeds that flourish in myriad ways, benefiting not only the traveler but also those who share in the stories and lessons gleaned.

By embracing thorough planning, nurturing open-minded engagement, and acknowledging the profound potential for growth inherent in every expedition, travel in the post-career years can become a defining feature of a meaningful life path. It stands as both a tribute to the decades of work that enabled such freedom and a testament to the ceaseless capacity for adventure that underscores human nature. The journey becomes more than a collection of destinations stamped in a passport; it evolves into a record of personal evolution, perseverance, and curiosity, woven into memories that endure. Through the ups and downs of navigating foreign streets, savoring local flavors, or encountering unexpected marvels, each voyage exemplifies the boundless possibilities that await those who dare to step beyond their usual confines. Even as time advances, there remains an abundance of new horizons beckoning exploration. By answering that call, retirees seize the chance to live their later years not as a final chapter but as an unfolding narrative of discovery and wonder, bringing renewed color and vibrancy to each passing day.

Part V: The Art of Thriving – Making the Most of Your Golden Years

Chapter 13: Cultivating Happiness and Fulfillment

Retirement offers a rare and often long-awaited opportunity to reexamine the fundamentals of what it means to feel whole, content, and deeply fulfilled. During previous decades, responsibilities such as earning a living, raising children, and navigating career demands may have shaped the way individuals measured success. Now, with those pressures modified or diminished, a quieter space emerges, allowing the mind to pose questions about what truly matters in daily life. It can feel liberating to step back from the pace of paid work, but in this new openness also lies the challenge of defining personal benchmarks for progress and happiness. When these benchmarks are not governed by deadlines or performance targets, the responsibility of self-direction can both empower and unsettle. Yet by taking time to clarify values, establishing healthful routines, and practicing reflection and gratitude, one can transform this phase of life into a joyful, meaningful, and constructive experience.

Defining success in the absence of structured career milestones requires honest introspection about personal strengths, passions, and objectives. The notion of success in a post-working world no longer revolves around promotions, pay raises, or the completion of large-scale projects. Instead, it takes on more nuanced forms, possibly encompassing creative development, family connections, or the pursuit of lifelong dreams sidelined by earlier commitments. This transition is seldom automatic. It often entails relinquishing ingrained notions of success that revolve exclusively around productivity in the marketplace. By consciously forming a new frame of reference, individuals can shape meaningful aspirations that align with deeper motivations, rather than letting them be dictated by outside expectations. While retirement does not render prior achievements irrelevant, it does open the door to new dimensions of identity that can flourish when given attention and care.

For some, success might be equated with building or strengthening relationships. Time once devoted to professional obligations can be reallocated to maintaining closer bonds with family, old friends, or community networks. Sharing life stories, lessons learned, and everyday experiences can help define success in a realm where emotional richness overshadows purely financial or professional endeavors. Others might find fulfillment in learning new skills—perhaps taking up a musical instrument, learning a new language, or delving into an academic subject long considered too time-consuming before. In these cases, success manifests as growth and personal evolution. Rather than focusing on external markers, such as accolades or awards, the measure of progress is an internal gauge of well-being, mastery, and intellectual stimulation.

Amid this process of redefinition, it can be helpful to recall how fluid one's sense of success has been throughout life. In childhood, achievement might have meant mastering a bicycle or spelling test. In early adulthood, it may have centered on forging independence or pursuing higher education. In the heart of one's career, success revolved around recognition, promotion, or the completion of significant projects. Recognizing that success is not static, and that it adapts to life circumstances, can soften the anxiety that may surface when the familiar environment of a career ends. Instead of perceiving a void, a retiree can view the situation as a catalyst for forging an identity that suits who they have become, complete with all the experiences, wisdom, and dreams that now define them.

Another crucial factor in understanding success in retirement relates to health and wellness. While many people focus on finances or social engagements, there is profound gratification in feeling physically capable, emotionally steady, and cognitively engaged. For some, this translates to scheduling regular exercise routines, whether walks in nature, group fitness classes, or low-impact workouts that protect joint health. For others, it might mean paying closer attention to nutrition, weaving in a diet that supports sustained energy and vitality. There can also be a mental health dimension that underscores the importance of mindfulness, therapy, or meditation, all of which can help one stay resilient when facing the unpredictability that arises in later years.

Emphasizing health as part of personal success ensures that the dream of a fulfilling retirement remains grounded in physical and emotional capacities to enjoy each day. This holistic approach to well-being can transform what might otherwise be considered mundane habits into daily affirmations of self-care and self-worth.

Even with a clear idea of success in mind, turning that notion into a reality demands an assortment of daily habits that encourage joy and purpose. Small actions, repeated consistently, can have an outsized impact on mood, motivation, and overall satisfaction. The day's beginning often sets the tone, so developing a short morning routine can launch one into a mindset of calmness and positivity. Some choose to start the day with a meditative practice, focusing on breathing or reciting a brief mantra that centers the mind on gratitude and readiness to engage with the hours ahead. Others prefer a mild stretch or slow walk outdoors, paying attention to the transition from night to morning and the subtle sounds of birds or rustling leaves. These gentle moments reinforce the idea that each day is a gift, creating a sense of spaciousness and anticipation that readies the spirit for whatever tasks or interactions may follow.

Another habit that supports a life brimming with purpose involves consciously mapping out how one's time is used. Without the obligations of a job, it can be surprisingly easy to lose track of the hours. Leisure can spiral into a sense of aimlessness if not balanced with purposeful engagement. Allocating segments of the day to creative pursuits, social connections, or self-improvement can dispel the feeling that time drifts away unproductively. At the same time, the schedule need not feel rigid. One of the gifts of this stage is the flexibility to adapt, to linger over a conversation, or to spontaneously explore a new interest if it arises. The key is to maintain a loose but intentional structure that ensures a variety of activities, while allowing freedom for those unexpected moments that enrich the day.

Nurturing meaningful relationships can be seen as an ongoing daily habit. Whether it is reaching out to a grandchild through a video call, texting a friend to share an interesting article, or inviting neighbors for a casual afternoon chat, these small gestures strengthen social connections that bring emotional warmth and security. Human beings are, by nature, relational creatures, and the sense of belonging that arises from supportive networks has been shown in numerous studies to contribute to longevity and happiness. For individuals who find themselves geographically distant from family, technology can bridge the gap, providing an easy avenue to check in on each other's well-being or share photos of daily triumphs. Even writing a letter, a seemingly antiquated practice, can yield deep satisfaction by transforming ephemeral thoughts into tangible words on paper. These moments of exchanging care and affection become the threads that weave a supportive tapestry in the day-to-day fabric of retirement.

Physical activity is another daily habit that can anchor well-being. Retirement is sometimes depicted as a time of reduced mobility or energy, but many older adults find that consistent exercise routines actually enhance stamina and morale. Whether it involves walking through a park, riding a bicycle, practicing yoga, or joining a local swimming group, the gentle stress on muscles and heart fosters both physical and mental robustness. A regular exercise habit can regulate mood, reduce anxiety, and even contribute to better sleep quality. The importance of rest and recovery grows with age, but rest is often more rewarding when balanced by physical exertion. Such habits can serve as a reminder that vitality is not solely the domain of youth; it can be sustained through mindful care of the body. Each workout or movement session might also be an opportunity to celebrate small victories, such as completing a few more steps than usual or holding a stretch for an extra breath, reinforcing a sense of progress that parallels the broader aim of a fulfilling retirement.

Intellectual stimulation offers a parallel track of daily enrichment, one that can protect cognitive sharpness and nurture curiosity. For some, reading widely or working through puzzles can serve this purpose. Others discover that volunteering, tutoring, or enrolling in courses at a local institution stimulates the mind and fosters new friendships. This stage in life is ideally suited for exploring subjects or fields that once seemed out of reach. Without the constraints of a work schedule, an individual might study a new language, delve into historical research, or pick up an instrument for the first time. The determination and insight garnered from a lifetime of experiences often speed the process of acquisition. Though the brain may not process new data as swiftly as it once did in early adulthood, many older learners exhibit enhanced creativity and problem-solving skills, partly attributable to their rich background of knowledge. This marriage of discipline and exploration can bolster a sense of purpose, reminding an individual that growth does not cease upon leaving the workforce.

Practicing mindfulness in daily activities further enhances the quest for joy and presence. Even mundane tasks such as washing dishes, tidying a room, or preparing a meal can transform into opportunities for gentle focus on the present moment. Paying attention to the scent of the soap, the temperature of the water, the texture of the dishes, or the colors in a bowl of ingredients can ground the mind in the here and now, alleviating mental chatter about past regrets or future worries. These micro-moments of mindfulness reduce stress and cultivate a meditative mindset that complements any formal practice of seated meditation. Over time, noticing small details of daily life and appreciating them as they unfold fosters an enduring sense of wonder.

Achieving a state of fulfillment also depends on limiting habits that detract from wellness. A life oriented toward purpose and peace might be undermined by excessive screen time, unbalanced consumption of news, or indulging in perpetual worry. By curating what one reads or watches, distinguishing between healthy information gathering and compulsive anxiety triggers, a retiree can protect mental well-being. Moderation in media exposure allows for better sleep, improved mood, and a more optimistic outlook. Similarly, adjusting diet and limiting the use of intoxicants or addictive substances can strengthen the body's capacity to enjoy retirement fully. Although many people equate retirement with relaxation and indulgence, a daily discipline that wards off overindulgence fosters both short-term energy and long-term health.

Above all, a key to daily life that feels simultaneously purposeful and unhurried is learning to engage deeply with each chosen activity. Whether reading a novel, painting a landscape, playing a musical instrument, or gardening, the mind stands to benefit most when immersed without distraction or multitasking. Such immersion transforms the activity into a flow experience, during which individuals often describe a sense of timelessness, heightened pleasure, and complete concentration. Flow states have been correlated with improved mood, enhanced creativity, and even a sense of spiritual fulfillment. For those who worried about boredom in retirement, discovering flow states through personally meaningful tasks provides a wellspring of emotional nourishment, even in seemingly simple pursuits. This sense of deep engagement, repeated daily, can sustain a gratifying lifestyle that unfolds at a pace determined by personal preference rather than external pressures.

Alongside habits that reinforce day-to-day vitality, the practice of gratitude and reflection plays a fundamental role in ensuring that happiness is not merely episodic but deeply rooted. Gratitude, as both a concept and a ritual, invites individuals to acknowledge the positive elements within their lives, whether major or minor. It can be as straightforward as keeping a small journal in which one writes down a few things that went well or felt inspiring. This gentle exercise reframes the mind's natural tendency to fixate on problems or regrets, steering attention instead toward blessings that might otherwise go unnoticed. Over time, documenting these moments of appreciation, whether it is the kindness of a neighbor, a delicious meal, or the warmth of sunlight after days of rain, accumulates into a convincing narrative of abundance. This practice does not deny that challenges remain. Rather, it calibrates perspective, preventing difficulties from overshadowing the significant, if quieter, joys of daily existence.

Reflection extends beyond a gratitude list, involving a broader look at how one's time, choices, and emotions align with stated values and desires. Many find that journaling or letter writing helps them articulate insights gained from each day's experiences. Reflecting on mistakes or disappointments can unveil lessons about resilience and adaptation, while identifying moments of pride or delight clarifies which pursuits resonate most profoundly. This reflective habit does not require elaborate or formal writing skills; it rests on sincerity and consistency. Some prefer an introspective conversation with themselves—perhaps a gentle mental review before sleep—rather than pen and paper. Regardless of the format, the key is to create a space in which thoughts and feelings can be acknowledged, assessed, and integrated, allowing for incremental personal growth.

Gratitude and reflection can also serve as antidotes to the occasional loneliness or disorientation that might arise in retirement. When leaving the workforce, certain social networks may grow distant, and the daily rhythm that once dictated when to wake, commute, and interact may dissolve. This abrupt loss of structure can lead to an emotional slump if the retiree has not found alternate frameworks or communities in which to invest time and energy. Through gratitude, one can remain attuned to the resources still available—family connections, neighborhood ties, newfound friendships in social clubs or volunteer organizations. Reflection complements this by helping the retiree see how each day can evolve into a meaningful, if less regimented, schedule. Together, they instill confidence that, while the scenery of life has changed, there is still beauty to be discovered in uncharted territories.

In many cultural traditions, gratitude and reflection are deemed essential to spiritual life. Retirement can be an opportune time to explore or deepen spiritual practices, whether through religious attendance, interfaith discussions, or personal contemplative exercises. Some discover comfort and reassurance in the rituals of their faith community, while others find spiritual resonance in nature, artistic creation, or the act of compassionate service. Whichever path feels most genuine, including it in a daily or weekly routine can introduce a sense of transcendence that cuts across mundane concerns. Such spiritual engagement, grounded in gratitude, anchors personal fulfillment in a dimension that surpasses the ephemeral. The result can be a lasting sense of peace, as the retiree interprets life's twists and turns through the lens of a broader existential framework.

Even for those who do not adhere to a specific spiritual tradition, practicing gratitude and reflection fosters emotional resilience. This resilience is particularly valuable in the face of unexpected health challenges, financial worries, or interpersonal conflicts that may occur in later life. Age can bring certain vulnerabilities. Yet gratitude reveals that even in moments of limitation or adversity, there remain sources of solace—caring professionals, supportive loved ones, or cherished memories that sustain hope. Reflection, in turn, allows individuals to acknowledge pain or loss without becoming mired in it, gleaning insights that may shape wiser decisions or open the heart to new forms of connection. These practices collectively ensure that retirement is not solely about relaxation, but also about inner evolution and the refinement of one's worldview.

Another important function of gratitude is its capacity to enrich relationships with others. Offering genuine thanks to family members, neighbors, or healthcare providers fosters mutual respect and recognition. Human empathy expands when individuals publicly acknowledge the kindnesses they receive. Even in casual circumstances, a heartfelt expression of appreciation can uplift the giver and the recipient alike. In retirement, when social interactions might diminish without the constant contact of an office environment, appreciation can become an essential social currency, ensuring that the retiree remains woven into the community's fabric. These moments of expressed gratitude make daily life more harmonious and underscore that support and goodwill flow in multiple directions, reinforcing bonds that nourish everyone involved.

Reflection on personal history and the broader timeline of one's life can also deepen a sense of identity and accomplishment. Retirement often provides the time and mental space to contemplate how earlier periods laid the groundwork for current experiences. Some people revisit diaries, photo albums, or genealogical records to better understand the forces that shaped their trajectory. Others might choose to write a memoir, not necessarily for publication, but as a personal project that clarifies how events, relationships, and choices interlinked over the years. This retrospective process promotes self-compassion, illuminating moments of adversity that were overcome and highlighting patterns of resilience that can be applied to new challenges. It also broadens empathy for others, given that reflection often yields a deeper acknowledgment of how random or uncontrollable circumstances can alter a life path. By placing present concerns in the context of a longer narrative, individuals who practice reflective thinking may find themselves less perturbed by trivial setbacks.

Examining one's life through a reflective lens can also prompt decisions about how best to spend the time that remains. If the first half or two-thirds of a lifespan were devoted primarily to building a career or raising a family, some retirees awaken to a yearning for creative expression or community service. Reflection highlights areas where unfulfilled aspirations linger, granting the impetus to move forward with neglected dreams. Perhaps it is a desire to paint, to learn pottery, to serve as a mentor for at-risk youth, or to champion environmental causes that once seemed too time-consuming to tackle. Embracing these goals, with the perspective and patience acquired over the decades, can be profoundly rewarding. It affirms that growth continues no matter one's date of birth, and that the joys of achievement and purpose are not confined to any particular stage of adulthood.

A sustained sense of gratitude is likewise beneficial for managing transitions that extend beyond the cessation of professional life. This period can include altered family dynamics, the birth of grandchildren, or the loss of loved ones. Gratitude helps ground the mind in an awareness of what remains steadfast or new blessings that arise, offsetting the sorrow that may accompany certain events. If one's children relocate for career opportunities, for example, maintaining gratitude for the communication tools that enable regular updates or video calls can mitigate feelings of loss. If an old friend or spouse passes away, remembering the shared joys and the support received from other caring individuals can provide a buffer during bereavement. By dwelling in the space of what one still has, rather than fixating solely on what has vanished, it becomes more feasible to navigate these ups and downs with emotional equilibrium.

Individuals are often surprised by the extent to which gratitude can reshape their outlook on mundane tasks. Cooking a simple dinner can transform into a moment of appreciation for the senses: the aroma of sautéing vegetables, the satisfaction of a wholesome meal, and the knowledge that one's body is still able to savor such nourishment. Gardening, even if limited to a small container on a windowsill, can foster gratitude for the wonder of growth and the patience required to nurture life. By recognizing that these experiences need not be taken for granted, an otherwise routine day is illuminated by an atmosphere of wonder and discovery. This shift in mindset can be especially valuable in retirement, when the line between the extraordinary and the routine may begin to blur.

Just as each new morning can be a chance to set positive intentions, each evening can be an opportunity to reflect with gratitude on the hours gone by. A gentle mental or written review of the day cements the lessons learned and acknowledges the bright spots of kindness, beauty, or personal progress. If interpersonal tensions arose, reflection can clarify ways to address them or, if necessary, to let them go. If a surprising act of generosity brightened the day, writing about it underscores its significance. This bedtime ritual can enhance sleep quality by reducing mental clutter, leaving less room for ruminations. The mind, entering the realm of rest, is soothed by awareness of gratitude and reflection, providing a stable emotional background that carries into the next day.

For many, this posture of reflective gratitude illuminates a desire to give back. Retirement offers the time to volunteer, mentor, or otherwise engage in community or charitable initiatives. Participation in these efforts expands one's sense of meaning by actively improving the lives of others or safeguarding the environment. Whether it is serving at a local shelter, contributing skills to an educational program, or offering support at cultural events, such endeavors heighten the recognition of shared humanity and reliance on communal efforts. The positivity derived from altruism can merge with personal growth, illustrating that giving and receiving are twin facets of a rich life. Retirees often remark that the satisfaction gained from volunteering transcends any fleeting pleasure found in solitary leisure. The knowledge that one's energy and empathy continue to make a difference fosters confidence and optimism about the future, even in the face of societal or personal challenges.

Much like success itself, gratitude and reflection are fluid practices that can adapt to personal style. Some people find creative ways to make these routines more tangible, such as establishing a gratitude corner in the home, decorated with meaningful tokens or photographs that evoke pleasant memories. Others might incorporate music, lighting candles, or reading poetry to facilitate a reflective mindset. The important factor is to maintain consistency, ensuring that each day includes at least a brief moment to pause and appreciate the path taken so far. In doing so, retirement emerges not as a static endpoint but as a transformative passage in which the deeper layers of self-awareness and personal fulfillment can be revealed.

In cultivating these practices, an individual can also uncover a renewed sense of agency over mental and emotional states. Rather than feeling powerless when negative thoughts arise, the habit of gratitude provides a ready tool for redirecting focus. Each instance of appreciating a supportive friend, a safe home, a functioning body, or a captivating hobby can counterbalance worries or regrets. Reflection helps integrate these impressions, lending them permanence in the mind's ongoing narrative. While aging can bring uncertain physical changes, the capacity to shape emotional well-being through conscious intention often grows sharper, bolstered by a lifetime of experience. This emotional empowerment enhances the sense of self-reliance in a stage that can sometimes evoke apprehension about diminishing capabilities.

Of course, no practice, however beneficial, ensures perpetual serenity. Emotional turbulence is part of the human condition, and retirement does not exempt individuals from crises, be they health-related, financial, or interpersonal. Nevertheless, gratitude and reflection serve as reliable companions during dark moments, reminding the heart that adversity can coexist with hope. They encourage a balanced perspective that acknowledges difficulty while refusing to let it monopolize awareness. By continuing these practices even when circumstances seem bleak, a retiree can glean the humility and adaptability required to endure hardships. Through reflection, one can better understand personal responses to stress and heartbreak, potentially unveiling new coping mechanisms or new angles for confronting problems.

In tandem with daily habits that promote physical vigor and mental acuity, the synergy of gratitude and reflection can give rise to an authentic sense of autonomy in defining success. Rather than marching to a societal script or succumbing to pressures that prioritize productivity above all, retirement can be recast as a richly creative period. Each morning offers a fresh slate to choose meaningful engagements: strengthening connections with loved ones, honing an artistic talent, volunteering for a social cause, or simply sitting beneath a tree and immersing oneself in the beauty of an autumn afternoon. These choices accumulate over weeks and months, painting a portrait of a life that is deeply attuned to one's innermost values. Success, in such a framework, ceases to be about external comparisons and becomes an inward measure of how closely one's actions align with cherished aspirations.

Occasionally, an individual may discover a dormant passion or find that the seeds of an earlier interest can now flourish. Reflection might reveal a love of gardening overshadowed by years of office work, or a fascination with history once overshadowed by deadlines and obligations. Retirement grants not just the time but also the psychological space to pursue these neglected enthusiasms. Cultivating these passions can be seen as a daily act of self-honoring, affirming the notion that it is never too late to kindle new forms of accomplishment or enjoyment. Even if the skill set is not fully developed, the learning process itself becomes an adventure. By infusing each day with small steps toward mastery, a retired individual can experience the incremental thrill of discovery that once might have characterized earlier phases of life.

At times, defining success may lead to bridging generational gaps by passing on knowledge to younger relatives, friends, or community members. The expansive perspective gained over decades of work and personal trials can serve as a guiding light for others forging their way. Whether by teaching a craft, offering career or life advice, or simply demonstrating empathy in a mentor-like capacity, retirees can channel their reflections to help shape the next generation's outlook. In return, being around younger minds invigorates many older adults, keeping them curious about new technologies, cultural shifts, or inventive problem-solving approaches. Gratitude becomes mutual in these relationships, each side recognizing the benefits of shared wisdom and fresh energy.

A frequent concern among those entering retirement is the fear of stagnation—of letting the days blur into an unremarkable routine lacking in novelty or growth. Maintaining daily habits that nurture body and mind helps avert the trap of monotony, but so does setting forth personal challenges. These could be modest, such as learning five new words in a foreign language every day, or more ambitious, such as training for a community marathon. Having set goals fosters a sense of momentum and anticipation. Reflection ensures these goals align with personal passions rather than arbitrary standards. Gratitude infuses each step of the journey with a sense of privilege for having the time and ability to chase new milestones. Taken together, these practices eradicate the stereotype of retirement as a slow fade and replace it with a dynamic framework that fosters continual evolution.

For many, the path to happiness and fulfillment lies in a delicate equilibrium of planning and spontaneity. The daily structure that fosters health and productivity is vital, yet the willingness to deviate from that plan in response to invitation or inspiration ensures that life retains a sense of discovery. Those who adhere too rigidly to a regimen may miss out on the spur-of-the-moment joys that retirement makes possible, while those without any routine at all risk drifting into disorganization. Gratitude supports a healthy balance, as it highlights how each unplanned moment of delight adds variety and richness to life, while reflection ensures that an overall sense of direction remains intact. From day to day, this interplay between intention and openness can yield experiences that feel simultaneously grounded and enlivened.

A further dimension of fulfillment is often found in the acceptance of the aging process itself. Society's fascination with youth can generate an undercurrent of resistance to the physical changes that come with age. Yet defying age is a hopeless pursuit, and can hamper the serenity that retirement is poised to bring. Instead, by practicing daily health habits, reflecting on past achievements, and nurturing gratitude for the present, an individual can cultivate a sense of dignity and pride in having arrived at a stage of life endowed with wisdom. This acceptance does not preclude self-improvement; on the contrary, it fosters a realistic perspective that both respects limitations and recognizes ongoing potential. In merging health consciousness, open-minded learning, and an appreciation for life's fleeting nature, the retiree can radiate an inner confidence that is difficult to obtain through external validation alone.

As the years advance, many individuals also confront the topic of legacy: the sum of values, stories, and tangible impacts they will leave behind. This concern can come to the forefront, not out of a sense of finality, but as part of a broader understanding of one's place in the continuity of family or community. One meaningful approach involves recording personal histories, either in written form or through audio or video, ensuring that the lessons gleaned from a lifetime do not disappear with the passage of time. Others might focus on philanthropic goals, such as establishing scholarships, supporting local arts, or championing conservation. Gratitude becomes the wellspring for such endeavors, as it reminds the individual of the many gifts that shaped their own journey, instilling a desire to pass similar opportunities to others. Reflection ensures that the chosen legacy aligns with core values. This confluence of introspection and appreciation can turn retirement into an active, purposeful period that resonates well beyond one's immediate circle.

Finding fulfillment also necessitates respecting the pace at which personal transformation unfolds. Some individuals adjust to retirement quickly, slipping comfortably into new roles and routines. Others experience a period of disorientation, especially if their identity was closely entwined with their career. Patience is essential during these transitions. Gratitude can soothe the frustration that arises when new routines do not feel natural right away, while reflection can illuminate subtle progress in clarifying values or finding fresh sources of satisfaction. In the end, acceptance of this ongoing, often nonlinear growth alleviates the pressure to have everything figured out immediately. The knowledge that each day can yield further insight underscores the continuing journey, enriching it with a sense of momentum and optimism.

The reciprocal power of these practices becomes evident over time. Defining success in personal terms cultivates a mindset of empowerment, allowing retirees to see infinite possibilities where they might previously have seen only constraints. Daily habits reinforce that sense of direction and well-being, weaving physical vitality, social connections, and intellectual curiosity into a harmonious routine. Gratitude and reflection anchor both the sense of purpose and the moment-to-moment experience of joy, reminding individuals that they have the capacity to choose their reactions and shape their emotional landscapes. The synergy of these elements fosters an overarching sense of coherence: a life that feels undeniably one's own, guided from within rather than dictated by external pressures or outdated societal narratives.

All of these dimensions—clarifying one's definition of success, establishing healthful and mind-enriching practices, and sustaining a spirit of gratitude and reflection—converge to form the essence of contentment in later years. They address the multifaceted nature of being human, acknowledging that emotional, physical, intellectual, and spiritual well-being must coexist for genuine fulfillment. By integrating them into daily life with consistency and adaptability, an individual not only finds joy in the present but also strengthens the capacity to handle future uncertainties. The result is a retirement experience that matures into a tapestry of significant moments, satisfying relationships, ongoing learning, and heartfelt appreciation for the passage of time.

The ultimate power in these practices lies in their accessibility. Neither gratitude nor reflection demands special resources; they only require a willingness to observe, a few minutes of quiet, and the courage to probe deeper feelings. Likewise, defining success does not hinge on external validation, but on self-discovery and the confidence to honor personal truths. Daily habits for well-being can be simple or complex, from a short breathing exercise to a more elaborate regimen that involves scheduling volunteering, reading, and physical workouts. The possibilities are virtually endless, yet every choice is anchored in the fundamental notion that a meaningful retirement is not automatically bestowed but consciously crafted.

Over the course of this continuous evolution, individuals often discover that the sense of purpose emerging from daily life radiates outwards. Family members, neighbors, and even strangers feel the calm and generosity that stem from a person genuinely at peace with their stage in life. Acts of kindness multiply. One might spontaneously help a neighbor with a chore, share advice gleaned from reflection, or simply offer warm conversation to someone feeling lonely. This ripple effect exemplifies the broader societal impact of those who approach retirement with mindful self-assurance and compassion. Although each personal journey is unique, collectively, these efforts coalesce into healthier communities in which wisdom and kindness flourish across generational lines.

For those concerned that adopting a calmer lifestyle might lead to complacency, the interplay of daily purpose, reflection, and gratitude dispels that fear. Ambition can still thrive in retirement, manifesting as the pursuit of new hobbies, philanthropic efforts, or even entrepreneurial endeavors tailored to personal convictions. The difference is that these aspirations serve the retiree's chosen definition of success, rather than being driven by the hustle of professional competition. By sustaining a reflective approach, evaluating which efforts align with deeper values and which are remnants of old habits, one maintains clarity about the significance of each pursuit. Gratitude then enriches the journey by celebrating every milestone, no matter how small, ensuring that ambition remains balanced by appreciation.

Perhaps the greatest reward of weaving all these elements together is an abiding sense of serenity. External factors may still bring disruptions: markets fluctuate, loved ones move away or pass on, and health conditions can change. Yet a life rooted in self-defined aims, nurtured by daily positive habits, and illuminated by gratitude and reflection can weather such storms more gracefully. Stability arises from the knowledge that, whatever the outside world may bring, one's internal framework for well-being remains firm. This quiet confidence enables a retiree to greet each new day with openness to possibility, trust in personal resilience, and a readiness to find meaning in the smallest of events. It is, in many ways, the culmination of an entire lifetime's worth of experience, distilled into a profound awareness of what it means to live fully in the present while forging a bright vision for the future.

In all these respects, shaping a fulfilling retirement becomes an ongoing act of authorship: each person holds the pen to craft a narrative that resonates with who they are at their core. Instead of measuring success by prior standards, a person can select priorities that elevate personal growth, relationships, physical health, and spiritual well-being. Everyday routines, properly tended, evolve into powerful supports that foster a joyful and meaningful life. Gratitude and reflection, far from being mere mental exercises, become vital sources of perspective and emotional nourishment. The resulting mosaic, unique to each individual, highlights the incredible variety and creativity that human beings can display when given the freedom and courage to determine their own path.

When examined as a whole, these practices speak to a universal longing shared by many who have spent years absorbed in duties and ambitions: the longing to celebrate life's intrinsic wonders, to discover renewed purpose in their own gifts and curiosities, and to nurture bonds with others in a spirit of generosity. Retirement, once envisioned simply as an end to work, emerges as a threshold to an enriched existence that consciously honors both past achievements and ongoing potential. The true measure of success in this realm lies not in acclaim or wealth, but in a sustained appreciation for everyday miracles and a heartfelt dedication to living in harmony with the knowledge, passions, and values one has accumulated.

Such an evolution is rarely instantaneous or effortless; it unfolds through deliberate choices and the willingness to remain open to new lessons. Yet with each passing day of mindful routine, each moment of gratitude, and each reflective insight, the distance narrows between what is hoped for and what is experienced. Over time, a retiree may come to realize that the contentment and sense of accomplishment they once sought from career accolades now bloom from simpler, more authentic sources: a morning walk in the crisp air, a conversation with a loved one that reaffirms connection, or the peaceful realization that each year has contributed to a deeper understanding of life. This inner stillness and joy expand outward, coloring all interactions and providing a gentle radiance that encourages others to embark on similar paths of self-discovery.

However one chooses to integrate these elements, the essence remains the same: a retirement guided by inner-driven definitions of success, fortified by nourishing daily habits, and enlivened through the transformative power of gratitude and reflection. The promise that emerges is not merely one of personal benefit, but of participating in a wider tapestry of kindness and empathy. Each person's journey, strengthened by the purposeful decisions made each day, becomes a testament to the resilience and grace that can accompany aging. Whether a moment's delight is found in sharing a heartfelt laugh with a grandchild or indulging in a beloved creative pursuit, the core message stands firm: retirement is not a sideline but a fertile arena for flourishing in ways that reaffirm the beauty, complexity, and infinite possibility of human life.

Chapter 14: The Legacy You Leave Behind

Crafting a lasting place in the tapestry of family and community is often a natural endeavor after the major obligations and busyness of work life taper off. During this stage, an individual can find the time, and perhaps the courage, to reflect on the path that led to the present moment. The desire to preserve personal experiences or to offer guidance for the benefit of others often ripens with age, strengthened by the sense that wisdom should not vanish when one's own journey nears its twilight. Part of this recognition involves capturing the essence of a life story and passing it on through memoirs or recorded recollections. A parallel component lies in establishing and perpetuating traditions that carry significance across generations, so that family and friends can recall and reenact meaningful customs long after one's direct presence has faded. Equally powerful is the aspiration to shape the future in a positive way, ensuring that children, grandchildren, and indeed the broader community profit from one's efforts and insight. In pursuit of these aims, each day can be seen not only as a time for personal satisfaction but as an opportunity to build a living legacy that resonates in the hearts of those who follow.

Conveying the details of a personal history through memoir writing has a transformative potential that goes beyond leaving a few words on paper. The process of crafting one's story can bring clarity and resolution to memories that have lingered only partially formed. It serves as a journey of self-discovery, granting the writer the chance to revisit triumphs, losses, regrets, and turning points in a methodical manner. By sorting through the events of childhood, adolescence, professional accomplishments, friendships, love, and loss, an individual may piece together the pattern that shaped who they have become. Through that very act of reflection, the author can find closure for old wounds and a renewed appreciation for the lessons gleaned along the way. On a purely emotional level, the sense of having shaped random threads of memory into a coherent narrative can provide comfort, especially for those who once feared that the details of their experiences would slip into oblivion.

Memoirs differ fundamentally from daily journals or diaries, for they carry an intention to communicate a larger story to an audience—often composed of family members, close friends, or even a broader readership if one chooses to publish. Rather than a raw log of events, a memoir typically weaves together scenes, dialogue, and personal interpretation to portray the essence of a life or a particular period within it. The style can range from conversational to literary, but the key is authenticity. What readers often value most is the candid voice of the author, unencumbered by the desire to impress or conform to conventional expectations. A sincere recounting of personal highs and lows can illuminate universal truths about resilience, love, and humanity's capacity for transformation. Whether one describes a journey across continents, the trials of raising a family, or the subtle emotional arcs of a quiet life, the genuine tone resonates.

For many, the idea of writing a memoir feels daunting at the start, especially if they have never written a lengthy narrative. Yet the process can be approached with incremental steps. One might begin by drafting brief anecdotes or recollections that stand out vividly in the mind. Later, these pieces can be assembled into a chronological arc or grouped by thematic relevance. Some prefer to begin with a childhood memory and move forward, while others choose to start in the middle, capturing a climactic episode— perhaps a life-altering decision, a sudden tragedy, or an epic adventure—and then branching out in various directions. The format is flexible, since the ultimate purpose is to capture the essence of a life lived. Along the way, individuals can seek feedback from loved ones, incorporate photographs or letters that spark additional insights, and remind themselves that perfection is not the goal. What truly matters is preserving the authenticity of the personal voice.

Preservation methods can vary. Traditional pen-and-paper manuscripts carry a nostalgic appeal, while typing on a computer facilitates editing and reorganization. Some retirees find that audio or video recordings suit them better, especially if writing feels cumbersome. They might sit down with a recording device, speak freely about the recollections they cherish, and later transcribe or share the recordings in digital form. These different approaches all converge on the same outcome: preserving life's defining stories for the benefit of others. Relatives who may not have known certain aspects of an individual's childhood or early struggles can gain fresh insight into the family's history and the forces that shaped it. This knowledge fosters empathy between generations, especially if younger descendants see echoes of their own aspirations or dilemmas in these stories from an earlier time.

Completing a memoir can also inspire conversations that bring families closer. Adult children who previously knew only fragments of a parent's background might encounter the unfiltered realities of that person's joys, fears, or sacrifices. These revelations can lead to respectful dialogue, opportunities for forgiveness, and a deeper admiration for the hurdles once faced. In turn, the memoir's author often discovers that the retelling sparks a renewed bond with younger family members. Rather than being seen solely through the lens of old age, they are recognized as the sum of their experiences, a living archive of resilience and knowledge. Such recognition can break down generational barriers and counter any stereotypes that aging implies irrelevance. Far from being superfluous, the older voice becomes a linchpin that binds past, present, and future.

However, leaving a personal legacy is not confined to memoir writing alone. Traditions—those repeated rituals, customs, or celebrations passed on through the years—function as another vital strand in the fabric of what one leaves behind. While the modern world has witnessed shifting social norms and changing family structures, traditions hold an enduring power to create continuity. They can be grand, elaborate ceremonies or small, intimate gestures. Some families mark the changing of seasons with gatherings that incorporate music, special meals, or storytelling around the fireplace. Others maintain a simpler practice, such as making a specific dish on birthdays or writing each member of the family an annual letter to reflect on the year's growth. These practices transcend mere repetition when they carry a sense of purpose, whether it is gratitude, remembrance, or unity.

Creating a meaningful tradition often begins with identifying the values and experiences a person wants to emphasize. If an individual cherishes the outdoors and the beauty of nature, a tradition might revolve around an annual camping trip in a beloved location, complete with certain songs sung at the campfire or an early-morning hike followed by a communal breakfast. If the goal is to honor cultural heritage, the tradition might involve learning and passing down folk dances, holiday recipes, or handcrafted items emblematic of a family's ancestral home. By knitting these customs into regular practice, each year or season gains an anchor point, something to look forward to and reflect upon. Over time, these repeated acts accrue emotional depth, recalling memories of past gatherings and strengthening a collective sense of identity.

Traditions can also serve as a mechanism for imparting wisdom to younger generations. Some traditions revolve around moral or ethical teachings, inviting participants to discuss topics like empathy, compassion, or perseverance. Others focus on imparting practical skills, such as weaving, carpentry, or storytelling. In many communities, traditions exist for passing on knowledge about nature's cycles, local agriculture, or sustainable living, ensuring that children grow up with an appreciation for the delicate balance that sustains human existence. In urban settings, these might be adapted to align with contemporary lifestyles, but the principle remains: traditions serve as vehicles for transferring knowledge and values across time. As retirees or older adults define or refine these customs, they play a direct role in shaping the worldview and character of the next generation.

One obstacle to sustaining family traditions lies in the geographic dispersal of modern families, with relatives living across cities, states, or countries. Yet even distance need not be an insurmountable barrier. Digital tools can facilitate collective participation. A family cooking tradition, for instance, might be upheld through virtual gatherings where each household prepares the same recipe while connected via video chat. Parents and grandparents can share the history or symbolism behind the dish, and younger participants might add their own flourishes or ask questions in real time. Similar solutions apply to annual ceremonies or discussions, allowing multiple generations to interact in creative ways. It might not feel exactly like being together in person, but it preserves the essence of communal warmth and shared intention, ensuring that traditions remain alive in changing circumstances.

As time passes, some traditions naturally evolve. The meal that once included recipes from a distant homeland might expand to feature new foods introduced by a relative's spouse or friend. A holiday gathering that initially revolved around certain songs or prayers may blend with alternative cultural elements, reflecting the richness of a blended family. While certain individuals might lament these changes as a dilution of heritage, it can be helpful to view them as a sign of vitality. A tradition that adapts while retaining its core meaning can reach more people and resonate across cultural lines. If the essence—family unity, respect for elders, honoring ancestral roots—remains intact, transformations can be seen as expansions rather than erosions. Those who initiate or sustain traditions can help guide such growth, ensuring the inclusion of new participants while guarding the heart of what made the custom special.

Parallel to writing memoirs and sustaining traditions is the desire to make a positive impact on future generations more broadly, extending beyond one's immediate circle of relatives. In this sense, leaving a legacy involves not just preserving personal stories and customs, but also championing values or initiatives that improve society as a whole. Some people engage directly in mentorship, offering their knowledge and experience to younger professionals or community groups. Others channel resources toward scholarships, charitable programs, or grassroots organizations that align with their deeply held convictions. Retirement can free up time to serve on boards, volunteer regularly, or even launch small projects in the realm of education, environmental conservation, or youth development.

Such contributions need not be grand in scale. Small gestures of generosity or activism can inspire wider changes when performed consistently. A volunteer who offers literacy support at a local library may not make headlines, but the children who learn to read more confidently under that guidance might go on to shape their neighborhoods in meaningful ways. A person who organizes a neighborhood group to plant trees could spark an appreciation for sustainability that resonates with children who pass by the newly formed grove each day. Over time, these seeds of community engagement can propagate far beyond the individual's immediate efforts. In reflecting on the legacy that emerges from such endeavors, many discover that the satisfaction derived from passing wisdom, uplifting lives, or protecting the environment surpasses any fleeting pleasure that material accumulation might bring.

Even the realm of creative arts presents paths for positively influencing future generations. Those with a flair for painting, sculpture, music, or drama can establish small workshops that nurture emerging talents. Sometimes, creativity flourishes late in life once the demands of a career recede, allowing the mind and spirit to explore artistic pursuits deeply. Sharing the resulting artworks, whether by donating them to community spaces or hosting local exhibitions, broadens the cultural landscape for others to enjoy. For those whose talents lie in performance, organizing or sponsoring a local choir, theatre group, or dance ensemble fosters intergenerational collaboration. At times, older adults who have honed their craft for decades can guide newcomers around pitfalls and help them refine their technique, ensuring that the spark of creativity is passed on rather than extinguished.

Another avenue for positively impacting future generations involves the wise stewardship of resources, both financial and environmental. Some individuals use estate planning or trusts to secure a robust platform for their descendants, earmarking funds for educational pursuits or entrepreneurial ventures. Such actions require careful consultation with legal and financial advisers, but they have the potential to uplift entire family lines. Others emphasize the importance of environmentally responsible living, a topic of increasing urgency in the global conversation. They might impart methods for composting, recycling, or conscientious consumption. In a more public sphere, they might advocate for protection of local ecosystems, sponsor green initiatives in schools, or introduce sustainable practices in community centers. The concept of legacy extends to the natural world when elders demonstrate a commitment to ecological balance, illustrating that the well-being of tomorrow's citizens depends on choices made today.

The passion to build a better future can also manifest through direct engagement in policy or governance at the local level. Certain retirees choose to run for positions on school boards, city councils, or community committees, bringing with them a wealth of experience and an empathetic perspective on social issues. By helping shape decisions about education, infrastructure, and public resources, they lay groundwork that benefits the children and families who will live there long after the older generation has passed on. While politics can be fraught with disagreement, a calm, reflective voice that draws upon lived experience and prioritizes community well-being often finds respect across diverse groups. In such roles, personal legacy becomes woven into the structural framework of a neighborhood or region, manifested in improved parks, safer roads, or more inclusive educational curricula.

At the heart of these efforts lies a recognition that one's lifespan is finite, and that the measure of a life well-lived often involves the imprint left on others. A stable community, a thriving environment, and cherished family relationships serve as living memorials more enduring than any plaque or monument. While it is natural to be concerned about the continuity of the intangible—memories, values, personal stories—one can take heart in the cumulative influence of written records, traditions, and mentorship. As time marches on, the specifics of an individual's name might fade, but the ripples created by that life continue to shape attitudes and opportunities. By anchoring memoirs, customs, and altruistic involvement in authenticity and genuine care, one ensures that the essence of that life resonates well beyond its earthly span.

In weaving together these different strands of legacy, it becomes clear that none exist in isolation. Writing or recording personal stories provides context and inspiration for the traditions one might found or uphold, which in turn can serve as catalysts for philanthropic or community-minded endeavors. The reflection that emerges from looking back on one's life tends to spur a desire to give back, while the practice of shaping traditions fosters a sense of cohesion that may fortify the community relationships needed to enact broader social changes. In this interconnected tapestry, each endeavor amplifies the effect of the others, creating a synergy that leaves a lasting and multifaceted imprint.

Those who worry about not having enough notable accomplishments to warrant a memoir or who feel uncertain about the significance of their traditions might be reassured by remembering that everyone's personal narrative carries value. A life story does not need to include public recognition, dramatic events, or extraordinary feats to be worth sharing. An honest portrayal of everyday resilience, the quiet joys of raising a family, or the evolution of a community through decades can inspire humility, gratitude, and hope in those who read or hear it. It is the warmth of human connection, the universal elements of struggle and perseverance, and the nuanced insights gained from ordinary experiences that resonate most universally. Indeed, many of the most touching memoirs are those that capture the textures of daily life and transform them into lessons on love, determination, and moral courage.

On the practical side, one can consider how best to store or publish these memoirs for posterity. Bound, self-published volumes can be gifted to family members, while digital formats allow for broader distribution without incurring high printing costs. Online platforms for personal storytelling also cater to older adults seeking an audience beyond family, with some choosing to share their reflections in blogs or forums dedicated to memoir writing. Likewise, traditions can be recorded through video or photography, capturing the atmosphere of gatherings and the instructions for meaningful rituals. Digital tools can ensure that decades later, when younger participants have grown older themselves, they can revisit the voices and images that shaped their childhood. These archived resources hold the potential to reawaken dormant family ties and reignite the impetus to carry on traditions that may have waned.

The emotional dimension of creating a legacy cannot be overstated. Many older adults find solace in the knowledge that their stories will not end in silence and that cherished traditions will flourish beyond their direct involvement. This perspective can alleviate some fears about mortality, offering reassurance that a person's identity and influence are not extinguished by the cessation of physical existence. Furthermore, the emotional reward extends to the recipients. Younger relatives frequently express gratitude and admiration when they receive a well-crafted memoir or guidance in upholding a treasured custom. The sense of belonging to a lineage, to a continuous thread of narrative, can instill confidence and moral grounding in children and grandchildren. They internalize the notion that their own aspirations rest upon a foundation of experience and effort laid down by those who came before.

At times, the question arises of how one should handle sensitive content in personal stories or traditions. Families often have dark chapters or unresolved conflicts, and an older adult might worry that airing those details could cause hurt or upset. The choice of whether to omit certain elements or to broach them openly belongs to the individual, ideally balanced with empathy for others involved. Some find that naming these difficult experiences in a compassionate, non-accusatory manner can encourage healing discussions. Others opt to keep certain matters private, focusing on the uplifting or instructive aspects of their story. There is no single correct approach. What matters is preserving integrity and ensuring that the overall message remains guided by a spirit of honesty and goodwill. A carefully worded memoir can acknowledge hardship and nuance while leaving room for reconciliation and growth.

Another subtle layer of legacy-building emerges in everyday interactions, the small gestures of kindness or integrity that imprint themselves on the memories of younger observers. Whether one is aware of it or not, each moment of generosity, patience, and warmth resonates with impressionable hearts. As family members reflect later in life, they often recall not so much the exact words of a grandparent's memoir or the schedule of an annual ceremony, but the tenderness of a shared smile, the presence of someone who listened without judgment, or the consistent example of a person who practiced ethical principles. These intangible, near-invisible demonstrations of care can be as powerful as any formal tradition. Embodying one's values through daily conduct may inspire children or neighbors more deeply than a single grand event. Knowing that these small acts accumulate into a broader legacy can motivate people in retirement to continue leading by example, even if they sense their circle of influence has narrowed.

Still, the impetus to consciously codify that legacy remains vital, lest ephemeral moments of kindness dissipate without a guiding framework for continued impact. Memoirs, in their own way, function as testaments that link fleeting experiences to enduring lessons. Traditions anchor family life, ensuring that the next generation not only inherits a set of values and practices but understands the significance behind them. Broader community projects, whether philanthropic or creative, establish a structure for carrying forth the generosity of an individual into the lives of many. Woven together, these strands embody a life's meaning, demonstrating how each step, from personal introspection to communal collaboration, enriches the totality of what we pass along.

The journey toward constructing a resonant legacy might spark unforeseen transformations within the individual. By delving into the tapestry of personal memory, a person may realize that certain narratives they believed to be resolved remain emotionally charged. Writing about them, or discussing them in the context of tradition, can lead to healing or shifts in perspective. Similarly, taking an active role in philanthropic or educational initiatives could awaken an unexpected passion or skill. Retirement is often portrayed as a phase of winding down, yet focusing on legacy can fuel a sense of vibrant purpose, reminiscent of earlier life stages filled with ambition and creativity. The difference is that now, the aim is less about personal success and more about communal thriving and generational continuity.

Sometimes, the fear of not leaving behind something deemed significant impedes the process of legacy-building. Individuals may compare themselves with those who have left large sums for philanthropic institutions or who have authored best-selling autobiographies. Yet a legacy's worth is measured not by size or public recognition, but by genuineness and alignment with one's true self. An honest account of a modest life that demonstrates steadfast moral commitment or depicts the quiet heroism of daily perseverance can resonate powerfully. Likewise, the creation of a simple tradition—like an annual family poetry reading, a shared walk through a local nature trail, or even a weekly communal meal—can shape the emotional climate of a household for decades. The depth of impact is not always apparent immediately, but unfolds as children grow, carry these customs into adulthood, and infuse them with their own interpretive touches.

An older adult aiming to foster a more outward-facing legacy might consider bridging generational gaps beyond family confines. Engaging with local youth groups, civic organizations, or mentorship programs can extend one's influence to a wider set of beneficiaries. Stories of personal triumph over adversity can motivate a teenager struggling with self-doubt or a young adult wrestling with career anxiety. Traditions that revolve around community celebrations—cultural festivals, neighborhood clean-up days, or seasonal art fairs—can catalyze unity in an era where digital connection sometimes overshadows face-to-face camaraderie. One's knowledge about sustainable gardening, for example, might be invaluable to a local school project that aims to teach students how to grow their own food. In these interactions, older adults not only share knowledge but also gain fresh perspectives, revitalized by the curiosity and energy of youth. The reciprocal nature of such engagements forms a shared legacy, built by multiple generations working in tandem.

Ultimately, the quest to leave a meaningful mark on the world can be seen as an integral part of the human experience, rather than a separate pursuit begun only in late life. The seeds of personal narrative are planted early on, each formative experience shaping identity and moral compass. Traditions often find their first expression in childhood or young adulthood and evolve over the decades. Acts of altruism or mentorship, big and small, can weave through different life stages, culminating in a more focused approach once retirement permits deeper commitment. What changes in later years is the sense of urgency and clarity—an awareness that time is finite and that every thoughtful act can ripple forward. This awareness intensifies the desire to preserve stories before they fade, to bequeath traditions before they become hollow, and to offer wisdom before it becomes lost in the noise of a fast-paced era.

For those who find themselves struggling with health issues or reduced mobility in retirement, the mission of building a legacy need not be hampered. Writing can be adapted with voice recognition software, enabling the memoir process to continue even if hands tire easily. Traditions can be carried on by delegating certain responsibilities to younger family members, with the elder acting as a guiding presence and moral backbone. Community involvements can be facilitated by online platforms, video calls, or phone trees, ensuring that distance or physical limitations do not sever the threads of influence. Far from being diminished by physical constraints, a person's determination to share experiences and better the world can become even more poignant, as it showcases resilience and the resolve to remain actively engaged regardless of circumstance.

In the end, every moment offered to shaping personal stories, preserving or evolving traditions, and building a kinder tomorrow contributes to the grand mosaic of a life's legacy. The process can be both humbling and empowering, reminding individuals of the trials they have overcome and the joys that once illuminated their days, while also showing them how these pieces of memory, ritual, and service can outlast physical presence. When a grandchild, decades from now, cooks a meal following a recipe passed down through family lines, or when a new homeowner plants flowers in memory of the local gardener's teachings, or when a young mentee references the guidance received during a pivotal crossroads—these are the quiet echoes of a life that endures. By realizing the potential of memoir, tradition, and community engagement, an older generation becomes a conduit for hope, knowledge, and continuity.

The sense of completion and peace that often accompanies these endeavors stands as a testament to their worth. To see one's life made coherent in written or spoken form, to observe the younger ones practicing and celebrating inherited customs, and to witness community improvements tied to one's ongoing or past involvement—these experiences affirm that existence has meaning and that time was spent wisely. Even if certain dreams went unfulfilled or mistakes remain uncorrected, the active decision to shape what is left behind can redeem much of what was lost. This redemption is not purely for the individual, but for everyone whose journey intersects with that person's story. In acknowledging that the measure of a legacy lies in the positive changes it leaves in hearts and communities, the older generation can rest assured that their influence does not stop at the boundaries of a single lifespan.

The beauty of this approach is that it does not rely on perfect circumstances or extraordinary resources. A humble home can become a backdrop for yearly gatherings that connect family scattered across distances. A handwritten notebook or typed manuscript can hold the weight of decades' worth of laughter, sorrow, triumph, and regret. A conversation with a neighbor's child can spark a sense of wonder about what is possible when generations collaborate. These small acts, taken collectively, forge a powerful current that weaves empathy, knowledge, and moral courage into the social fabric. By freely sharing these gifts, older adults shape the world they leave behind, ensuring that the essence of their experiences endures beyond memory's natural fade.

No single formula prescribes how best to assemble a personal narrative, carry out a treasured tradition, or champion a cause for future benefit. Each path is as diverse as the people who walk it. Yet the unifying theme is intention: the decision to invest in creation and preservation, rather than allow life's treasures to scatter unheeded. Some individuals pour their energies into a carefully honed memoir, expecting that future generations will be guided by the reflections it contains. Others prefer to instill robust communal traditions that teach cooperation, gratitude, or love of beauty. Still others take an active role in shaping the future, whether through volunteerism, philanthropy, or policy engagement. Countless variations exist, but each emerges from the same conviction that life's gifts—stories, lessons, skills, and compassion—become more profound when passed on.

As the years unfold and personal vitality shifts, these efforts may take on new forms. The devotion to writing might evolve into assisting others in drafting their stories. The family tradition of an annual reunion might blossom into a larger community festival that celebrates cultural heritage and local art. The philanthropic mission might extend to forging alliances that amplify collective impact. Through every iteration, the core remains unwavering: a willingness to extend oneself beyond immediate concerns, ensuring that the next generation can trace its roots and glean guidance from those who came before. This continuity defies time's impermanence, cultivating a sense of shared humanity that links present needs with future promise.

On a personal level, the impulse to shape a legacy can imbue daily existence with renewed meaning. Rising each morning, one might ask, how will today's choices contribute to the story my grandchildren hear, or the tradition my neighborhood celebrates, or the philanthropic project that has become my passion? Such questions provide gentle direction, a reason to remain engaged and alert. They counter any tendency to drift aimlessly when freed from the rigors of the nine-to-five routine. Instead, each hour can be threaded with purpose: gathering old photographs, cooking a special meal, writing a page of memoir, or brainstorming with fellow volunteers about a new initiative. The scope of these tasks might be small or far-reaching, but together they form the bedrock of a life that resonates well beyond personal borders.

In the closing phases of this journey, it is common to experience both satisfaction and longing. Satisfaction arises from witnessing the tangible manifestations of effort: the well-worn storybook that younger family members read with awe, the local tradition that has become a cherished event, the scholarship that enabled a promising student to flourish. Longing may persist for those undertakings that never fully materialized, or for the relationships that remain unresolved. This duality speaks to the imperfections inherent in life. Yet by having engaged actively in sharing stories, fostering traditions, and uplifting future generations, one has illuminated a path of hope, continuity, and generosity. Few achievements offer a more enduring testament to a life's significance.

In accepting this delicate balance of closure and incompletion, many find a sense of peace. The understanding that not every dream achieves its final form does not negate the preciousness of what has been accomplished. Indeed, it reminds us that legacy is a collaborative effort, one that generations refine, expand, or redefine in their own era. A memoir may inspire a new perspective on family history, a tradition might adapt to the mores of a changing society, and a philanthropic act might spark a movement beyond its initiator's imaginings. Thus, the legacy evolves even after its originator's role has ended, carried forward by those who glean energy and inspiration from it.

When viewed from this expansive vantage point, writing memoirs, creating traditions, and influencing future generations coalesce into a unified act of faith in humanity's collective promise. It is the quiet assertion that each life carries inherent worth, each tradition can harness the power of belonging, and each step taken to nurture the next generation lights a small candle in a world sometimes overshadowed by darkness. Retirement, rather than a period of diminishing relevance, becomes a portal to deeper engagement. While the face in the mirror may bear the marks of years gone by, the inner flame can shine brightly with a purpose linked to something greater and more enduring than the self. In that flame lies the essence of legacy: a humble, resolute offering of love and knowledge to those who step into tomorrow's dawn.

Conclusion

Life's unfolding chapters do not halt at the threshold of retirement or at the moment one steps away from earlier responsibilities. Rather, each new day offers an invitation to remain fully engaged in the world. There is a freedom in setting aside old limits—self-imposed or otherwise—and discovering the vast potential that still lies ahead. The beauty of this stage in life rests in the conscious choice to greet each morning with renewed curiosity, determined to shape a future that aligns with evolving values and desires. Prior phases may have been devoted to intense work, raising a family, or simply establishing some sense of security; now the opportunity arises to weave that foundation into a more self-directed tapestry. Whatever path led to this moment, the essential truth remains that personal growth continues as long as the mind and heart remain open to what tomorrow may bring.

Living with intention becomes the lifeblood of this journey. Gone are the days of rigid schedules imposed by external forces; in their place, a more individualized pace emerges, guided by interests, passions, and the pursuit of purpose. The decisions made each day—whether modest or far-reaching—provide evidence that autonomy can flourish under the right mindset. Some may find renewed meaning in creative endeavors, resurrecting latent artistic talents that once seemed overshadowed by professional or domestic tasks. Others discover fulfillment in guiding the next generation, whether as mentors, educators, or simply wise voices in their families and communities. The key lies in recognizing that living intentionally does not require monumental gestures. Small acts, repeated diligently, speak volumes about the determination to leave each corner of the world better than it was before. These gestures might revolve around nurturing relationships, contributing to local projects, or cultivating personal growth in areas long unexplored.

Learning does not cease once a certain age is reached, and neither does the capacity to evolve. Indeed, the process of embracing each day with strength and confidence may involve challenges, as all meaningful pursuits do. Physical, emotional, or logistical hurdles sometimes loom large, testing the ability to adapt. Yet it is precisely this element of risk and uncertainty that bestows richness on the later chapters of a lifespan. Facing difficulties head-on can strengthen self-belief and reaffirm that even in the midst of shifting circumstances, an indomitable spirit can persist. Tending faithfully to health—physical and mental alike—transforms into a core commitment, ensuring that the body can still rise to adventures and that the mind remains lucid enough to perceive new horizons. Rather than resigning oneself to passivity, it is possible to greet obstacles as catalysts for fresh insights and deeper resilience.

Confidence at this time of life blooms from a perspective that only experience can shape. The struggles and triumphs, the changes and opportunities, the heartbreaks and joys of previous decades together weave a tapestry of wisdom that now takes center stage. This hard-earned knowledge informs balanced decision-making, fosters empathy, and deepens comprehension of human interconnectedness. Such clarity might guide an individual to participate more vigorously in social causes or to approach personal relationships with patience and compassion. The acceptance of vulnerability—whether physical or emotional—does not undermine confidence; rather, it testifies to an understanding that true strength arises from authenticity. By acknowledging both limitations and possibilities, one can harness an inner power that transcends the superficial constraints commonly attached to aging.

The sense that the best years are still ahead can thrive in the mind of anyone willing to greet the unknown with trust. Milestones traditionally linked to youth—graduations, marriages, the birth of children—often come earlier, but that does not negate the potential for fresh milestones of a different kind. An older adult may choose to explore countries never before visited, delve into digital platforms and technological developments that transform how we communicate, or embark on an entirely new vocation that reflects personal passions. In an era of constantly changing landscapes, there is immense possibility in forging unexpected paths that earlier generations might never have envisioned. At this juncture, it becomes clear that self-limiting beliefs and societal stereotypes can be firmly dismantled, making room for a sense of vibrant purpose that erases any arbitrary time limits on ambition.

As the years accumulate, so does the capacity for reflection, enabling one to draw on memories that are replete with nuance and context. Reflective contemplation can awaken gratitude for both the grand adventures and the quiet accomplishments that comprise a lifetime. The realization that new opportunities await does not erase what has come before; rather, the tapestry of earlier experiences enriches every forward step. Even the regrets or missed chances of the past can inform future directions, acting as signposts that clarify what resonates most with one's core identity. Embracing a broader viewpoint on life's arc infuses the present with an appealing immediacy, inviting a deeper awareness of what each hour brings and how best to cherish it.

There is a paradox in these later years: it is often a period when one sees, more sharply than ever, both life's fragility and its grand possibilities. The recognition that time is finite imparts urgency, but not necessarily fear. It can focus attention on what truly matters, prompting deliberate care of one's wellbeing, treasured relationships, and the ongoing pursuit of growth. Savoring the sunrise with eyes full of awe is no small feat when each moment feels newly precious. Infusing days with love for others grows more paramount as illusions of endless longevity fade. The heart, guided by empathy derived from a lifetime of joys and sorrows, can manifest compassion in everyday gestures, building a sense of unity that defies generational divides.

Choosing to believe that the next phase of life can be the most fulfilling is more than mere optimism; it is an act of conscious will. Such conviction urges individuals to shape each day thoughtfully, to cultivate the habits of resilience and curiosity, and to reach out when support or inspiration is needed. This is not to claim that difficulties vanish. Health can falter, personal loss may occur, and the complexities of society remain. Yet the vantage point of maturity offers a profound counterbalance. Each day of adversity carries seeds of growth, and each challenge invites creative solutions grounded in the wisdom gleaned from former trials. If worry arises, it can be met with the knowledge that transformation is always possible. If loneliness emerges, it can be countered by discovering or forming communities attuned to shared interests or experiences. In these ways, believing in the promise of what lies ahead begins to reshape reality.

Though there is no universal blueprint for how to live this stage wholeheartedly, the broad principles are anchored in authenticity and compassion. The individual learns to inhabit the present without apology for who they are, acknowledging that every layer of the past—each success, mistake, or lesson—has contributed to the person facing tomorrow's sunrise. This self-acceptance paves the way for forging deeper connections with others, free of the masks that once served as armor in more competitive environments. The simplicity of a heartfelt conversation, an act of generosity, or a quiet moment observing nature's splendor can resonate more powerfully than any fleeting ambition once did. Cultivating presence in this manner, day by day, year by year, reveals that no part of life's tapestry is wasted if the individual embraces it with open eyes and a willing heart.

This perspective resonates across all the different themes that have woven through the broader discussion: maintaining financial security without letting money overshadow joy; keeping physically and mentally active so that personal independence remains as robust as possible; investing in loving relationships that sustain emotional vitality; and sharing wisdom through community involvement or creative outlets. Each dimension of a well-rounded existence underscores the notion that longevity by itself is not the end goal, but rather living richly and with purpose, however one defines it. There is immense satisfaction in devoting time to what one truly values, be it scholarship, art, volunteerism, or forging deep bonds with friends and family.

For many, the newly unlocked freedom can awaken the adventurous spirit. This need not manifest as globe-trotting, though it certainly can. It might also be found in the quiet challenge of learning a new language, mastering a musical instrument, or honing the skills to craft a memoir. Even adopting a meditative practice can transform the interior landscape. Each fresh endeavor stands as proof that age imposes no permanent barrier to innovation or self-discovery. Curiosity, indeed, is an ageless gift, and retirement or any ensuing period unburdened by rigid obligations can become a platform to chase the joys and callings that once lay dormant.

Trust in the future flourishes when one aligns daily actions with a clear sense of personal mission. Whether the mission is to bring kindness to others, to protect the environment, to strengthen communal ties, or to leave creative legacies, it confers direction and animates the spirit. Each sunrise then appears as a resource—an interval of precious hours in which one can write, connect, learn, or simply reflect on the blessings that shape the day. Through this lens, the concept of best years references neither the illusions of youth nor the presumed decline of old age, but rather a state of mind that unites experience with enthusiasm.

In a broader context, living with intention, embracing each day confidently, and believing in the promise yet to come serve not just the individual. They radiate outward, touching family members, neighbors, and even strangers who observe the vitality that comes with a genuine dedication to what remains possible. Younger people witness that a lifetime of trials can yield empathy, resourcefulness, and humor; that relationships can flourish and knowledge can expand long after conventional deadlines have passed; and that the essence of a spirited existence transcends any single role or period. They learn that a life lived on purpose does not taper into insignificance but rather evolves into a deeper, more nuanced chapter, guiding those who follow.

Aging, therefore, becomes less an act of diminishing and more a continuous unfolding, in which each year grants permission to refine personal priorities and choose meaning over superficial concerns. What arises is not a swan song but a new stanza in the melody. Each note is informed by what came before, yet resonates uniquely because perspective has shifted, revealing subtleties unappreciated in earlier times. It is a phase rich with possibility and depth, one that can carry as much excitement as the early leaps of young adulthood, but shaped by the steadiness gained from decades of living.

For the individual reading these words, there is the reminder that nothing stands in the way of this forward momentum except, perhaps, the inclination to believe otherwise. A subtle mental shift can transform worry or regret into impetus for exploring fresh horizons. Embracing each dawn as another chance to refine how one moves through the world creates a life of ongoing progression. Encounters once seen as obstacles may reveal themselves as hidden opportunities for service, self-development, or forging ties that might otherwise remain unattainable. At every turn, the realization deepens that one has more control than expected over the tone and substance of life's latter pages.

Resting in that recognition, the heart finds reassurance that the best days do not belong solely to memory or idle fantasy. The best days can come forth whenever curiosity triumphs over complacency, compassion over isolation, and perseverance over doubt. Whether dedicating mornings to new knowledge, afternoons to cherished pursuits, or evenings to laughter shared with loved ones, one weaves a routine distinguished by authenticity and joy. The future becomes not a place of fear or loss, but a domain in which hope and resolution intertwine, revealing that age is, above all else, an invitation to keep discovering how vast human potential can be.

The winding road of life, from early aspirations through varied triumphs and trials, culminates in a vantage point that offers perspective both wide and deep. The story unfolds with new purpose each time a person decides to invest energy in what sparks creativity and nurtures well-being. Perhaps the greatest gift of the years is the freedom to bestow attention where the soul finds nourishment. Some might call this late blooming; others see it as an ongoing harvest of seeds planted long ago and now ready to flourish. By choosing not to settle into inertia, one reaffirms that the best chapters remain unwritten, poised for whichever themes the heart deems worthy.

The choice to keep dreaming, to keep creating, to remain compassionate and open, marks the essence of a life continuing forward with intention. Boundaries once believed insurmountable can soften, replaced by a quiet confidence that even if challenges arise, they serve as catalysts for deeper engagement with the fullness of being alive. And so, in the gentle light of each morning, the voice within whispers that there is more to see, more to contribute, and more to appreciate. From day to day, that promise remains the unbreakable thread linking a lifetime of experiences to an unfolding future.

With trust in one's capacity to adapt, with optimism that adversity can kindle growth, and with gratitude for the moment at hand, it becomes evident that there is no endpoint to the quest for fulfillment. This is the enduring truth that carries one from the first glimmers of possibility long ago into the expansive realm of yet-to-be-realized dreams. Grounded in that understanding, each individual can rise to greet every sunrise with calm assurance, stepping forward with lively energy and bright vision for all that still awaits. In that spirit, life endures as a work in progress, guided by purposeful action and buoyed by hope. The journey, ongoing and ever-evolving, will continue to summon a sense of wonder and promise, renewing itself perpetually in the rhythms of days yet to come.